Religious Mythology and the Art of War

Contributions to the Study of Religion
Series Editor: Henry W. Bowden

Private Churches and Public Money: Church-Government Fiscal Relations
Paul J. Weber and Dennis A. Gilbert

A Cultural History of Religion in America
James G. Moseley

Religious Mythology and the Art of War

COMPARATIVE RELIGIOUS SYMBOLISMS OF MILITARY VIOLENCE

James A. Aho

Contributions to the Study of Religion, Number 3

GREENWOOD PRESS
Westport, Connecticut

Library of Congress Cataloging in Publication Data

Aho, James A
    Religious mythology and the art of war.

    (Contributions to the study of religion ; no. 3
ISSN 0196-7053)
        Bibliography: p.
        Includes index.
        1. War and religion.   2.   War (in religion, Folk-
lore, etc.)   I.   Title.   II. Series.
BL65.W2A38   291.1'7873   80-23465
ISBN 0-313-22564-8 (lib. bdg.)

Library of Congress Catalog Card Number: 80-23465
ISSN: 0196-7053
ISBN: 0-313-22564-8

First published 1981

in the United States of America by Greenwood Press, a division of Congressional
Information Service, Inc.
88 Post Road West, Westport, Connecticut 06881

in Great Britain by
Aldywch Press Limited
3 Henrietta Street, London WC2E 8LU

Printed in the United States of America
10 9 8 7 6 5 4 3 2 1

Copyright Acknowledgments

I am grateful to the following two journals for permission to use parts of my previously published articles as chapters in this book:

From "Huitzilopochtli's Feast: Sacramental Warfare in Ancient Mexico," *Sociological Symposium*, no. 18, Spring 1977, pp. 84-105, copyright 1977 by Virginia
Polytechnic Institute and State University, Blacksburg, Va. Reprinted by permission
of the publisher.

From "The Protestant Ethic and the Spirit of Violence," *Journal of Political and
Military Sociology*, vol. 7, no. 1, copyright 1979 by Northern Illinois University,
DeKalb, Ill. Reprinted by permission of the publisher.

To Margaret

CONTENTS

MAPS AND TABLES

War has a necessary place in human affairs. Whether we judge specific campaigns to be successful in achieving objectives or merely a waste of life and materiel, major civilizations have inevitably resorted to armed conflict. And instead of negating their religious influences during wartime, each civilization has drawn on its mythological heritage to inform its military practices. This important volume shows for the first time how religious symbolism has shaped a distinctive military ethic in significant cultures. Eight connected studies demonstrate the dialectical relationship between mythologies and martial codes.

Earlier writers have tended to stress the importance of ideas and then reasoned deductively to issue statements about behavior. Too often they have ignored important variables, yielding either an unrealistic understanding of religious content or inaccurate descriptions of actual practice, or both. James A. Aho has set new standards for comprehensive coverage and thorough analysis in the field. He has gathered together a wide range of source materials on religious outlook and military behavior from ancient Mexico, India, China, Japan, ancient Israel, Europe, and the Moslem world. Moreover he provides insights into how Aztec beliefs, Hinduism, Confucianism, Zen Buddhism, Judaism, Catholicism, Protestantism, and Islam affect the conception as well as the conduct of war.

Not the least of Aho's contributions is a hypothetical scheme that places religious systems and cultures into two general categories. One, the immanentist type, derives from a framework exemplified by the Aztecs and medieval Catholics who fought to order affairs according to a divine plan discerned in the cosmos. The other, a transcendent type, pertains to Israel, Islam, and Protestant Christianity that seeks to establish in historical reality the personal wishes of a heavenly deity. Both typologies help explain broad similarities between divergent cultures and their conduct in life-or-death struggles for survival.

Through comparative analysis and a selective overview this significant survey breaks new ground. The study brings fruitful insights to bear on a field not known for order and coherence. Professor Aho's schematic interpretation of isolated material brings out relationships not mentioned earlier. After making the case that mythological structures affect attitudes about collective violence, he explicates the sense behind normative military codes. As long as men make war, we should learn more fully how they give cognitive content to such struggles and act in them to achieve personal and public redemption. This volume represents a significant step toward understanding how different martial ethics comprise varying attitudes, motives, and ways of fighting.

Henry Bowden

PREFACE

This book grew from a conviction that the way in which man does violence to man in warfare is as much a philosophical, or better a spiritual problem, as it is a problem of technology and political economy. If we are ever to overcome the bane of modern military violence, we must reexamine certain mythological notions deeply imprinted in our souls as Occidentals: Christian, Muslim, and Jew alike. That this belief runs counter to conventional social scientific wisdom is obvious to me. Nevertheless, three events in the 1970s force Westerners to recognize that violent spiritual energies continue to thrive, perhaps as explosively as ever, beneath the fragile superstructure of our smugly enlightened world. I refer first to the horrifying spectacle of religiously motivated mass suicide-homicide that ended in a flash the quasi-Christian utopia of Jonestown. I refer next to the successful Muslim-inspired revolution that shattered, at least temporarily, plans of Western technologists to mold Iran after a secularized American image. I refer finally to the last armed confrontation (at this writing) between Israel and Egypt when, upon crossing the Suez Canal, Muslim infantry were heard collectively to expostulate the ancient *takbir*, "Allah is the greatest!" —thus expressing their view of the invasion as a *jihad*. (To this event might be added another, the 1968 six-day blitzkrieg by Jewish armored cavalry against the Muslim world, followed on the seventh day by Sabbath, in accordance with the Deuteronomic criteria of holy war.) We can neither truthfully nor safely continue to overlook the spiritual component of war, in favor of admittedly more easily apprehended material factors.

The theory informing these pages arose from reflection on my own experience. Its source was a deeply personal confrontation with my own propensity to self-righteousness and rage. The religious mythologies I studied were each chosen less for abstract methodological considerations, than for the insights I felt they could provide me in dealing with this personal specter. Each was analyzed in its uniqueness with an attitude of sympathetic understanding. Figuratively (and sometimes literally) I "became" a confessor of the cult about which I was writing at that particular time: an Aztec flowery warrior, a *kshatriya* knight, a sword-wielding samurai, a donkey-riding nomad, or one of Cromwell's dragoons. Intellectually, morally, and spiritually, I traveled over several years immense distances in giving birth to this work. The chapters of the volume are arranged in approximately the order in which this journey in self-discovery was made. It began in the cults and mysteries of ancient Mexico and India; that is, in the "womb of unconsciousness." It continued through the intriguing allure of Chinese and Japanese ritual propriety and serenity. It ended with investigations of ancient Judaism and Islam, of medieval Christianity, and finally Reformation Protestantism, some of the world's first celebrations of self-directing individualism. In other words, in the course of searching for the roots of my own personal violence, I was led by fate or design back to my own spiritual roots: to the teachings of Luther, Calvin, and Wesley, with which I had been engrained as a child, and which I had rejected as a youth. The last section of chapter 11 on Protestant mysticism and violence is as close to a self-confession as a sociologist can make while still calling himself a scientist.

This project could never have been contemplated, much less completed, without the help and sustenance of many other people, living and dead. At the risk of failing to mention an individual crucial to my development, I feel I must acknowledge my debt to the encyclopedic vision of Max Weber, whose work I sought to emulate, to Albert Camus for his example of the morally engaged artist, and to Peter Berger for his intellectual integrity in dealing with the sacred.

On a more concrete level, I would like to thank Dean Davies who, as an English graduate student when I was embarking on this project, introduced me to the writings of the mythologist Joseph

Campbell. Thanks should go also to Michael Bybee who, as a graduate student, opened to me his magnificent library and world of Oriental philosophy and the martial arts. I am grateful to my father-in-law John W. McMahan, who baptised me in medieval Catholic philosophy and who critically but sensitively read an early version of this manuscript. I also want to thank Charles Africa of Idaho State University and his student Amando Alvarez for their careful translations from the Spanish and Gabrielle Patty for her translations from the German. I am indebted to the Idaho State University Faculty Research Committee for the grant that allowed me to reimburse them for their services. Thanks also go to Idaho State University for unconditionally awarding me the sabbatical that gave me the opportunity to collate a disheartening mass of data under memorable circumstances. To both the University of New Mexico and particularly the University of Washington I am thankful for giving me privileges as a visiting scholar to peruse and use their excellent library holdings. Finally, I must thank my wife Margaret, not only for her constant emotional support during the difficult times, but more importantly, for her intellectual inspiration. It was my wife who, although not mentioned in the bibliography, must take credit for my finally coming to understand the nature of symbols and the esoteric rendering of the mythology of sacred combat, and who therefore enabled me to make theoretical closure on this subject; she enabled me to see that, after all, I am the warrior about whom the myths of holy war speak. I dedicate this book to her.

Religious Mythology and the Art of War

CLAIMS, DEFINITIONS, AND CONFESSIONS

1

THE PARAMETERS OF THE STUDY

This study concerns the religious symbolism of war. My aim is to demonstrate how, in selected cases, a society's military ethic and its dominant religious mythology constitute a single, unified structure of meaning. A society's *Kriegethik*—its preferred style of collective raping, looting, burning, and killing—is often "dialectically" or "reflexively" interrelated with its prevailing religious mythology. The mythology legitimizes a certain ideal of military practice, and this in turn "confirms," as it were, the validity of the mythology. I shall, furthermore, suggest that in the history of civilizations there have evolved two types of religious symbolisms of warfare: one seeing it as an act which reorders the divine cosmos, the other as the forcible reestablishment of a god's law in history.

This book deals solely with the subject of "civilized" warfare. Discussion of armed combat in primitive societies has been purposely avoided. There are two reasons for this. The first is that I was simply uninterested in studying armed violence among the Nuer of North Africa, for instance, or the natives of the New Guinea Highlands. Secondly, there is a serious question of whether primitive combat is in a strict sense warfare at all. Some anthropologists indicate that it is really an institutionalized means of retribution for private torts which appears wherever there are no such political bodies as states.[1]

By "war," we are referring exclusively to the violent struggle between organized states, regardless of the various excuses—slaves, territory, equality, salvation, or power—that have been used to justify such struggles. By "state," we mean at the very least, a relatively closed nonkinship group of armed persons that "taxes" and "protects" those residing in a fairly delimited territory, ignoring for now the widely divergent ways those taxes can be collected or "justice" administered. Territorial states and warfare, as so defined, are institutions unique to peoples whose surplus production is sufficient to support in some comfort a body of nonproductive tax collectors, judges, police, and soldiers. But such wealth can be produced only by populations whose economies enjoy inventions like irrigation, crop rotation, fertilization, and extensive markets, the very things commonly associated with the word "civilization." Thus, the data collected by ethnologists on primitive violence, however intriguing they may be in other respects, were judged largely superfluous to our objectives.

By the term "religious mythology," we mean a body of stories dealing with supernatural beings, forces, ancestors, or heroes told among a people. We are employing the term in a completely neutral sense without begging the issue of the veracity of such tales. While there are many different types of mythologies, this study will deal only with those having an essentially *religious* subject matter. For our purposes, religious myth and ritual will be distinguished from other human activities by two necessary and sufficient criteria: by its ultimacy and by its reference to holy phenomena.

Paul Tillich writes that the peculiarity of religion is to be found in its relationship to the "ultimate concerns" of man's existence.[2] Man's final concerns comprise the substance of his faith. Religion makes unconditional demands on the confessor's time, wealth, energy, and perhaps even his life. In exchange it promises fulfillment of his yearnings for security, immortality, bliss, and meaning. Religious faith in this sense is paradigmatically represented by the Deuteronomic commandment: "Thou shalt love the Lord thy God with all thine heart, and with all thy soul, and with all thy might" (Deut. 6:5).[3] Tillich's characterization of religion is compatible with the subject matter under investigation here. As we shall see, the "ultimate concern," so to speak, of the ancient Mexican, to which he willingly sacrificed everything including his own heart, and which he anxiously awaited each dawn, was the victory of light over darkness. By the same token, the ultimate concern of the Japanese samurai was in large part his own death, as expressed in the saying: "When all things in life are false, there is only one thing true, death.'' And finally, the ultimate concern of ancient Judaism and Islam seems to have been with God's justice and man's participation in its sometimes terrifying administration.

As fruitful as Tillich's definition is, by itself it is insufficient to isolate with precision the phenomena examined in this volume. As Tillich himself admits, success, social standing, the Party, and nationalism may all under certain circumstances be considered the object of a people's ultimate devotion and thus their religion.[4] For this reason he finds it helpful to distinguish between ''true'' and ''false'' ultimacy, between an ultimacy where, to use his words, the object of devotion ''transcends'' subject and object and is consequently authentically religious and an ultimacy which involves worship of a manufactured idol or ideology.[5] Following Tillich's suggestion, in this work the adjective ''religious'' will refer only to those artifacts, myths, and liturgies which relate to a genuinely religious experience, to what Rudolf Otto has called the ''holy'' or ''numinous.''[6]

In his classic work on the subject, the numinous is described by Otto as an experience which totally transcends the normal everyday consciousness of reality. It is portrayed in the last chapter of Job, in Arjuna's vision of Vishnu in the Bhagavad-Gita, in Pascal's diary, or in the descriptions of the *satori* experience of the Zen monk. It breaks unexpectedly through the humdrum daily routine and leaves the subject awestruck and mesmerized. Compared to its majesty he senses profoundly his own insignificance. And yet he is fascinated by it. Transcending conventional experience, the phenomenon of the holy supersedes as well the realm of mere ethical and aesthetic judgement. It is a spellbinding experience before which all conceptualization seems trivial, inadequate, and irrelevant.[7]

It is not my place here to inquire into the validity of the holy experience. For our purposes, it is only important to appreciate that in principle, anything in man's *Existenz*, from rocks, thunderstorms, or mountain peaks, to birth and death, can be an occasion for the numinous experience—even a sword. Consider, for example, the samurai Inazo Nitobe's poetic depiction of the feelings evoked by the *daitō*, the long sword.

Its cold blade, collecting on its surface the moment it is drawn the vapours of the atmosphere; its immaculate texture, flashing light of bluish hue, its matchless edge, upon which histories and possibilities hang; the curve of its back, uniting exquisite grace with utmost strength—all these thrill us with mixed feelings of power and beauty, awe and terror.[8]

There has never existed a people immune to the religious experience, nor a society without religious myths and rituals in the sense defined above. However, we will study only the relationships between the mythologies of selected *world* religions and the art of war, world religions being those which, to use Max Weber's definition, "have known how to gather multitudes of confessors around them."[9] Not all the recognized world religions will be discussed in this volume. Nor will the social history of any single confession be studied exhaustively. This would have been inappropriate given my initial interest, since many religions, including Jainism, Mithraism, Manichaeism, and Nestorian Christianity, appear to have had no unique military ethic.[10] Only those world religions are included which have had unquestionable influences on specific martial arts. And only that period in the evolution of each of them is surveyed during which a peculiar martial ethic arose.

A single chapter has been devoted to each of the following cults and their ideals of military practice: Aztec Nahuatlism, Vaishnite Hinduism, Confucianism (particularly of the Han dynasty), Tokugawa Zen Buddhism, ancient Hebraism, Islam, medieval Catholicism, and Reformation Protestantism.[11] The Greco-Roman popular religions (as opposed to the "civic religions") are not studied in this book because they appear to have had little direct bearing on the Greco-Roman martial ethic. But the Greco-Roman *Kriegethik* did have a discernible influence on both Islamic and Christianized European military thinking, and will therefore be discussed in the appropriate chapters.

The mythologies and military ethics of these various cults are classified under several analytical types. Naturally, any classification system is only a hypothesis, and other investigators may interpret these religions in contrary ways. Nevertheless, the canons of science do not require complete consensus, but insist only that any proposed taxonomy be supported with adequate documentary evidence. In this context it is necessary to make a few technical points. Our content analysis will be based largely on the subjective meanings the mythologies and martial ethics seem to have had for their proponents. Thus, we assume that the most fruitful way of coming to understand the significance of myths or ethics to their believers is to observe them sympathetically "from within," through their eyes and imaginatively to experience reality as they themselves might.[12]

The application of *verstehende* sociology to the study of ancient religions entails a serious methodological problem. Ordinarily, ethnographic accuracy can be assessed by inquiring whether the subjects can identity themselves in the investigator's report. But how can one validate claims concerning the psychological meaning of a myth when its believers have long since died? There probably is no satisfactory answer to this question. However, three things can be said: (1) Notwithstanding the difficulties normally associated with primary reliance upon formal mythological documents—they do not always reflect the beliefs of the commoner—given the lack of any other source of information, it would be highly presumptuous not to rely upon them. The priestly documents are in general the best and in some cases the *only* data source for dead religious worlds. This is why we place so much emphasis on the content of the standard holy books and original literatures of violence of the cults in our sample. (2) The actual meanings for believers (or even for priestly authors) of passages from their holy books are not revealed directly in a simple reading by an outsider to the confession. The investigator must attempt sensitively and accurately to place the passages and selections in question in a larger social-historical context. If, for example, we are concerned with interpreting the real meaning of *herem*, the biblical ritual of liquidation of the stranger in God's Land, to the Hebrew, we must at the very least examine the political and military situation of Judaism in 500 B.C., and the tradition of Semitic culture in regard to military extermination in general. But to do this, particularly if, like myself, the investigator has little background in the religion at issue, he must rely upon the previous researches and secondary monographs of considered experts in the field. Although the authorities upon whom I rely will be dutifully noted at the appropriate points later, honesty demands that I mention the two who have had an unmistakable influence on my basic theoretical perspective: They are Max Weber and Joseph Campbell. While obviously they cannot be held responsible for any inaccuracies in this work, their well-argued insistence that Judaism, Islam, and particularly Protestant Christianity have had consequences for institutional life radically different from those of Buddhism, Confucianism, Catholicism, and Hinduism, was the starting point for this inquiry into religion and warfare. (3) Any religious text can be read either "exoterically" or "esoterically."[13] That is, any religious claim can be taken either literally as an empirically testable assertion about history or the cosmos, or as a vivid metaphor of a largely ineffable, psychological process. The concept of sacred warfare clearly illustrates this. Speaking generally, it appears that most confessors to the major world religions have understood holy war exoterically, as a public enactment of a religious duty to eradicate an objective evil from the world. In any cult, however, there have been mystics who have esoterically seen the notion of war as allegorical of a deeply personal struggle to eliminate subjective evil from their lives. One of the commonest errors committed in the popular study of comparative religions has been the suggestion that Judaism, Islam, and Christianity are exclusively exoteric in outlook, and that Buddhism and Hinduism are primarily esoteric. In fact, all "Western" religions have had their esoteric traditions, even in regard to the myth of the holy war: Sufism, the Kabbalist conventicles, and Christian mysticism. And "Oriental" religions have had their own exoteric beliefs and practices which, at least in terms of numbers of adherents, are much more significant than any forms of esotericism. I have tried throughout this study to be attentive to these facts so as not to bias my own understanding of the commonly shared meanings of the religious symbolisms of warfare.

THE BASIC HYPOTHESIS

Any complete religious symbolism of warfare contains two analytically distinct elements: Cognitive claims concerning the nature

of reality in general and warfare in particular and a program of preferred military conduct, a military ethic, a *Kriegethik*. Our object is
to examine the relationships that exist between these two elements
in eight different civilizations.

The first element defines the relationships between the divine and
the world. It specifies what evil means, how human pathos arises,
and proposes theoretical solutions to suffering. The second element
is the "operational" aspect of war's symbolism. It grounds the
mythology in a specific action orientation. Our hypothesis is that
these two elements are reciprocally interrelated, the mythological
meanings of warfare influencing the ways wars (ideally) should be
fought, and the practice of violence in turn determining the meaning it will have to its participants. In other words, the normative
military code serves both as a "plausibility structure" which, if
adhered to, will lend credence to the cognitive content of the war
myth[14] and as one of the recommended paths to public and personal redemption.

We shall find that any complete military ethic (the second
element) contains the following three components: a vocabulary of
acceptable motives for engaging in war and an inventory of legitimate goals toward which violence might be directed; the preferred
attitude or response to be assumed toward war; and approved ways
of fighting. In the last category, a further distinction can be made
between those prescriptions dealing more with the "style" of combat, including required costumes, music, prayers, and banners, and
those dealing directly with the "substance" of violence, such as
allowable weapons and tactics. Table 1 provides a diagram of the
basic theoretical model.

AN OUTLINE OF THE ARGUMENT

Social order is a "shield against terror," harboring each individual from the preeminent evil, the specter of nothingness.[15] Without
social order there can be no psychological order, only madness.
"The man who is isolated [anomic] is no part of the *polis*," taught
Aristotle, "and must therefore be either a beast or a god." Every
society, intuitively understanding this as the basic principle of

**TABLE 1: The Dialectical Relationship between the Two Elements of
Warfare's Religious Symbolism. (The bidirectional arrow
indicates that the elements are dialectically or reciprocally
related.)**

A. The mythological or cognitive aspect of war's religious symbolism.	B. The operational aspect of war's religious symbolism. The military ethic as both path to salvation and plausibility structure.
1. What kind of reality war represents	1. Appropriate motives for war
2. Why there are wars ◄———►	2. Preferred attitudes toward war
3. What evil is and how it is caused	3. Approved ways of fighting
4. How man's suffering can be redeemed	a. style
	b. substance

social life, takes elaborate pains to preserve social order (the
nomos) from threats to its integrity. Historically, one of the major
institutional preventatives against chaos has been warfare. The ultimate and universal meaning of sacred combat—from the Aztec
guerra florida, to the Islamic *jihad*; from Christianity's "pilgrim's
wars," to the martial arts of the Far East—has been to sustain
social order and sanity, to preserve *nomos* in the face of *anomos*.

Naturally, the use of violence to keep anomie at bay is fraught
with terrible dangers. The intentional destruction of human beings
always contains the potentiality to devastate mankind's fragile cultural creations and thrust him into total darkness. And yet, killing
and dying, particularly when done "well," when done courageously in the name of an ethical principle, are among man's most convincing witnesses to the facticity and solidity of social order. In the
sacrifice of the warrior, the reality of society is symbolically cleansed
of any taint of chaos and its members are persuaded of its immortality.

All holy wars have as their final goal the protection of the world from nothingness. But order, and by implication the violent struggle to eradicate chaos, have been mythically conceived in radically different ways throughout history. In some mythologies, chaos is viewed as a disruption of the historical order and sacred warfare as an act reestablishing a faithful relationship between man and his god. Such a myth posits the divine to be an ethereal Person inhabiting a realm separate from the world of natural affairs, which is "fallen," that is, not sacred. We shall call this holy war myth the transcendent-historical type. It is approximated in ancient Hebraism, Islam, and Protestantism. In other mythologies, the divine is said to be an impersonal *pneuma*, spirit, or Law intimately pervading the material world. In this case, chaos is understood as an interruption of the cosmological order, and the holy war as an act reunifying man and the divine. This we shall call the immanentist-cosmological myth of holy war. It is exemplified in varying degrees by Buddhism, Hinduism, Confucianism, Nahuatlism, and medieval Christianity.[16]

Each of these holy war myths is associated with a particular type of military ethic. The major task in the following chapters is to trace the nuances of these associations for each of the major world religions in the sample. A schematic anticipation of what we shall find is presented in Table 2.

THE BIG PICTURE

A society's myth of war is not the only variable influencing the content of its military ethic. In many cases, the power position of the society's military elites relative to its priests and the frequency and intensity of its wars together determine more of the content of the *Kriegethik* than does the society's dominant religious mythology. (Of these two "extraneous" variables it appears that the degree of dependency of the military upon religious institutions is more important causally than the frequency and intensity of warfare.)[17] However, the correlation between specific war myths and particular military ethics does not disappear when the extraneous

**TABLE 2: Hypothesized Characteristics of Military Ethics
          by Type of Holy War Myth**

	TYPE OF HOLY WAR MYTH	
	Immanentist-Cosmological	**Transcendent-Historical**
Major Characteristics of the Military Ethics	1. ATTITUDE: Warfare is play. It is an end in itself. Killing and dying in war are glorified as absolute ends. Avoidance of death is an indication of attachment to self.	1. ATTITUDE: Warfare is work. It is a means to an end other than itself. Death and injury in war are considered liabilities to be avoided if at all possible.
	2. CONDUCT: Warfare should be pursued "religiously," with reverent devotion and meticulous attention to ritual detail. Intricate ritual proscriptions are placed around all aspects of military conduct from the initiation of hostilities to the treatment of prisoners.	2. CONDUCT: Warfare should be pursued "scientifically," i.e., on an exclusively utilitarian or Machiavellian basis. No *ritual* restraints are placed on military conduct, although utility alone may dictate the necessity of restraint.
	3. MOTIVE: Warfare if done properly leads to full human maturity and to salvation, i.e., return to the "cosmic womb."	3. MOTIVE: Warfare if done properly leads to full human maturity and to reestablishment of a faithful relationship between man and god.

variables are held constant. The dialectical relationship that we have posited to exist between the two elements of war's religious symbolism is not, in other words, spurious. For example, General Sun Tzu's *Art of War* was composed during the Era of Warring Principalities in China (463-221 B.C.) when the ritual imperialism of the Chou dynasty had disintegrated into military anarchy. Still the

Art of War posits doctrines highly congenial to orthodox Confucian military principles such as "bloodless victory," victory through superior virtue, and adherence to the Middle Way. Again, Kautilya's largely Machiavellian *Arthashastra* was written during a period when (321-296 B.C.) and in a location where (the Buddhist Mauryan Empire) the *kshatriyas* had liberated themselves from the control of Hindu *brahmana*. All the same, it promotes political and military practices compatible with an immanentist-cosmological *Kriegethik*. In the chapter on "Wonderful and Delusive Contrivances," for example, Kautilya reveals to the budding spy how to fast like an ascetic, miraculously alter his skin color, pass through fire unharmed, see at night, and make himself invisible. In the latter case he should first fast for three days following the death and immolation of a *brahmin*, then on the day of the star Pushya, after forming a sack from the corpse's garment and filling it with its ashes, he should don it.[18]

When the two extraneous variables—the power position of military elites, and the frequency and intensity of war—are controlled, the mutual influence of war myths and military ethics upon one another sometimes increases. For example, the effect that an immanentist-cosmological myth of sacred combat has on a playful liturgical ideal of the martial arts will be thrown into sharp relief when the society in question is both in a state of relative peace and its military leaders are under the sway of ecclesiastical authorities. On the other hand, the ties existing between a transcendent-historical notion of holy war and an opportunistic work-oriented *Kriegethik* become even more obvious when the society is involved in frequent, ferocious warfare and its military elites are freed from the constraints of the priestly colleges.[19]

In this volume our interest is only in the religious symbolism of warfare and not in the influences of other variables on martial conduct. Thus, research is limited primarily to those cases where the interrelationships between the two elements, the myths of war and the military ethics, are most clear-cut. These are represented by the cases in the far left- and right-hand columns of Table 3. The remaining cases in the two center columns will be treated only peripherally to throw light on the major hypotheses.

TABLE 3: Actual Historical Cases, Their Approximate Dates and Typical Document Consulted, by Religious Mythological Type, Power Positions of Military and Religious Elites, and Frequency and Intensity of Warfare*

MILITARY ELITES SUBORDINATE TO RELIGIOUS ELITES DURING TIMES OF RELATIVE PEACE		MILITARY ELITES INDEPENDENT OF RELIGIOUS ELITES DURING TIMES OF CONSTANT, INTENSE WARFARE	
Immanentist-Cosmological	Transcendent-Historical	Immanentist-Cosmological	Transcendent-Historical
Aztec (1400-1521) (*Florentine Codex*)	Jewish, post-Davidic (1010-586 B.C.) (*Kings, Samuel, Chronicles*)	Indian Buddhist (500 B.C.-A.D. 330) (*Arthashastra*)	Hebraic, Deborah-Barak (1250-1020 B.C.) (*Joshua, Judges*)
Vaishnite Hinduism (330-1192)** (*Mahabharata, dharmashastras*)	Shiite Muslim	Chinese (460-221 B.C.) (*Sun Tzu, Art of War*)	Sunna Islamic, esp. Arabic (620-700) (*Qur'an*)
Confucian (200 B.C.-A.D. 1912)** (*Spring and Autumn Annals*)		Japanese (1300-1600)	Protestant (1560-1750) (*Swedish Discipline*)
Tokugawa Buddhist (1600-1867) (*Hagakure Bushidō*)			
Medieval Christian (900-1350)† (*Tree of Battles*)			

*This table includes only those military ethics discussed in this volume. It is arranged in such a way that both extraneous variables, the power position of the military elites and the frequency and intensity of warfare, are held constant.

**There were periods during this time span when other military ethics prevailed. These are only very approximate dates.

†There is a serious question of whether medieval Christianity truly represents a form of divine immanence. In this volume, we take the position that in regard to warfare, it does. See footnote 14.

This book is divided into two parts. Part I deals solely with the immanentist-cosmological symbolism of war, part II exclusively with the transcendent-historical symbolism of war. Each part is introduced by a theoretical discussion of the particular symbolic ideal-type. Each discussion is followed by detailed studies of the several historical cases which best approximate the particular ideal-type. The final chapter of the book briefly summarizes the findings and comments on their ethical significance.

NOTES

1. Joseph Schneider, "Primitive Warfare: A Methodological Note," *American Sociological Review* 15 (1950): 772-77.

2. Paul Tillich, *Dynamics of Faith* (New York: Harper & Row, 1958), pp. 1-4.

3. Unless otherwise indicated, all biblical quotations are taken from the King James Version.

4. For an example of a recent use of "religion" in this broad sense, see Patrick H. McNamara (ed.), *Religion American Style* (New York: Harper & Row, 1974).

5. Tillich, *Dynamics of Faith*, pp. 11-12. Likewise, others who have borrowed Tillich's definition have added the further specification that for ultimacy to be strictly religious, it must refer to the "supernatural" or to the "sacred." For example, see J. Milton Yinger, *The Scientific Study of Religion* (New York: Macmillan, 1970), pp. 13-14 and McNamara, *Religion American Style*, pp. 4-5.

6. Rudolf Otto, *The Idea of the Holy*, trans. by John W. Harvey (London: Oxford University Press, 1973 [1923]).

7. Otto's use of the phrase *das ganz Andere*, "the totally other," to describe the *numinosum* has led to a number of unfortunate misunderstandings concerning the intent of his work. Neo-Calvinist theologians have used *das ganz Andere* to signify the utter transcendence of God relative to man. But according to John Harvey, Otto's translator, Otto never intended his words to be taken this way. Otto was a phenomenologist of religion, not a theologian (Otto, *The Idea of the Holy*, p. xviii). The numinous experience is just that, a pre- or trans-cognitive experience. Indeed, in his seminal empirical study of mysticism, Otto uses *das ganz Andere* not only to depict the Protestant religious experience, but also the atheistic mystical poetry of Shankara (See Rudolf Otto, *Mysticism East and West: A*

Comparative Analysis of Mysticism, trans. by Bertha L. Bracey and Richenda C. Payne (New York: Macmillan, 1932).

8. Inazo Nitobe, *Bushido: The Soul of Japan* (Rutland, Vt.: Charles Tuttle, 1969 [1899]), p. 134.

9. Max Weber, "The Social Psychology of the World Religions," in *From Max Weber*, trans., ed., and intro. by Hans H. Gerth and C. Wright Mills (New York: Oxford University Press, 1958), p. 267.

10. Mithraism once constituted the major challenge to infant Christianity in the eastern marches of the Roman Empire. It flourished for some centuries in the camps of the imperial army from Gaul to Mesopotamia, where some of its icons and altars may still be found. But this was at a time when the classic Roman military ethic was already long established and in fact was on the wane. See C. M. Daniels, "The Role of the Roman Army in the Spread and Practice of Mithraism," in *Mithraic Studies*, ed. by John Hinnels, (Oxford Road: Manchester University Press, 1976), vol. 2, pp. 249-74.

11. Comparative religionists, as a rule, restrict the application of the term "world religion" exclusively to confessions of the Old World. Whether this is based upon careful analytic procedure or (more likely) trained professional oversight, one does not often hear serious students claim for Mesoamerican religion the status of a world confession. But even a cursory examination reveals that it meets the *criterion definiendum* of "world religion." While Mesoamerica was comprised of a plurality of autonomous nations each with its unique cultural traditions and separated by fierce rivalries, there existed prior to the Spanish onslaught a relatively uniform religious structure uniting the whole of the Mexican people into a homogeneous mythological world involving the same ritual calendars, human sacrifices, and even rubber ball games. The very facility with which the Spanish, at least superficially, imposed their version of Christianity on these peoples was a consequence of this fact. At the time when the *conquistadores* landed at Vera Cruz, no single name had evolved for the Mexican world's religious system. But, after all, "Hinduism," which can in no way be considered a solitary body of myth and ritual, much less a single ecclesiastical organization, was originally only a term applied by various Western conquerors to the confusing welter of sects that shared little more than their location "beyond the Hind", east of the Indus River. One might do far worse, then, by dubbing the universal Mexican cult "Nahuatl-ism" after the name of the linguistic world that stretched from modern Utah to the Yucatan with its center in the Mexican plateau. The names of the major Nahuatl gods still varied from city to city in A.D. 1500. The celestial god, for example, went

variously by the address of Quetzalcoatl, Tezcatlipoca, Huitzilopochtli, or Mixcoatl. (This may be compared to the prevalence of diverse local names for Shiva and Kali in "Hinduism.") But systematization of the Nahuatl pantheon under one ultimate godhead was unquestionably in progress in Tenochtitlan when the Spanish made their unannounced visit. See Alfonso Caso, *The Aztecs: People of the Sun*, trans. by Lowell Dunham (Norman: University of Oklahoma Press, 1958), pp. 7-8 and Octavio Paz, *The Labyrinth of Solitude: Life and Thought in Mexico*, trans. by Lysander Kemp (New York: Grove Press, 1961), pp. 89-96.

12. Joseph Michael Ryan, "Ethnoscience and Problems of Method in the Social Scientific Study of Religion," *Sociological Analysis* 39 (Fall 1978): 241-49.

13. Ralph Slotten, "Exoteric and Esoteric Modes of Apprehension," *Sociological Analysis* 38 (1977): 185-208.

14. For the notion of "plausibility structure," I am indebted to Peter L. Berger, *The Sacred Canopy* (Garden City, N.Y.: Doubleday & Co., 1969), pp. 16, 45-47, 48, 58, 78-79, 123, 124-25, 134-35, 150.

15. Ibid., pp. 23, 26, 49-50, 90.

16. For the distinction between transcendent and immanent mythologies, I am indebted to Max Weber, *The Sociology of Religion*, trans. by Ephraim Fischoff (Boston: Beacon Press, 1963), pp. 166-83.

It should be clear that as *religious* mythologies, both types ultimately refer to an experience which "transcends" common-sense reality. The difference between the two mythologies is that one maintains this "transcendent" element to be immanent in the world of natural affairs, while the other maintains that the "transcendent" is separate from this world.

Although the reasons for considering medieval Catholicism to be a form of immanentist-cosmologicalism should become clearer in chapter 5, it will be helpful to make some preliminary comments at this point. It would be foolish of course, to deny the existence of historical consciousness in medieval Christianity. Near the end of the first Christian millennium in particular, popular anticipations of the historical fulfillment of the Second Coming were flourishing. The First Crusade, a mass penitential pilgrimage undertaken not only to mitigate the harshness of God's imminent judgment, but also to cleanse the Holy Land in preparation for His coming, was simply the most well known of these movements.

However, the Church by this same time, through her syncretic assimilation of pagan folkways and legislative pronouncements, was well on the way to sacralizing the totality of European personal and public life. Ignoring the intercessory functions of the Church pantheon and the introduction of the idea that all social estates are essential parts of the unified body of Christ, the two clearest examples of this are: (1) The institution of the seven sacraments, which meant that hereafter each of the major passages in an individual's life would be ritually regulated, legitimized, and given meaning in terms of the Resurrection. (2) The introduction of the liturgical calendar. Each day of the holy year would become a feast day celebrating still another divine mystery of the Church. These two institutions had the effect of rendering the experience of personal and public time for the average Christian confessor into a cosmic cycle, having its beginning and end in God the Father. One of the most revealing expressions of this idea was the evolution of the popular devotional cult to Mother Fortuna. Art-forms of the period picture her slowly and relentlessly spinning the eternal wheel of fortune, at the hub of which is the face of *Deus in rota*. He who yields to the Great Mother, it was taught, resisting not, but moving with the wheel, sacrificing his wishes to her way (perhaps, in imitation of Christ who submitted himself to the tree, the universal symbol of the creative-destructive powers of Femininity) will transcend the fleeting tribulations of this life and find eternal peace in the Lord. See H. R. Patch, *The Goddess Fortuna in Medieval Literature* (Cambridge, Mass: Harvard University Press, 1927) and A. O. Lovejoy, *The Great Chain of Being* (Cambridge, Mass: Harvard University Press, 1936).

17. For an excellent discussion of this subject, see S. N. Eisenstadt, "The Protestant Ethic: An Analysis," in *The Protestant Ethic and Modernization*, ed. by S. N. Eisenstadt (New York: Basic Books, 1968), pp. 3-45.

18. *Kautilya's Arthashastra*, trans. by R. Shamasastry, intro. by J. F. Fleet (Mysore: Mysore Publishing House, 1960 [1915]), chapt. 14, sec. 3.

19. Statisticians would say that in these two situations the other two variables "specify" the original correlation between war myths and military ethics. Technically, it means that they are more closely related to one of the two elements of war's religious symbolism than to the other. See Hubert M. Blalock, *Social Statistics* (New York: McGraw-Hill, 1960), pp. 337-43.

PART I

THE IMMANENTIST-COSMOLOGICAL SYMBOLISM OF WAR

THE IMMANENTIST-COSMOLOGICAL WAR MYTH AND MILITARY ETHIC

2

THE MYTH OF WAR

"Feminine" symbolism and art-forms occupy a major place in immanentist-cosmological religions.[1] The Magna Mater is the Alpha and Omega. Male divinities recede into the background as auxiliary actors in the drama of creation. Through hierogamy with the goddess, either as the sun or rain, they may perform as fecundators; but she, not they, is considered the creatrix. "The doorway of the Mysterious Female," sings Lao-tzu, is the source of all things seen and unseen.[2] Indeed, in immanentist doctrines, the male gods themselves are invariably said to have been given life by the Great Mother.[3] Thus whatever her name—Ishtar (Astart), Inanna, Hathor (Isis), Kali, or Coatlicue—she is pictured everywhere holding to her breast her first son, the storm and sun god: Marduk, Enlil, Horus (Osiris), Surya, or Huitzilopochtli.

The Great Mother is not just the womb of life; she is also the tomb of death. She consumes the very children she births. Her sign, the earth, symbolizes not only the source, but the final resting place of all things, including the sun and storm gods who return to her upon completion of their tasks. This is why Kali, the Hindu goddess-supreme, is painted black, the hue of rich soil and fertile womb, but also the color of death. She is seen bloody-toothed, standing on dismembered corpses, wearing a skirt of human arms and a necklace of human skulls.[4]

In immanentist mythologies, this paradoxical duality of the Great Mother is said to be the Way of the cosmos. In a highly abstract form, it is represented as the Primordial Round, the "cosmic egg", *dharma, tao, michi,* or *arta,* as it has been variously called. Like the Magna Mater herself, the Way is considered the source, the sustenance, and final encompasser of the cosmological order.[5] All human suffering, from psychological neuroses and economic catastrophes, to floods and earthquakes, are viewed as disruptions of this order. They are all understood as symptoms of chaos. And chaos is the direct consequence of mankind's failures, either through ignorance or sin, to adhere to the cosmic Way. It follows that for one's own inner peace, as well as for the sake of reality as a whole, each must conform to the Way peculiar to his position in the cosmos. Each, in his or her own way—merchant, farmer, wife, or prince—must submit meticulously to the eternally given duties incumbent upon his or her status in the world to keep it from slipping into nothingness.

Sacred warfare is one such duty. Seven related mythological truths follow from this fact: (A) Holy war preserves the cosmic world from chaos. (B) Therefore, holy war is one of mankind's highest callings. (C) The victory over chaos is attained only by means of sleight and magical weapons. (D) Perhaps as compensation for this, the righteous must themselves suffer a grave wound. (E) But this very wound guarantees the individual warrior a type of divinization. (F) Because of their negative *mana,* holy warriors are taboo. Let us examine each of these mythological propositions separately.

(A) Apart from its alleged material causes, sacred warfare in a cosmological world has as its primary meaning the preservation of reality from chaos, and by implication the redemption of personal misfortune and public calamity. It has the effect of atoning for man's transgressions against the cosmic Way, thereby mythically reestablishing "at-one-ment" with the divine order. Ideally, the holy war will be staged during crises, moments when collective anxiety concerning the viability of the normative and psychological orders is most prevalent. This can result from any number of circumstances, an anticipated change in the seasons (particularly, from Winter to Spring), a misplay of an important liturgical obligation by a high public official, the coronation of a new monarch, or even a natural catastrophe like a comet or volcano, interpreted by the masses as a sign of impending doom. In the largely playful and highly stylized military sacrifice of the victims impersonating the forces of *nomos* and *anomos*, the cosmological world is symbolically secured against threats to its existence. In a sense, they reenact the victory of the fecundating sun and rain gods over lifelessness on earth.

Why in the final analysis is violence employed as the vehicle of world maintenance and not some other less spectacular device? A paradoxical psychological truth may shed light on this mystery. In many cases, the greater the effort, the treasure, or the lives expended in accomplishing a goal, the more cognitive and emotional value it has. Deep conviction seems to demand symbolic failure, even crucifixion, as its witness. This is why, "whenever man has thought it necessary to create a memory for himself, his effort has been attended with blood, torture, and sacrifice."[6] Neither the discernment of omens, admonitions, the exchange of insults, nor gambling so compellingly certifies the validity of divine decisions or augurs so convincingly fate's course, as the outcome of ceremonial combat.

(B) The Greco-Romans, the Teutons, and the Aryans of India and Persia all viewed the struggle, life-risking agony, as sanctifying. In the very pathos of uncertainty and physical pain, ultimate value was created. This is why for the *kshatriya* knight, peaceful death at home in bed was considered the ultimate evil.[7] Warfare, in other words, was for them an end in itself, a form of play in the strict sense of the word. Indeed, the English term "play" is derived from the Anglo-Saxon *pflegan*, which means to pledge for, to stake, to risk great things in battle. As Johan Huizinga has shown: "In all Germanic languages and in many others besides, play-terms are regularly applied to armed strife as well. Anglo-Saxon poetry . . . is full of such terms and phrases. Armed strife, or battle, is called *heado-lac* or *beadu-lac*, literally 'battle-play,' or *asc-plega*, 'spear-play'."[8]

It is often in their visions of heaven that men reveal their conceptions of the highest good. Thus, it is worth recalling that German warriors falling in combat were not promised eternal repose in Wodan's Valhalla, but endless strife and the daily possibility of violent death. Each dawn they would awake, feed on mead and flesh provided by the sacred boar and goat, and then gird themselves once more for battle.[9]

(C) Typically, in cosmological mythologies the victories of the various sun and storm gods over nothingness are said to have been achieved by resorting to unfair strategies. A classic example in Indo-Aryan literature occurs during the epic battle between Indra and Vritra.[10] The two antagonists solemnly agree to kill one another "neither by day nor night, neither with the dry nor with the wet." Acting with the greatest duplicity, Indra assassinates Vritra "at the departure of night, but before the rising of the sun," with a magical lightning bolt (*vajra*) supplied to him by his allies. To be sure, insofar as Indra has only eluded, but not directly contravened the sacred compact (*rta*) with his enemy, he does not strictly sin. And yet in the Hindu holy war, the righteous will henceforth be viewed as tainted. In the Mahabharata, for example, the Pandus, who with their white skins and association with Krishna stand for virtue, are repeatedly pictured as having a demonic streak. Outwardly, they represent *nomos*, but inwardly they seem as evil as their black-skinned opponents, the Kuru brothers. One of the most sacred vows of the *kshatriya* is never to strike a woman in battle. Knowing that Bhishma, the most stalwart Kuru prince, would never breach this convention, the Pandus are ordered by Lord Krishna himself to reveal to Bhishma that the Pandu warrior, Shikandian, is really just a woman disguised as a man. Knowing this, the chivalrous Bhishma will not raise his arms in his own defense even as Shikandian kills him.[11]

Why should the forces of light, truth, and goodness be compelled in the holy war to employ questionable means? The answer given in the Mahabharata is simple: Even "if ye [the Pandus] had put forth all your prowess," says Krishna, "then ye could never have slain them [the Kurus] in battle by fighting fairly! King Duryodhana [the Kuru leader] . . . could never be slain in fair encounter!"[12] The reason for this is that the Kurus themselves are treacherous in both peace and war. It is they who cheat in the dice game that occasioned armed strife in the first place. It is they who commit the wrong of stripping Draupadi, the wife of the five Pandu patriarchs, in the

TABLE 4: Mythological Genealogy of the Mahabharata

King Vasu = fish-nymph

Parashara[1] = Satyavati[2] = Santanu[3]

Vyasa[4]   wife = son[5]   wife = son[6]

Vyasa[7] = widow[8]   Vyasa = widow[9]

Dhritarashtra[10]   Yudhisthira[11]

1. A wise old yogi, he has intercourse with Satyavati halfway across the river of life.

2. Daughter of Truth, she works as a ferry pilot on the river of life. The near shore is that of illusion; the far, that of disillusion. She mates with both Parashara and Santanu.

3. Great old king.

4. The alleged author of the Mahabharata, he was born on an island halfway across the river of life. The Epic is thus like *maya*, simultaneously half-true and half-false. Or more accurately, it both hides the truth, if understood literally (exoterically), and reveals the truth if understood esoterically. Properly read, the Epic is thus closer to a psychological account than accurate history.

5. He is killed in battle.

6. He dies of consumption.

7. As an old, ugly, smelly man, he has intercourse with the widows of both sons of Santanu.

8. She closes her eyes in horror of Vyasa's appearance. Thus, her son will be dark-skinned.

9. She turns pale when confronted with Vyasa. Thus, her son will be light-skinned.

10. The Kuru patriarch.

11. The Pandu patriarch.

hall during her "season." It is Kuru Kanika who advises them to burn the Pandus to death while they sleep at home, so as to avoid having to meet them in open combat.[13] The ancient teaching is: "If the enemy fights aided by deceit, he should be met with the aid of deceit." He who out of fear of sinning allows evil to follow its wicked way untrammeled, commits thereby an even greater sin.[14]

But the fact remains that in defeating evil, the righteous have become evil. The opposition between good and bad, victory and defeat, in the cosmological holy war becomes more apparent than real. In the end, the antagonists are pictured as collaborators, or more accurately, as blood relations. The Pandus and the Kurus are both said to be the offspring of Vyasa, himself the son of a wise old yogi and the daughter of Truth, Satyavati (see Table 4). Osiris and Seth, the epic representatives of life and death, are portrayed in Egyptian mythology as the "divine twins" born of Geb and Nut. The gods of Olympus and their cosmic antagonists, the Titans, all are said to have been mothered by Gaia. Huitzilopochtli (the sun) and Coyolxauhqui (the night), it was taught, were both given life by the same mother Coatlicue.

(D) Holy war saves the world, but only at a terrible price; its saviors suffer a cosmic injury. In the Mahabharata, for example, all but five survivors of the Pandu family are totally annihilated during a treacherous night attack before they can finally overcome the Kuru brothers. In the very act of slaying the serpent, the Pandus themselves must be slain first. This is the significance of Arjuna's vision in the Bhagavad-Gita of all the warriors on both sides simultaneously being consumed by Vishnu, the god of *nomos*, maintainer of the world illusion.[15] This is also the meaning of the sacrifice of Horus's (the sun god's) eye, as he emasculates and thus renders powerless Seth (the devil), during their struggle for the earth.[16]

Exoterically, this myth may be read as expressing the inevitability (and perhaps, the justice) of the indignities all parties must experience in war. But esoterically, it seems to symbolize the "psychic wound" suffered by the righteous when they realize their own unwitting complicity in evil. Thus, upon hearing Krishna's indictment (above), the Pandus are struck with shame and grief. "Although victory hath been ours, O Krishna," confesses Pandu Yudhisthira, "our heart, however, is yet trembling with doubt. . . . The course of events is difficult to be ascertained even by persons endued with spiritual insight," agrees Pandu Arjuna. "The foe who were vanquished have become victorious! . . . Misery looks like prosperity, and prosperity looks like misery!"[17]

This latter interpretation of the theme of the suffering savior provides insight into yet another feature of the cosmological symbolism of holy war: The hero always attains victory by resorting to a magical weapon against which all resistance is hopeless. And characteristically, this implement exudes fire, a blinding flash, a shock, or all three. Zeus (and Jupiter [a corruption of Zeus + *pater*]) has his thunderbolt; Huitzilopochtli, his *xiucoatl* or fire serpent; Thor, his hammer; and Indra, his diamond-lightning *vajra*. Again, this symbol can be and usually has been taken literally. The Aztecs, to cite just one case, futilely employed a consecrated fire-arrow against the Spanish during the final days of the siege at Tenochtitlan. But the symbol can also be understood esoterically as the irresistible power of truth which shatters any illusions one may harbor concerning his own purity. This is the preferred meaning of the *vajra* bolt in Tantric and Mahayana (particularly Zen) Buddhist teachings.[18] The shocking flash is the religious experience which suddenly awakens the righteous one to the terrible truth of the darkness within his own soul. Thus, "the warriors in the [Pandu] camp beheld Death-night in her embodied form, black, of bloody mouth and bloody eyes . . . standing before their eyes." Earlier, the Pandus had objectified sin as being other than themselves, belonging to the enemy "out there." Now they realize that it resides in their midst, lives in their own natures, no longer as a stranger but as an essential part of themselves.

(E) "Lightning is followed by a roar and tumult of awakening life and rain—the rain of grace" according to Joseph Campbell. Analogously, in the painful acknowledgment of his own sin, the righteous one is reconciled to his "shadow aspect." This is why Krishna's words to the Pandus regarding the necessity of their own evil are accompanied by visions of drum-beating angels, flowers falling from heaven, and lapis lazuli sparkling on the horizon. In other words, in cosmological mythologies holy war not only preserves the public world from nothingness, it is also a type of "yoga"; yoking each combatant together with the divinity immanent within himself (in both its benevolent *and* malevolent aspects).

"Death in battle," guarantees the Mahabharata, "is the womb of heaven." Exoterically, this promise can be understood as referring to the largely visible process of physical demise, burial (that is, return to the Earth Mother, the Source from which all things issue), decay (consumption or assimilation by the Great Mother), and rebirth into a different, perhaps eternal, life-form. This, apparently, was what most ancient Mexican warriors had in mind when proclaiming: "There is nothing like death in war, Nothing like the flowery death, So precious to Him who gives life; Far off I see it: My heart yearns for it."[19] But "death in battle" can also be taken esoterically, as the killing of illusions and rebirth to a new vision of oneself. In this case, each warrior is like the universal hero who, dying to his righteous persona, descends into the earth's bowels, the cellar of his own soul, to confront darkness alone and returns to the surface with the gift of gods: full maturity.[20] In whatever way the promise is read, if one engages in the holy war with sincerity and correctness, calming his own fears and desires, he is guaranteed personal salvation.

(F) Because of the maturity earned through suffering, his association with death, and the potentiality his work has for destroying the world, the warrior is both fascinating and terrifying. Mythology depicts him harboring a negative *mana* or charisma in his person. This is confirmed when, possessed by Wyrd or Brut, the Norwegian and Anglo-Saxon warrior spirits, the warrior becomes berserk, no longer a man but *ein Untier*, a monster. (*Berserkir* is a Scandinavian term, "having a bear envelope," that is, having the appearance of a bear.) Mythology thus gives him a name, a totem, a banner, and a legendary heredity, all symbolizing this alleged fact.[21] And it treats him as taboo, admonishing the community ritually to exclude him from its midst, often for several months following combat. The universal existence of exclusive men's barracks segregated from the community is not simply for disciplinary purposes. It also has authentic religious motives.[22] Notwithstanding the documented practice of barracks' homosexuality, precautions will often be taken to prevent the warrior from polluting and thus endangering himself through inordinate contact with his own religiously charged body. In Deuteronomy, for example, explicit prohibitions are placed upon nocturnal emissions while on campaigns, and the soldier is obligated by law to bury his own excrement outside the war camp (Deut. 33:9-14). Reentry into the world of ordinary men must be preceded by the performance of intricate lustral rites and in some cases even purification by fire.[23]

THE MILITARY ETHIC

An immanentist-cosmological military ethic has three analytically distinct components, all of which can be derived from the myth of the holy war: appropriate motives for participating in combat, a preferred attitude toward military violence, and a set of norms defining how the enemy should be engaged.

The Motives of War

There are countless reasons that could be given for engaging even in ostensibly holy wars. It would be a mistake to idealize all the combatants as religiously motivated. Although many, particularly the elite troops, have fought for the "right" reasons, some have been forcibly conscripted to bear arms against their better judgment. Others have been mercenary hirelings unemployable elsewhere, and some have been adventurers entertaining dreams of glory. Still others have been present only to maintain personal friendships. In brief, we are safe in assuming that the average ancient soldier, like his modern counterpart, was essentially uninformed, nonidealistic, vaguely afraid, and somewhat resentful of this intrusion on his life. "Minister of war, You have acted without discrimination. Why have you rolled us into this sorrow, So that our mothers have to do All the labour of cooking?" asks a nameless Chinese infantryman.[24]

However, we are not concerned with these other motivations, but only with the ideal vocabulary of motives implied in the mythology of the cosmological holy war: how warfare *should* present itself to the participants' minds, not how it actually does in fact. Fundamentally, cosmological military symbolisms direct that an individual take part in war to save the world from evil and to earn, as a matter of course, either manhood or eternal life in heaven. This is not to say that warfare in cosmological symbolisms is considered a vehicle of world improvement. Strictly speaking, social progress is inconceivable in any but transcendent-historical war myths. Nowhere in Nahuatlism, Hinduism, or Buddhism, and only cursorily in Confucianism is social advancement even suggested as a possible goal of organized violence. Nor, it is crucial to note, are we arguing that the *intention* to rescue world and soul from the snares of nothingness was necessarily the *cause* of ancient Mexican, Chinese, or Hindu strife. To attribute causality to human action is logically quite different from empirically assessing the meanings that the actors are expected to give to that action.[25] Our interest is exclusively with the latter question.

In cosmological military symbolism the preferred motive for fighting is simply to preserve the cosmos from chaos. But insofar as social order and sanity are said to be predicated upon adherence to a particular Way, an important ethical implication follows from this fact: In cosmological military symbolisms the end or the *telos* of combat is not divorced from the military means to attain this end —at least not to the same degree as in transcendent-historical symbolisms. As we shall observe repeatedly in our case studies, the proper use of a specific tool of force in the desired frame of mind is identical to the end sought by the warrior, namely, unity with the divine Way. This appreciation reaches its high point in Japanese *bushidō* wherein combat becomes a contemplative act annihilating illusion and eliminating pathos. Still, this is just another way of saying that cosmological martial arts are closer to play-forms than they are to types of work. Playfulness thus becomes the preferred attitude of the cosmological warrior. Another ethical orientation follows directly from this: To the extent that cosmological symbolisms ground world maintenance upon observance of a single imperishable Way, then warriors are expected to struggle against the forces of anomie within the rigid bounds of ritual propriety. If they do not, then all will "sink into deep and limitless hell without a raft."[26]

The Preferred Attitude toward Military Violence: War as Play

Arjuna, generalissimo of the Pandu army, arrives on the field of battle in a chariot, his limbs quaking, his mouth dry, and his hair standing on end. Krishna, his driver, consoles him with these words: Only the body is destroyed in combat. But the body is transient. It is born, ages, and dies. Thus, it does not truly exist anyway. Only Self (Atman) truly is, and as such, It is eternal. Consequently, "He [Atman] is not slain when the body is slain. . . . Weapons do not cleave to this self, fire does not burn him; waters do not make him wet; nor does the wind make him dry" (Bhagavad-Gita 2:13-24). "In reality . . . no one slays and no one is slain" in war.[27]

In the Mahabharata, the killing in war (and even the opposition between enemies, as we have seen) is an illusion (*maya*).[28] But this means that in Hinduism the violent contest, properly viewed, is a form of play to be neither rebuked nor avoided, but to be joyfully and unself-consciously entered as one might a game or dance. (Hinduism is unique neither in associating the illusory with play, nor warfare with illusion. The Latin *illudere*, "to mock or jeer at" [*im* = against + *ludere* = to play] has as its root *ludes*, "game," or *ludens*, "player." All struggles, athletic and violent, were known by the Latins as types of "playing against.")[29]

Krishna recommends that *kshatriyas* act "as if" they have objective enemies, "as if" they are doing the killing and dying. Because in reality, "by me [Vishnu] alone are they slain already" (Bhagavad-Gita 11:32-34). The warrior, if he plays his role well, can only submit to Fate in an attitude of detachment toward ego: by playing the game according to the rules, with neither sorrow nor fear.

It must not be thought that if warfare is a game, then the players are allowed to proceed in an attitude of hilarity and nonseriousness. *Jocus* and *jocari* in the sense of joking and jesting, do not mean "play" proper in classical Latin.[30] For the Romans, Hindus, Germans, and Chinese to consider war a form of play was to count it among the most solemn and significant of man's affairs. For above all, unlike its antithesis "work," "play" refers to those activities engaged in as ends in themselves.[31] Play is not some "servile" art whose value is found in its utility relative to ends apart from itself. On the contrary, it is the essence of sacred liturgy, the ritual celebration of the highest end.

If in cosmological symbolisms the holy war is play, then no expense in either treasure, life, or limb need be spared in its performance. The crucial thing is not, after all, the practicality of the ceremony but its compelling reenactment, the maintenance of the world in the face of chaos. This is why sacred warriors will don lavishly embellished costumes and use weaponry that may actually impede their offensive capacity when struggling against the foes of order. European knights literally destroyed themselves financially in order to adorn their persons, their horses, and their retainers in the most conspicuous manner possible during the Hundred Years' War. Humphrey, duke of Gloucester, wore gold-encrusted armor and shot silver-tipped arrows; the Black Prince of Wales had his swan-embroidered velvets; Sir John de Hawkwood's company had its white uniforms.[32] It is not beyond the realm of plausibility to suggest that one of the major motives behind Aztec warmaking was the need to obtain quetzal feathers, jewel lip-plugs, and other colorful regalia that Mexican warriors employed to bedazzle their opponents and impress Yaotl, their war god. At the high point of Aztec ascendancy, the annual tribute to Tenochtitlan included 33,000 handfuls of quetzal feathers.[33]

The Approved Manner of Fighting: War as Ritual

True play will be demarcated from the work-a-day world by boundaries of various sorts, spatial, temporal, and normative. The game of holy war is no exception. For a violent struggle to be considered in the eyes of its participants an authentic test of the strength of men and gods, it must be fought on the appropriate "holiday," on sacred ground, and with ritual propriety. "To obtain victory in battle without cunning or stratagem is the best sport," Pandu Yudhisthira tells us, "those that are respectable never . . . adopt deceitfulness in their behavior. War carried on without crookedness and cunning—this is the act of men that are honest. . . . Even enemies should not be vanquished by desperate stakes in deceitful play."[34]

It is essential to appreciate that this recommendation by Yudhisthira to be chivalrous is perfectly consistent with the mythological truth just recounted, that military victory is tainted with sin. In Hindu military ethics, the constraints placed upon martial conduct are predicated upon the truth that warfare contains the risk of terrible crimes. But other things being equal, those awakened to their own insidious capacity to commit evil are more just, merciful, and temperate in the treatment of the enemy than those deluding themselves in their absolute innocence. Indeed, one of the fundamental differences between cosmological and historical symbolisms of warfare is precisely this: The Hebraic, Muslim, and Reformation Protestant soldier, in identifying his cause with the perfect righteousness of God, uses the very ferocity of his violence as a confirmation of his own purity. The Mexican, Hindu, Confucian, medieval Christian, and Buddhist warrior, on the other hand, in being asked to recognize himself in the enemy and the enemy in himself, is thus bound to deal with him within the limits of ritual propriety, using only a restricted inventory of relatively harmless weapons and strategies.

Since the ritual proscriptions circumscribing the cosmological holy war are described later we need not enumerate them here. Let us instead address two other related issues: To what degree is one justified in inferring the actual behavior of warriors from codifications of martial law authored primarily by priestly literati? Upon what are such codifications based?

It is impossible to determine precisely the extent to which warfare in now dead civilizations conformed to the ideals of their religious leaders. Undoubtedly, a significant minority of the ancient combatants failed to achieve the state of "egolessness" preferred in theory, and when faced with the choice of either death or deviance from the code of chivalry, took the sinful but safe path. Nevertheless, this assumption must be tempered by two other considerations: In the first place, cosmological military ritual ordinarily is considered legally binding only when the enemy himself is judged worthy of restraint and honest dealing. If he exists beyond the pale of the civilized world, either as an alleged demon or mere animal, he can be treated accordingly. The criteria typically used for purposes of identification of humanity naturally vary: shared language (Mexico), shared faith (Christian Europe), or formal membership in a brotherhood of states (China). However, as a rule one condition is always necessary for judgment as a human being, adherence to the appropriate military ethic. In a situation of *apattikala*, say the Hindu law books, where righteousness is transgressed by the enemy, the *raja* is permitted any scheme to preserve the world. Consequently, practical considerations alone would favor obedience to military convention.

As a second consideration, where the military role is given a cosmic meaning, the mere thought of warfare contrary to the eternally given Way might have consequences analogous to the panic homosexuality conjures for Anglo-American males. Just as the thought that one may himself be a homosexual provokes existential terror that one is "unnatural," a "being thrust into the darkness that separates one from the 'normal' order of men,"[35] so it might have been for a soldier to resort to forbidden tactics and weapons in ancient Mexico, China, or India.

In the European Middle Ages, for example, chivalry was considered a virtue. "Virtue" comes from the Latin *virtus*, "manly" or "strong" (from *vir* = man). By implication the unchivalrous, even if victorious, knight could lose his claim to manhood if he were to circumvent the rules of war. Even after its efficacy had been demonstrated in numerous encounters, the Christian knight was reticent about adopting the longbow, as it was an unreliable measure of fortitude. It could be wielded effectively by those fearful of directly clashing with the enemy. "Cursed be the first man who became an archer; he was afraid and did not approach," reads a famous inscription.[36] Accordingly, its use was relegated to less virtuous, less virile persons called sergeants, a title having the same root as the Latin *servus*, slave.

Upon what is the Way of the warrior based? Cosmological worlds consist typically of three levels: the macrocosm, the planets and stars; the mesocosm, the public affairs of society; and the microcosm, the life and psyche of each individual. If world order is to be preserved and the individuals within it find happiness, then mesocosm and microcosm must align themselves with the *T'ien Tao* (the Way of Heaven): "On earth as it is in heaven." This is why, from Mesopotamia to ancient Mexico, social life and personal biography became miniature reenactments of astrological cycles.

Thus it was also for military affairs. The characteristic Mesopotamian fortress-city, for example, was surrounded by four walls, each facing one of the four cardinal directions, with the ruler's ziggurat in the center, signifying the "fifth" direction, up-and-down, the position mediating relations between heaven and earth. (The five directions corresponded to the five planets visible to the naked eye.)[37] In China, each wall was protected by an army unit designated by the appropriate directional totem and color. The north army was under the black tortoise or serpent of the north, the south army under the red bird, the west under the white tiger, and the east, the green dragon. It was precisely in this way, by the dictates of the compass, that Chinese armed forces until 1912 arrayed themselves both for the march and for encampment with these additions and alterations: Insofar as the commander-in-chief was considered the emperor's representative in the field, then he camped beneath the color of the fifth direction, yellow. And as the color black was considered a bad omen, the north battalion was provided in emergencies with a blue banner.[38]

Universal to immanentist-cosmological military ethics are "heavenly" weapons, with magical efficacies alleged to be like those employed by the various sun gods in their battles against the night: the Japanese *daitō*, the German battle-axe, the Hindu *vajramushti*, or the Chinese bow. There is also a preferred army size, determined in some cases by calculations of the precession of the equinoxes. There is even an auspicious moment for departure of an expedition. "That king," says Bhishma, "who sets out under a proper constellation and an auspicious lunation always succeeds in winning victory."[39]

And by implication, there is also a time when the positions of the planets foretell military disaster. Perhaps the most tragic example of this occurred in 1519 in Mexico. Legend had it that Huitzilopochtli, the Aztec national god, had exiled the white Tezcatlipoca, also named Quetzalcoatl or the Feathered Serpent, along with his retainers on a reed raft into the eastern ocean. Astrologers held that he would return to resume sway over his people in the year "One Reed." But the year that the white-skinned Cortés arrived from the east on *his* "raft" was exactly One Reed.[40] According to the *Florentine Codex*, Montezuma II, the last Aztec ruler, employed soothsayers, wizards, and magic to trick the Spanish general into defeat, just as Huitzilopochtli had done five centuries earlier to Quetzalcoatl. Seeing these fail, Montezuma despaired and greeted Cortés as a god, placing the mantle of Quetzalcoatl upon him.[41] The Aztecs apparently knew, before the war was ever fought, that there was no hope of victory; the Feathered Serpent, as written in cosmic law, had come to replace Huitzilopochtli (and his people) as lord of men.

CLOSING THOUGHTS

The immanentist-cosmological symbolism of war, then, has both an intellectual and an active component: a myth of holy war and an operationalization of the myth in a specific *Kriegethik*. The content of the *Kriegethik* follows directly from the nature of the myth, and the plausibility of the myth (both exo- and esoterically) is in turn supported by conformity to the ethic. If victory is achieved playfully and fairly, the victors in the holy war will recognize—they will collectively "re-know"—the truth of their shared mythology, and the cognitive world that is based upon it will thereby be sustained. If instead the holy war is lost, then assuming the losers have fought unself-consciously and correctly, they can be confident of having attained manhood (and, perhaps, even individual salvation).

This symbolism of war prevailed in Nahuatl Mexico, Hindu India, Catholic Europe, Confucian China, and Buddhist Japan.

NOTES

1. By "feminine," we are referring to a general symbolic "archetype." For an examination of this mythological system, see Erich Neumann, *The Great Mother: An Analysis of the Archetype*, trans. by Ralph Manheim, Bollingen Series 47 (New York: 1955).

2. *The Way and Its Power*, trans. by Arthur Waley (New York: Grove Press, 1958), poem 25.

3. Thus, proclaims a Tantric psalm: "Oh Mother! Cause and Mother. Thou art the One primordial Being, . . . Creatrix of the very gods; even of Brahma the creator, Vishnu the preserver, and Shiva the destroyer" (*Hymns to the Goddess*, trans. by Ellen and Arthur Avalon [London: Luzac & Co., 1913], pp. 32-33).

4. Likewise, the Mexican Coatlicue has a serpent's head, lion's claws, and is dressed in a shirt of human hands, a serpent-skin skirt, and a belt the buckle of which is a human skull.

5. *Dharma*, for example, has as one of its elements the Sanskrit term *dhr*, "throne," "support." It is, thus, that upon which the cosmos rests.

6. This is quoted from Friedrich Nietzsche, *Toward a Genealogy of Morals*, Doubleday-Anchor edition, p. 192 in Berger, *The Sacred Canopy*, pp. 191-92 n. 13. See also p. 40.

7. *Bhishma-parva*, VI, *Mahabharata*, trans. by Pratap Chandra Roy (Calcutta: Datta Bose & Co., 1919-33), xvii: 2.

8. Johan Huizinga, *Homo Ludens: A Study of the Play Element in Culture* (Boston: Beacon Press, 1955), pp. 38-41, 46-49, 52-75.

9. Georges Dumézil, *The Destiny of the Warrior*, trans. by Alf Hiltebeitel (Chicago: University of Chicago Press, 1970), pp. 111-14.

10. Ibid., pp. 65-81.

11. *Bhishma-parva*, xiii: 3-8; xiv: 15; xcix: 34-39. It might be pointed out that Shikandian is really Amva Kasi, a woman whom Bhishma raped and then refused to marry. As no other man would have her, she was forever ruined (*Udyodga-parva*, V, *Mahabharata*, cxciii-iv and clxxiii-iv).

12. *Salya-parva*, IX, *Mahabharata*, lxi.

13. For these incidents, see respectively, *Sabha-parva*, II, *Mahabharata*, xlvi-lxxiii; *Sabha-parva*, lxviii; *Adi-parva*, I, *Mahabharata*, cxliii. See also *Sauptika-parva*, X, *Mahabharata*, i.

14. *Santi-parva*, XII, *Mahabharata*, xcv, cix, lv, lvii, xv, xxii, xcviii.

15. "All yonder sons of Dhrtarashtra [the Kuru patriarch] together with the hosts of kings and also Bhisma, Drona, and Karna along with the chief warriors on our side [i.e., the Pandu side] too,—Are rushing into Thy [Vishnu's] fearful mouths set with terrible tusks. Some caught between the teeth are seen with their heads crushed to powder.

As the many rushing torrents of rivers race towards the ocean so do these heroes of the world of men rush into Thy flaming mouths. As moths rush swiftly into a blazing fire to perish there, so do these men rush into Thy mouths with great speed to their own destruction.

Devouring all the world on every side with Thy flaming mouths, thou lickest them up. Thy fiery rays fill this whole universe and scorch it with their fierce radiance, O Visnu.''

(Bhagavad-Gita, trans. by Sarvepalli Radhakrishnan, in *A Sourcebook in Indian Philosophy*, ed. by Radhakrishnan and C. A. Moore [Princeton, N.J.: Princeton University Press, 1957] 9:26-30). All subsequent quotations from the Bhagavad-Gita are from this edition.

The reader may compare this image with the picture of total destruction promised during the War with the Wolf in German mythology. See, for example, Joseph Campbell, *The Masks of God*, vol. 3, *Occidental Mythology* (New York: Viking Press, 1970), p. 486.

16. Joseph Campbell, *The Mythic Image* (Princeton, N.J.: Princeton University Press, 1974), pp. 114-21.

17. These quotations are found, respectively, in *Salya-parva*, lxiii and *Sauptika-parva*, x.

18. Campbell, *The Masks of God*, vol. 3, pp. 269, 480-81.

19. A. M. Garibay K., *Historia de la Literatura Nahuatl* (Mexico Editorial Porrua: 1953), p. 168.

20. For a good discussion of this mythological theme see Joseph Campbell, *The Hero With a Thousand Faces* (New York: Meridian, 1956).

21. Dumézil, *The Destiny of the Warrior*, pp. 139-47.

22. For the classic discussion of taboo in regard to war, see James G. Frazer, *The Golden Bough: A Study in Magic and Religion* (New York: Macmillan, 1951 [1922]), pp. 244-52.

23. And do ye abide without the camp seven days: whosoever hath killed any person, and whosoever hath touched any slain, purify both yourselves and your captives on the third day, and on the seventh day. And purify all your raiment, and all that is made of skins, and all work of goats hair, and all things made of wood. . . . Everything that may abide the fire, ye shall make it go through the fire, and it shall be clean: nevertheless it shall be purified with the water of separation: and all that abideth not the fire ye shall make go through the water.

And ye shall wash your clothes on the seventh day, and ye shall be clean, and afterward ye shall come into the camp (Num. 31:19-24).

24. *The She King* (*Shi Ching*) or *The Book of Poetry*, trans., ed., and intro. with notes by James Legge, *The Chinese Classics*, vol. 4, (Hong Kong: Hong Kong University Press, 1970 [1871]), part II, book iv, ode 1, stanza 3.

"At first, when we set out
The willows were fresh and green;
Now, when we shall be returning,
The snow will be falling in clouds.
Long and tedious will be our marching;
We shall hunger, we shall thirst.
Our hearts are wounded with grief,
And no one knows our sadness" (II, i, 8, stanza 6).

25. C. Wright Mills and Hans H. Gerth, *Character and Social Structure* (New York: Harcourt, Brace & World, 1964), pp. 112-29.

26. *Sauptika-parva*, xxv.

27. *Santi-parva*, xxv.

28. *Maya* is a Sanskrit word with the verbal root *ma*, "to measure, measure out, to form, to build." It denotes the power of a demon to produce illusory effects, "magic," and finally, the illusion superimposed upon reality as a consequence of ignorance.

29. Huizinga, *Homo Ludens*, pp. 35-36.

30. Ibid.

31. Josef Pieper, *Leisure the Basis of Culture*, trans. by Alexander Dru (New York: Random House, 1963).

32. M. M. Postan, "The Costs of the Hundred Years' War," *Past and Present* 27 (1964): 42-43. For striking photographs of comparable outfits, see Robert Laffont, *The Ancient Art of Warfare* (Paris: International Book Society, 1974), vol. 1.

33. Byam Nigel Davies, *The Aztecs: A History* (New York: G. P. Putnam's Sons, 1974), pp. 96-100, 164.

34. *Sabha-parva*, lix.

35. Berger, *The Sacred Canopy*, p. 24.

36. Richard Barber, *The Knight and Chivalry* (New York: Charles Scribner's Sons, 1970), p. 196.

"With his left hand he never did sustain

The shield, nor faced he the portended spear,

But with his bow, that weapon of a dastard,

Was still prepared for flight: such arms afford

No proof of courage" (Words of Lykus in *Herakles*

Distracted, quoted in A. T. Hatto, "Archery and

Chivalry," *Modern Language Review* 35 [1940]: 50).

37. In cosmological worlds, the number five became a basis for the principles of life: the five virtues, the five obligations, the five senses, the five colors, the five elements, the five major feast days, and so on. For an excellent analysis of this and related facts, see Joseph Campbell, *The Masks of God*, vol. 1, *Primitive Mythology* (New York: Viking Press, 1970), pp. 144-50; *The Masks of God*, vol. 2, *Oriental Mythology*, pp. 103-44.

38. T. F. Wade, "The Army of the Chinese Empire . . . ," *Chinese Repository* 20 (1851): 252-53 and Norman LaForce, "Chinese Classical Warfare," *Moves: Conflict Theory and Technique* (December 1972), p. 10.

39. On the eve of an armed engagement with Arab invaders, Rai, the Hindu King of Alor asked his house astrologer,

"I must fight today; tell me in what part of the heavens the planet Venus is and calculate which of the two armies shall be successful and what will be the result." The astrologer replied, "according to the calculations the victory shall be to the Arab enemy because Venus is behind him and in front of you." Rai was angry on hearing this. The astrologer said, "be not angered, but order an image of Venus to be prepared in gold." It was made and fastened to his saddle straps in order that Venus might be behind him and he might be victorious (Henry M. Elliot, *The History of India as Told by its Own Historians*, ed. by John Dowson [London: n.p., 1877], vol. 1, p. 169).

40. Campbell, *The Masks of God*, vol. 1, pp. 457-60.

41. *Florentine Codex*, trans. from Nahuatl by A. J. O. Anderson and Charles E. Dibble (Sante Fe: Monographs of the School of American Research; Salt Lake City: University of Utah Press, 1952), vol. 12, pp. 5-15. Davies, *The Aztecs*, pp. 258-59, questions the veracity of this story.

HUITZILOPOCHTLI'S FEAST: SACRAMENTAL WARFARE IN ANCIENT MEXICO

3

It is often true that the less a person knows of history, the more confidently he speaks of similarities between civilizations. As a consequence, sweeping historical analogies usually deserve the rebuke they suffer. It is thus with caution and reticence that we suggest several remarkable parallels in the social evolution of the Fertile Crescent of the Tigris and Euphrates rivers around 3000 B.C. and the valley of central Mexico approximately three millennia later.

Both Sumeria and Teotihuacán were originally ruled by priests whose arcane knowledge of writing and calendry and their monopoly over fertility rites provided them with sufficient leverage to seize the surplus product of wheat or maize.[1] But in the mountains and highlands surrounding these largely pacific peasant villages there resided nomadic peoples, the Semitic-speaking Akkadian tribes in Sumeria and those of the Nahuatl language group in Mexico. Stone fragments depict these tribes as terrifying Others who resided beyond what the city dwellers considered the pale of civilization. The Mexicans derisively called those living in caves and clothed in skins, subsisting on wild fruit and animals, *Chichimecs*, of the "lineage of the dog."[2]

Exactly how the Semites and the Chichimecs came to dominate those who farmed the lush alluvial plains, whether through outright military conquest or through a more complex process of usurpation, is not important to determine here.[3] The crucial point is that their political and religious ascendancy found expression in a characteristic mythological legend, that is, of a male god (the sun) represented by an eagle, defeating the consuming mother (black chaos) in an epic battle, and creating the world and man from her remains (cf., the *Enuma elish*). In Aztec Mexico the chief character of this mythic drama, the symbol so to speak of the banishment of anomie from existence, was called Huitzilopochtli. The *Florentine Codex* tells of his miraculous birth from Coatlicue, the Earth Mother. Sweeping one day, she came upon a ball of feathers which she picked up and hid in her bosom—"At that moment Coatlicue was with child." Insulted by the rumor that their mother was an adulteress, her sons and daughters, the heavenly bodies of night, conspired to kill her. But Huitzilopochtli overheard the plot. While still in the womb he comforted his mother saying, "I know what I must do." At the very moment that the powers of Darkness were about to destroy the earth, Huitzilopochtli issued from it (her). Taking his spear thrower and sacred fire-arrow in hand, he beheaded the female anti-god Coyolxauhqui in single combat, chased the "unnumbered ones" from the north and south heavens to the abode of death, and established the reign of light.[4]

Huitzilin ("humming bird") *opochtli* ("of the south") was originally a fisherman's god closely connected with Tlaloc, the Mexican water god. Indications are that at the beginning of their migration from the legendary "seven caves," each of the several clans comprising the Aztec nation had its own deity, just one of them worshipping Huitzilopochtli. At Coatepec around A.D. 1170, however, Huitzilopochtli's supporters won an intratribal dispute, and he was elevated in stature from a minor earth deity to lord of the sky and general Aztec patron.[5] His color, originally the blue of rainwater, now came to represent the summer sky.

The Aztecs were the last Chichimec migratory group to arrive in the valley where Mexico City is now located, and naturally were at first viewed as outsiders and accorded a subservient pariah status by their long established neighbors. Within a short period of time, however, reckoned by historians to be about A.D. 1400, they had thrown off the bonds of dependency and begun to assert themselves militarily. It was then that intellectuals within the community began to see Aztec history as a continuation of Toltec tradition, and urged adoption of the customary Toltec form of sacramental warfare. (Toltec civilization had flourished from ca. A.D. 950-1150 in the same area.) In the end, the Aztecs not only abandoned the bow and arrow, emblematic of their earlier life as rude scavengers, appropriating the dart thrower (*atlatl*) and the obsidian-bladed club (*macana*) into their own arsenal,[6] but their national god, Huitzilop-ochtli, took upon himself all the characteristics of the ancient Toltec divinity known as the Black Tezcatlipoca.

According to myth, the Black Tezcatlipoca had shamed the pre-eminent Toltec god, Quetzalcoatl, into exile first by getting him drunk and then deceitfully encouraging him to have sex with his own sister, thus breaking two of the most honored Nahuatl pro-scriptions. His (and now Huitzilopochtli's) epic victory, then, like that of Indra's over Vritra, was tainted with a criminal blemish. Founded on an act of mythic treachery, Aztec metaphysics would henceforth be imbued with an overwhelming pessimism for the future of the world, a fact which we have already observed was capitalized upon by the Spanish.

Quetzalcoatl had been a benevolent god, protector of wisdom and art, and inventor of calendry. His element, water, represented his intimate association with maize and fecundity. The Black Tezcatlipoca, on the other hand, was a monstrous warrior. And now Huitzilopochtli, like him, had become patron of military vio-lence. Lord of cold and ice, whose fetish is an obsidian knife, the Black Tezcatlipoca was said to be the rapist of Tlaloc's wife, Xochiquetzal. But he was also popularly known as the sun god whose totem was the solar eagle. Thus, in spite of his ferocity he was also known as the ultimate lord and giver of life.[7]

Each day, according to popular Aztec belief, Huitzilopochtli is reborn from his mother, Coatlicue, to whose womb he returns each night. Each evening, then, the cosmic war between light and dark-ness must be refought, and each dawn is a miracle to be celebrated joyously. But it is also to be vigorously worked for and coaxed into being. For if Huitzilopochtli is to presevere against the awesome-ness of night, he needs the nourishment of his favorite nectar, *chal-chihuatl*, human blood. This, then, was the vocation of the Aztec nation, to feed their god *chalchihuatl* in the form of fresh human hearts for the benefit of man and the maintenance of the world.[8]

It is to this calling and the institution that grew from it, the *xochi-yaoyotl* as it was called in Nahuatl, the "flowery war" (from *xochi* = flower + *yaotl* = war), that we now turn our attention. For present purposes the important fact to note concerning the *xochiyaoyotl* is that although it was a type of combat, it was even more a religious ritual. Thus, every step in its enactment, from the formal declaration of hostilities to the final consecration and sacrifice of captives, was rigidly circumscribed by rules. In order to expedite our presentation, we will trace an idealized flowery war from start to finish, concluding with an attempt to understand its meaning from the viewpoints of its celebrants.

THE FLOWERY WAR

The *Codex Ramirez* tells of a council of war among the Coyoacan, a Nahuatl people, concerning the most feasible manner to deal with Aztec depredations against them:

Some suggested that they invite the Mexicans to a feast and during the meal fall upon them unaware and kill them. To this the lord of Coyuhuacan answered: "That would be a most dastardly act, appropriate for common and low people," for not for a moment should anyone think of such a treasonable and evil act, because they would then assuredly be regarded as cowards and the neighboring nations would be offended.[9]

Public worship is formally announced among most peoples, and as this episode suggests, this was the case for the Nahuatl nations with their flowery wars. Custom required that any invitation to the enemy to join in the *xochiyaoyotl* be publicized by a diplomatic mission consisting of four persons, each holding in his right hand an arrow by the head with the feathers pointed upward, and in the left a small shield. The diplomats would communicate the intention to attack if the party which received their visit refused them tribute. This was done by anointing the enemy ruler's arms with white chalk, symbolizing his impending death, then sportingly placing upon him a feathered headdress, and putting into each of his hands a club and shield.[10] It is significant that even Cortés who was otherwise distinguished for his treachery, sent a taffeta hat, a sword, and a crossbow to Tlaxcala warning of the existing state of war between them and the Spanish.[11]

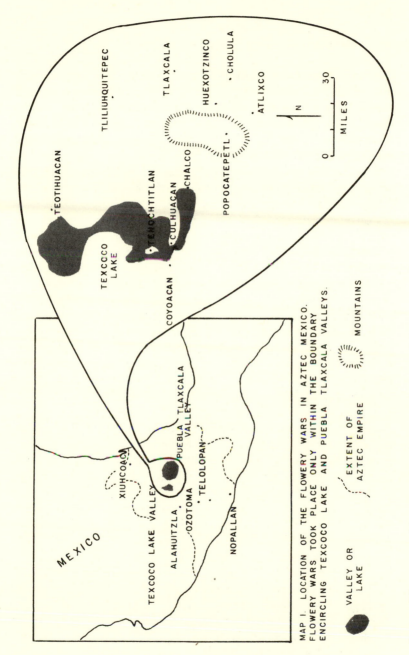

MAP I. LOCATION OF THE FLOWERY WARS IN AZTEC MEXICO.
FLOWERY WARS TOOK PLACE ONLY WITHIN THE BOUNDARY
ENCIRCLING TEXCOCO LAKE AND PUEBLA TLAXCALA VALLEYS.

VALLEY OR
LAKE

EXTENT OF
AZTEC EMPIRE

MOUNTAINS

Source: Map prepared by the author.

Ideally, three lunar months of twenty days each would follow this declaration, with the exact day of battle determined by the calculations of priests and astrologers who, although from warring cities, often worked together in this regard. Byam Nigel Davies reports one engagement in 1444 between Chalco and Tenochtitlan, the Aztec capital, where priests from the former nation pleaded with and received a five-day truce from the latter so that the final battle could be fought on the feast day of their war god, Camaxtli. Chalco wanted fresh prisoners for Camaxtli's sacrifices.[12]

Convention decreed that the arrival of diplomatic missions even with hostile intentions be immune from harm. Once the declaration of war had been issued, however, its members were fair game. Interesting stories are told of emissaries barely escaping death at the hands of enraged enemies,[13] or more often failing to do so. Montezuma I's ambassadors were suffocated to death in Cotaxtla in 1461 by means of smoking chilies, their bodies stuffed with straw, and then dressed in robes. Cotaxtla leaders perversely prostrated themselves before the effigies, communicating their contempt for the Aztecs.[14] Perhaps as a result of such manifest hazards, rulers often found it easier simply to send the required club, feathers, and shield by neutral courier.[15]

At this point it might be asked what caused Mexican elites to extend "invitations" to potential enemies to pay them tribute, requests which, by the way, were generally posed in such demeaning language that only rulers with absolutely no pride could reasonably accept.[16] A cursory examination of the accounts of Aztec history by such as Diego de Duran or Fernando Tezozomoc leaves one with the impression that all Aztec military campaigns were provoked by the insults and wrongs of enemy cities. Yet a closer analysis reveals that most of these incidents were either provoked by the Aztecs themselves or simply manufactured fictions: A group of Aztec women fetching water is insulted by the young men of a neighboring city and so Tenochtitlan declares war on that city. Or, people in a village refuse to give adequate service to the culinary and sexual demands of a passing Aztec column; thus its leaders are presented the shield and club by an Aztec delegation. The residents of Tlatelolco insult Tenochtitlan's public morals by parading its women nude in front of the city walls.[17] And in an almost inconceivable incident an Aztec king betroths a Culhua princess and invites her father to celebrate the wedding. Meanwhile, the princess is beheaded by her suitor, and her skin flayed from her body and donned by a priest. On the happy day the unsuspecting father is invited to view the bride. When approaching her with gifts, he discovers the grotesque parody and is suddenly overcome by nausea. In a frenzy he declares war on the Aztec community which is now justified in defending itself from aggression.[18] It is perhaps understandable why around 1450 Tlacaélel, the Aztec prime minister, proposed to the council of nobles to do away with such cumbersome contrivances altogether and simply declare once and for all that a state of perpetual flowery war exists between Tenochtitlan and selected cities in the Puebla-Tlaxcala Valley:

Because our god doesn't need an occasion of some insult to go to war, he finds himself a convenient market which will welcome our god with his army to buy victims and people to eat. And quite as in the mouth of a *comal* (cooking pot) he finds his warm tortillas when he wants and has desire to eat. And our people and armies come to these fairs to buy with their blood and with their heads and hearts and life the precious stones, emeralds and rubies, . . . for the service of admirable Huitzilopochtli.

This *tianguis* (market), . . . may be in Tlaxcala and Huexotzinco and in Cholula and in Atlixco and in Tliliuhquitepec and in Tecoac. Because, if we put it farther . . . those lands are very distant and the flesh of those barbarians are not pleasant to our god; he considers them brown and hard bread, tasteless and out of season, because, as I say they are of a strange language and are barbarian. . . . [However, in the six other cities named] our god will have warm bread which has just come out of the oven, soft and tasty . . . [the] victims will come warm and bubbling.[19]

The battle has been formally announced, and the two armies have arrived at the altar, the *yaotlalli*, the ground where the flowery war will be celebrated. The morning of the day determined by diviners to be propitious for securing a rich harvest of *chalchihuatl* has arrived. Spies from the respective armies have already reconnoitered the foe and calculated its size and strength. Finally, the young men have donned their battle regalia, a narrow loincloth called the *maxtlatl*, a small round shield worn on the left arm made of netted cane interwoven with cotton and covered with boards, and a sleeveless jacket worn under a cotton frock (*ichhuipilli*), which is adorned with splendid quetzal feathers and jewels.[20]

The warriors have been arrayed for battle. The vast majority are grouped on a clan basis fighting under their clan totems, just as Tenochtitlan is divided administratively into four quarters (*calpulli*) on a kinship basis. Each *calpulli* has its *teocalli* or "house of god," its own military barracks and academy (*telpochcalli*), and its own armory or "house of darts" (*tlacochcalo*). The male children of all free commoners are required to live in the *telpochcalli* from the ages of fifteen to twenty-two to learn the rudiments of religion and the art of war. Upon entry their heads are shaved but for a single lock (*piochtli*) around the nape of the neck. Heading the array of common conscripts are various ranks of captains, distinguished from their inferiors by having their hair bound up behind in red leather. They exhibit dazzling lip plugs and green stone pendants in their noses, and their legs and arms are ringed with golden bracelets and anklets. They carry small drums with which to communicate orders to their men.[21]

Two groups of warriors do not fit the standard array. First are the small numbers of berserks who, naked and unarmed but for a net, will seek to ensnare an unwary foe. A member of this honorary fraternity is designated by the name "master of cuts" (*tlacatec-catl*).[22] Other groups of braves are adorned with the heads of jaguars, ocelots, and eagles, signifying their membership in one of the several military orders. Entry into them is based solely upon courage in battle as demonstrated by the unaided capture of at least three prisoners. The Ocelot and Jaguar warriors ("beasts of prey") are, as their titles indicate, employed as scouts, in ambushes, and in flanking movements. The Eagles will administer the final shock to the enemy.[23] For these men is reserved the unique honor of having their own *piochtli* shaved off.[24]

The priests blow on conch shells and strike war drums to signal the beginning of the attack, and the masses of warriors converge on each other with whistles, screams, and war whoops. At first contact, hostilities take the form of an exchange of defiant epithets and challenges, along with barrages of missiles, pebbles, darts, and arrows. Several scores of braves tentatively advance and suddenly retreat, stop short, and continue their advance. Finally, the fight comes to close quarters and the melee is on. It consists of a series of personal combats between braves brandishing *macana* (war clubs) with razor-sharp obsidian blades.

[The *macana*] was tied to the wrist in order that dropping it they might seize an enemy . . . without losing the weapon. They had no style of fencing, neither did they charge directly, but skirmished and rushed back and forth. At first one party would turn to flee, as it seemed, the other pursuing, killing and wounding and capturing all those lagging in the rear. Then the party fleeing would suddenly turn back on the pursuers which fled in turn. Thus they proceeded as in a tournament, until they were tired, when fresh new bodies moved up to take up the fight.[25]

There are few organized tactics beyond the simple ambush, which apparently was employed so extensively throughout Mexico as to be considered a ritual expectation in its own right, a fact that was to spell disaster for the Aztecs during the Spanish invasion.[26] At a prearranged signal, the troops flee in feigned terror from the field. Ocelot warriors, meanwhile, have concealed themselves in pits or foliage behind the lines to pounce on the pursuing army as it passes, and the individuals are crippled and captured, but not killed. For above all, the object of the flowery war is not to slay the enemy, but to seize him alive so that his precious tuna flower, his heart, can be fed later to the gods. Ideally, the foeman is only stunned by a blow from a rock or club. And as he stumbles he is dragged away to be tied with leather thongs and to await transport to the prison camp. Thus, in spite of the ferocious masks and the howling and shrieking, those enacting the *xochiyaoyotl* show remarkable restraint so as not to harm the opponent more than necessary.[27] The only exception to this is the first unblemished captive whose heart is removed on the battlefield as an offering to the war god Yaotl to insure success in battle that day.[28] Warriors tainted with serious injuries, naturally, are not acceptable sacrificial victims, so their throats are slit and ears taken as trophies. Other than this, adherence to the obligation to treat the enemy with care was such that even the man who nearly killed the Aztec emperor Axayacatl was not himself killed in revenge, but honored as a captive.[29]

There is an ironically playful interaction between the captor and his prey in the *xochiyaoyotl*. It is a point of honor not to escape the ultimately horrible destiny awaiting the prisoner. So well engrained is he with this idea that he will later be allowed freedom of movement outside the prison barracks.[30] Only one who is not truly a "son of the sun" would take advantage of the situation to deny the gods their rightful feast. In the military academy legends had been passed on of the womanly Moquiuix who committed suicide to avoid capture and of the heroic Mixcoatl who, even after he had killed several opponents in gladiatoral combat (to be described below) and had earned his freedom, insisted on having his heart given to the gods.[31] On the other hand, the captor takes a personal interest in his prey, whom he will care for and fatten for the feast day. Presumably when he makes his capture, the brave seals this covenant with the words, "He is as my beloved son." His prisoner supposedly replies, "He is my beloved father." These are the same words the captor will ritually utter when, during the second month of the lunar calendar, at the height of the feast of Xipe Totec, he refuses the cooked flesh of his victim saying, "Shall I, then, eat my own flesh?"[32]

Capture, not killing, is the object of the flowery war, and only new recruits are allowed to achieve this with the aid of others. And only those who succeed in this harrowing task are granted the honors and privileges cited above. Understandably with the pressure placed upon each individual to capture his foeman, disputes arise over rightful ownership. Thus, a temporary military court is established on the field to adjudicate the claims. If the argument is not resolved, neither man receives rewards and the object of dispute is killed immediately.[33] The remaining captives are secured by leather thongs and wooden collars and led to the capital, to prostrate themselves there before the city god and view the altar where they will meet their fate. In the meantime, negotiations are conducted between victor and vanquished, the latter generally agreeing to pay one year of tribute in advance, thus ending the affair.[34]

THE EXTENT OF THE XOCHIYAOYOTL

It is important to appreciate that not all Aztec military campaigns fit this idealized typification of the *guerra florida*. While the wars against other Nahuatl peoples residing in the valley of Mexico and across the eastern mountains in Puebla-Tlaxcala did seem to conform to this pattern, engagements with the "uncivilized" tribes living in the distant marches followed quite another. As it was for Christian soldiers of the Middle Ages and the Chinese "flowery states," the rules of chivalry circumscribing the sacrament of warfare did not apply outside the Nahuatl world. Thus, we read of surprise attacks without prior announcement by Ahuitzotl in 1490 against the cities of Xiuhcoac and Telolopan, although even there the preponderant idea was to capture not kill.[35] This was not, however, the case with Ahuitzotl's treatment of Alahuitzla and Oxtoma where the adult populations were completely exterminated and the children seized as slaves.[36] Or consider Tezozomoc's description of an evening raid upon Nopallan and Tepatepec: Arriving at midnight, the warriors moved so quietly that they reached the royal house without being observed, counted the entrances and sallies, and ascended the top of the temple. Then the scouts returned to the main temple, reporting upon what they had found. When the morning star arose, "each body moving like a strong wall and with the swiftness of lightning . . . fell upon the settlement and they began to slaughter so furiously that neither old people, nor women, nor children were spared, and they set fire to the houses, also to the temples, so that the place looked like a volcano."[37] The Aztecs were able to justify such atrocities because the hearts of the Nopallanese who worshipped alien gods did not constitute a satisfactory meal for the Nahuatl pantheon. As Tlacaélel had said in his speech to the Aztec nobility, "Those lands are very distant and the flesh of those barbarians are not pleasant to our god; he considers them brown and hard bread, tasteless and out of season. . . ."

Historical evidence allows us to be even more precise than this in locating the exact territory within which the *xochiyaoyotl* was performed. In particular, Tlacaélel's intimation notwithstanding that Tlaxcala, Cholula, Huexotzinco, Tecoac, Atlixco, and Tlⅰliuhquitepec were all to enjoy the rite of flowery war with Tenochtitlan, they in fact did not have identical relationships with the Aztec capital. Tlaxcala and Tenochtitlan were antagonists in a long campaign to obtain *political* domination over one another, not just to nourish their respective gods. The fact that even with superior military resources the Aztecs did not succeed in conquering Tlaxcala, does not justify the inference that they "preserved this small nation in its mountain fastness as a source of food for the gods in time of peace."[38] The extremely high casualty rates in the armed confrontations between the two peoples alone would seem to militate against this conclusion. At any rate, any semblance of flowery war between them was formally ended by Montezuma II in 1504 when Tlaxcala was attacked in earnest, the campaign continuing until the arrival of the Spanish in 1518. The *conquistadores* found Tlaxcala economically stunned by these encounters, harboring a virulent hatred for the Aztecs, and anxious to establish an alliance with Cortés to destroy them.[39] A more likely explanation of the Aztec failure to defeat Tlaxcala is that the inhabitants lived in a formidably fortified military camp and the costs to be incurred by subduing it were greater than the anticipated tribute.

Even at the time of its greatest popularity, the *guerra florida* was confined to a relatively small, precisely demarcated zone. And, perhaps, by 1500 it was beginning to disappear altogether under the onslaught of Aztec brutality and practical politics.[40]

THE MEANING OF THE FLOWERY WAR

We are not interested in the question of the causes of the flowery war.[41] But it would be appropriate to address in more depth the meaning that the flowery war had for its participants. It is insufficient simply to say that the warriors were motivated to keep the world from slipping into eternal darkness and dismiss it at that. After all, people were sacrificed not just to Huitzilopochtli, the god of light and order, but also to Tlaloc, the rain god, and to Xilonen, the maize goddess, among others.

A close examination of the sacrificial rites reveals that the victim actually assumed the person of the god to whom he or she was given. If offered to Xipe Totec, the flayed god of death, he was anointed and painted in red stripes to resemble the god. Or he was painted black and white in recognition of night and day if he was fed to Huitzilopochtli. Or she was adorned in maize cobs and green feathers if she was beheaded for Xilonen. The victim danced and sang as the god himself had and was paid obeisance and granted the god's privileges by the community. The most striking example concerns the person selected for his beauty to impersonate the White Tezcatlipoca. For a year he was given concubines, tended, and worshipped until the day he was ritually martyred.[42] Indeed, it is the very fact of ritual imitation of a divine personage that explains the often enthusiastic participation of the victims in their own deaths. Thus, as he mounted the steps of the temple, the victim could presumably be heard to shout, "already here I come! You will speak of me in my home land."[43]

There is no reason to believe that all the actors were so taken in by the role they were required to play as this quote from the *Florentine Codex* suggests. We may safely assume that for the most part they adopted an attitude of helpless and horrified detachment to the goings-on around them. But the fact that the captive who is killed is playing the role of the god whose fiesta is being celebrated that month allows us to understand the meaning of the sacrifices in the first place. In ancient Mexico as in other primitive societies found in Indonesia, Oceania, or India, the basic mythological theme was an expression often in highly concrete imagery, of the awesome life-death cycle of the plant world, of the paradoxical monstrosity and yet benevolence of nature. Wherever man harvests and plants for his nourishment, the truth is clearly brought home to him of the interdependence of life and death, their complementarity as phases of a single state of being. Without death, without killing, there is no life. Nor can there be any shedding of blood or burying of flesh or vegetation without its becoming manifest later in life. This provides the nuclear idea of the mythology of the primitive planting peoples, the idea of the eternally dying and resurrected god. In the very act of the god being voluntarily wounded (tortured) and slain, so is life on earth made possible.[44]

In the pre-Homeric myth of Persephone, which typifies this world view, the beautiful maiden descends freely but in dread each

Fall for three months to Hades, that is, to Death, as a consequence of a bargain struck earlier between Zeus her father, and the lord of the underworld. In exchange for this divine death, Hades has promised that for the other nine months of the year Persephone may return to earth and life. In thankfulness, her mother Demeter, goddess of vegetation, has decreed that for those nine months the fields should flower and grain grow for the delight and benefit of men and gods. In the Spring feast of the Thesmophoria, Persephone's sacrifice and resurrection was replayed. The first day commemorated the downgoing (*kathodos*), wherein consecrated effigies, live animals, and, perhaps originally, human beings were thrown into a pit to be consumed by snakes. The second day was given to silent fasting and wailing as worshippers mourned the death of Persephone. On the third day, the maiden, represented by fresh stalks of grain, returned to earth (*anodos*) amid songs of thanksgiving by the joyous congregation.[45]

The continuity of this myth and ritual with those of ancient Mexico is striking. According to one ancient legend, for example, Quetzalcoatl sprinkled blood from his own mutilated penis on the bones left following the cataclysm that ended the last world, his act creating man. For this reason, men are called *macehuales*, "those brought back because of the penance of the gods."[46] In a related story, the gods, it is said, agreed to reproduce the sun to provide man with light and warmth. Nanauatzin, "the Pimply One," daringly threw himself on the cosmic fire. Not to be outdone, the other gods in suit immolated themselves, the fuel of their flesh feeding the sun's fire.[47] Because man also must eat, we read of Xilonen, the corn goddess, whose story is universal throughout pre-Columbian North America. She was beheaded, then flayed of her skin, buried, and her grave carefully tended, so that men could harvest maize from the spot.[48]

It was fitting, therefore, that those honored to reenact the mythology of the ancient Mexican pantheon should in turn give of their flesh and blood that there might be more abundant life. Thus, high priests in Quetzalcoatl's temple mutilated their own penises and pricked themselves with maguey thorns that the ground might be covered with their blood.[49] Thus, captives during the feast of

Tlaxochimco, the god of fire, were thrown alive into a fire, roasted, taken out, and their still-beating hearts were removed.[50] In addition, the prettiest female captive was, during the feast of Xilonen, dressed as a corn cob, beheaded, her flayed skin worn by a priest, and her body returned to the earth as food for maize.[51] "No wonder, we may say, if the Spanish padres thought they recognized in the liturgies of the New World a devil's parody of their own high myth and holy mass of the sacrifice and resurrection."[52]

In popular Nahuatl teachings the divine was said to be everywhere manifest in the world of natural events. However, since this was no doubt forgotten sometimes, and at other times perhaps even denied, it was necessary to impress indelibly its truth on men's minds. The pedagogic rituals employed by the Aztecs for this purpose were far from unreasonable. For what more effective way is there to teach the truth of divine immanence than to have men play, actually *be* the gods, or at any rate be the outwardly visible signs of these deities in the world? What more impressive way is there to be reminded of the love and mercy of these gods than actually to have men mimic their sacrifices in the most grotesque and painful ways? Thus, the captives from the *xochiyaoyotl* were washed and dressed at the appropriate time by their captors and brought before the sacrificial stone, tied to it with a rope, and armed with mock weapons. There they fought and lost to four Eagle and Ocelot warriors in gladiatoral combat to legitimize their presence at Huitzilopochtli's altar. When exhausted, their life fluid was drained and given to God just as He had given His to man at the beginning of time.[53] Finally, what more literal manner is there to convey the paradoxical notion of the divinity of man himself than ceremonially to consume the consecrated flesh of these sacrificed man-gods? During the second lunar month, the flayed bodies of the victims were apportioned to the various tribal temples, and a stew called *tlacatlaolli*, a mixture of tomatoes, peppers, and consecrated human flesh was prepared.[54] The original captor would be offered (and formally refuse the first time) the choice of the flesh. Then he was whitened with chalk, given quetzal feathers, and bedecked as the sun god. For twenty days he donned the skin of the sacrificed man-god, and as appropriate to his temporarily divine status was given tobacco, flowers, and honors. At the conclusion of the month the skin was removed and the victim's thighbone was suspended from a consecrated pole—the pole called, significantly, "of the playing of men." The thighbone was then clothed with paper and a mask of the god, and a fiesta was celebrated in his honor.

By means of the flowery war and the sacrificial feasts with which it culminated, the Aztec Indian re-knew the truth of Nahuatl mythology. And in this way he fulfilled his divine function to save the Mexican world from nothingness. In the playfully correct liturgy of human destruction the cognitive order was sustained in the face of *anomos*.

We must not delude ourselves in thinking that the use of ceremonial mass murder to save the world was (or is) unique to illiterate jungle folk. One of the highest, most mythologically sophisticated civilizations ever to grace this earth was that of the Hindus (ca. A.D. 300-1000). There also liturgical combat of an equally playful but bloodthirsty sort was consciously employed as a vehicle of cosmic preservation.

NOTES

1. For the best general archaeological history of Mesoamerica, see Michael D. Coe, *Mexico* (New York: Frederick A. Praeger, 1962). For the seminal work on Aztec history in particular, see Byam Nigel Davies, *The Aztecs: A History* (New York: G. P. Putnam's Sons, 1974).

2. Coe, *Mexico*, pp. 132-34.

3. William T. Sanders and Barbara J. Price, *Mesoamerica: The Evolution of a Civilization* (New York: Random House, 1968) seek to apply Wittfogel's theory concerning the rise of "oriental despotism" from control over irrigation to ancient Mexican civilization. Cf. René Millon, "Irrigation at Teotihuacán," *American Antiquity* 20 (No. 2). Coe leans toward the hypothesis that the Chichimecs established their position of rule through invasion and conquest, *Mexico*, pp. 134, 144-45, 152-54.

4. *Florentine Codex*, vol. 3, pp. 3-5. Cf. Miguel León-Portilla, *Aztec Thought and Culture: A Study of the Ancient Nahuatl Mind*, trans. by J. E. Davis (Norman: University of Oklahoma Press, 1963), pp. 42-43.

5. For an original rendition of this evolution in the status of Huitzilopochtli, see "Codex Ramirez," trans. by Paul Radin from Fernando de

Alvarado Tezozomoc, *Cronica Mexico*, "The Sources and Authenticity of the History of the Ancient Mexicans," in *University of California Publications in American Archeology and Ethnology* 17 (1920): 67-74.

6. Just as the Aztecs aped Toltec military arts and ideology, the latter borrowed in turn from Olmec civilization. Located near modern Vera Cruz (ca. 800-400 B.C.), Olmec excavations have revealed monuments of soldiers brandishing war clubs, bas-relief figures of sexually mutilated war captives, and frescoes of snarling Jaguar soldiers with spears (Coe, *Mexico*, pp. 88-96). Coe claims that the Chichimec bow never appeared in the art of civilized Mexico.

7. *Florentine Codex*, II, pp. 46-48.

8. "Codex Ramirez," pp. 67-74. Alphonso Caso, *The Aztecs: People of the Sun*, trans. by Lowell Dunham (Norman: University of Oklahoma Press, 1958), pp. 12-20. León-Portilla, *Aztec Thought and Culture*, pp. 33-38, 47-49, 61.

9. "Codex Ramirez," p. 100.

10. Davies, *The Aztecs*, p. 129. Adolf Bandelier, "Art of War and Mode of Warfare of the Ancient Mexicans," *Peabody Museum of American Archeology and Ethnology*, 10th Annual Report 2 (1877): 129. Although a century old, this is still an important source of information. Bandelier's hypothesis (pp. 127-28) that Aztec society was a "military democracy" has since fallen into disrepute. Cf. Lewis H. Morgan, "Montezuma's Dinner," *North American Review* 122 (April 1876): 265-308. Another helpful if brief article, is found in Robert Laffont, *The Ancient Art of Warfare* (Paris: International Book Society, 1974), vol. 1, pp. 406-15.

11. Bernal Diaz del Castillo, *The Discovery and Conquest of Mexico*, trans. by A. P. Maudslay (New York: Noonday Press, 1966), p. 122. See also Davies, *The Aztecs*, p. 249.

12. Davies, *The Aztecs*, pp. 90-91. According to the Spanish chronicler Juan Bautista Pomar, wars were executed without fail every twenty days, corresponding to the sacred lunar calendar which consisted of eighteen twenty-day months. See Eduardo Noguera, "Las Guerras Floridas," *Mexico Prehispanico: Culturas, Deidades, Monumentos* (1946): 363.

13. "Codex Ramirez," pp. 95-97.

14. Davies, *The Aztecs*, p. 103.

15. Ibid., p. 107.

16. Bandelier, "Art of War," pp. 128, 130.

17. "Codex Ramirez," pp. 101-2. Davies, *The Aztecs*, pp. 96-101.

18. Davies, *The Aztecs*, pp. 33-34.

19. Diego de Duran, *Historia de las Indias de Nueva España e Islal de la*

Tierra Firma, ed. by Angel M. Garibay K., (Mexico City: Editorial Porrua, 1967), vol. 2, pp. 232-33. Cf. "Codex Ramirez," p. 109.

20. Bandelier, "Art of War," pp. 108-12. For illustrations, see *Florentine Codex*, vol. 8, pp. 78-79 and Laffont, *The Ancient Art of Warfare*, vol. 1, p. 407.

21. Bandelier, "Art of War," pp. 119-26.

22. C. A. Burland, *Montezuma: Lord of the Aztecs* (New York: G. P. Putnam Sons, 1973), p. 109.

23. Bandelier, "Art of War," p. 106.

24. Burland, *Montezuma*, pp. 82, 86, 106. Davies, *The Aztecs*, pp. 189-90 and Bandelier, "Art of War," pp. 117-18.

25. Mandieta, *Historia Ecclesiastica Indiana* (Icazbalceta, 1870), Lib. II, cap. XXVI, quoted in Bandelier, "Art of War," p. 138.

26. Each day the Mexicans would sally forth to battle and then retreat to ensnare the Spanish in Tenochtitlan's winding alleys. But Cortés advanced cautiously, filling and guarding each passage, and leveling the buildings along the streets. In time, using the Mexican's own ritual tactic against them, the Spanish drove the defenders into a small space where, dying of thirst and hunger, they surrendered. "In this manner the favorite Mexican tactics of decoy and ambush were gradually overcome step by step, with little loss of life. Their treacherous sallies were not only not dreaded, they were desired, since each of them procured a new basis to the assailants, who thus reached, from three sides, the entrance to the pueblo" (Bandelier, "Art of War," p. 159).

27. Diaz del Castillo, *The Discovery and Conquest of Mexico*, pp. 124-26. "Codex Ramirez," pp. 102-3. Davies, *The Aztecs*, pp. 105, 140-41. Burland, *Montezuma*, pp. 73, 80-81, 106.

28. *Florentine Codex*, vol. 8, p. 53.

29. Davies, *The Aztecs*, p. 141.

30. Burland, *Montezuma*, p. 94.

31. For these two legends, see respectively, Burland, *Montezuma*, pp. 37, 61 and Caso, *The Aztecs*, . 59.

32. *Florentine Codex*, vol. 2, pp. 52-53.

33. Ibid., vol. 8, pp. 51-53, 83-86.

34. Bandelier, "Art of War," p. 140.

35. Davies, *The Aztecs*, pp. 164-65.

36. Ibid., pp. 174-76.

37. Fernando de Alvarado Tezozomoc, *Cronica Mexicana*, IX, *Kingsborough's Antiquities of Mexico*, cap. LXXXIV, p. 148, quoted in Bandelier, "Art of War," p. 142.

38. Burland, *Montezuma*, p. 83.

39. For clear statements of Tlaxcala hatred for the Aztecs, see Diaz, *Discovery and Conquest of Mexico*, pp. 119, 123, 142, 145, 156, and 16. For similar feelings of the Aztecs toward Tlaxcala, see pp. 162-63 and 170.

40. Byam Nigel Davies, *Los Senorios Independientes del Imperio Azteca* (Mexico City: Instituto Nacional de Anthropologiae Historia, 1968), p. 150. For a clear statement of the exact extent of the *guerra florida*, see pp. 139-49. Cf. Davies, *The Aztecs*, pp. 229-32 and Bandelier, "Art of War," pp. 140-41.

41. The reader interested in one theory concerning the cause of the *xochiyaoyotl* may wish to consult Michael Harner, "The Ecological Basis for Aztec Sacrifice," *American Ethnologist* 4 (February 1977): 117-35.

42. *Florentine Codex*, vol. 2, pp. 64-68.

43. Ibid., p. 47. Cf. Davies, *The Aztecs*, pp. 168-73.

44. Campbell, *The Masks of God*, vol. 1, pp. 135-225.

45. Ibid., pp. 183-90.

46. León-Portilla, *Aztec Thought and Culture*, p. 111.

47. Ibid., pp. 38-45.

48. Campbell, *The Masks of God*, vol. 1, pp. 224-25.

49. Burland, *Montezuma*, p. 83.

50. *Florentine Codex*, vol. 2, pp. 104-8.

51. Ibid., pp. 96-100. Cf. Campbell, *The Masks of God*, vol. 1, pp. 222-24.

52. Campbell, *The Masks of God*, vol. 1, pp. 224. Cf. Charles S. Braden, *Religious Aspects of the Conquest of Mexico* (New York: AMS Press, 1966 [1930]).

53. *Florentine Codex*, vol. 2, pp. 48-52.

54. Diaz del Castillo, *The Discovery and Conquest of Mexico*, pp. 229, 236-38.

THE *DHARMA* OF THE *KSHATRIYA*: THE CELEBRATION OF MILITARY VIOLENCE IN HINDUISM

As Semitic-speaking nomads descended upon the farming communities of Sumer another migration occurred that was even more significant for the world's religious history, the movement of Indo-Aryan peoples (ca. 2000-600 B.C.) throughout Europe, the Northern Middle East, and India.[1] They called themselves "Aryas," the name of the ancient Persians which survives to this day in the names "Iran" and "Ireland"; they were the direct ancestors of the Greeks, Latins, Teutons, and Hittites as well. Their mythologies, as reflected in *Beowulf*, the *Iliad,* the *Niebelungenleid*, and the Rig Veda, were consistent with the violent life of war-loving tribespeoples. Typically, the dominant figure was a male war god— Wodan, Zeus, or Indra for example—residing in the sky, who fought a last battle with a feminine archrival who was herself attended by a male consort. Following this god's victory over the forces of Darkness, he created the world and man from the stuff of the anti-god. Man, constituted of a substance other than this god, was estranged from the divine. Heroically but futilely, he struggled to find release from this sad condition.[2]

The social organization of the Indo-Aryans reflected their nomadic origins. Each tribe was headed by a military chieftain, variously called *rajan* (Sanskrit), *rex* (Latin), or *rig-yo* (Celt).[3] He seemed to have held his position by virtue of an election by a consociation of freemen known in Hindu mythology as a *samiti* or assembly. In the Rig Veda the term employed to designate a member of this body is *kshatra* or nobleman. It is from this term that the

Sanskrit word for warrior, *kshatriya*, evolved.[4] The *kshatriyas* comprise one of the four major castes in Hindu law, claiming a monopoly over the legitimate means of violence in the civilized world.

Attached to every Indo-Aryan military fraternity were shamans or priests. Their responsibility was to advise the high council concerning decisions affecting the tribe and to propitiate the gods for the benefit of the community. This seems to have been the source of the *brahmana* in India, the second of the four basic social groupings. Originally claiming, through utterances of the once secret formulas of the Rig Veda, an ability to manipulate local deities, the *brahmana* evolved into a closed caste of literati, the chief carriers of Indian intellectual culture.

With the development of patrimonial states out of the original tribal republics, the *kshatriyas* began losing their predominant position to royal administrators who were generally drawn from the *brahmana* caste. As the power position of the literati increased so did their pretensions—a situation that was not unique to India, as an examination of both Chinese and European Christian histories show. One consequence of this development was a systematic attempt to reinterpret military actions in sacred terms, to circumscribe the dealing in human blood with ritual proscriptions. This effort eventually found a prominent place in the major Hindu literatures; the Epics (including the Mahabharata and the Ramayana), the Puranas, and finally and most importantly, in the *dharma-shastras* or sacred lawbooks. Our intention in the following pages is to depict in some detail the classic Hindu idea of sacramental warfare.

THE GLORY OF RIGHTEOUS CONQUEST

The seeming appeal of Gandhi's program of nonviolent resistance for the Indian masses is commonly explained by invoking a supposed Hindu tradition of *ahimsa* or noninjury.[5] But in Hinduism, as opposed to Buddhism, *ahimsa* was a binding obligation only for particular castes. For the *kshatriya*, the ideal life anciently was held to be *dig-vijaya*, the conquest of regions. As it is brusquely stated in

The Laws of Manu: Yodha-dharma sanatanah, "War is the eternal law of kings."[6] "Like a snake swallowing up mice," says Usana "the earth swallows the king who refuses to fight. . . ."[7]

Like a fisherman who becometh prosperous by catching and killing fish, a king can never grow prosperous without tearing the vitals of his enemy and without performing other violent deeds. The might of thy foe as represented by his armed force, should be completely destroyed, by ploughing it up (like weeds) and mowing it down or otherwise afflicting it by disease, starvation and want of drink.[8]

In Hinduism, the confessor gains merit by performing various sacrificial austerities. Ancient teachings hold that he who does not shrink from battle, but kills and dies with concern for neither victory nor defeat, performs at once all four of the major austerities. Accordingly, he can look forward after his violent death to a beatific life in that heaven universally peculiar to warriors, populated by willing perpetual virgins:

> The men their lives who bravely yield
> To death upon the battlefield,
> Their fleeting pangs and suffering o'er,
> All straight to heavenly mansions soar.
> There nymphs divine these heroes meet,
> With witching smiles and accents sweet,
> Run up and cry in emulous strife,
> "Make me," "nay me," "nay me," "thy wife."[9]

Little wonder that with such promises as these the religious *kshatriya* sought death in battle soon after the birth of his son's son, lest he succumb peacefully in bed. "Death on a bed of repose, after ejecting phlegm and urine and uttering piteous cries, is sinful for a *kshatriya*. . . . The death of a *kshatriya*, O sire, at home is not praiseworthy. . . . Surrounded by kinsmen and slaughtering his foes in battle, a *kshatriya* should die at the edge of keen weapons."[10]

Notwithstanding these bloodthirsty injunctions, ideally the conduct of the Hindu military campaign was subject to stringent constraints. If the conquest of regions was the paramount duty of the Hindu knight, it was equally essential that this be done in a manner consistent with *dharma*. One must not ". . . attempt to gain the earth unrighteously, for who reveres the king who wins unrighteous victory?" asks Manu. "Unrighteous conquest is impermanent and does not lead to heaven."[11]

As to what righteous conquest entails, the Epics and *dharma-shastras* are explicit. In the first place, there must be an appropriate cause for attacking a neighbor. It is unnecessary to exhaust all the proper occasions for embarking on a righteous campaign, such as the royal consecration or the ritual of royal rejuvenation. Let us consider only the pageant-filled Horse Sacrifice (*asva-medha*), a public reassurance that the king, the *dharmaraja*, enjoys supreme power over the earth which, as a consequence, is guaranteed against anomie. From the royal stables an unblemished stallion is chosen to stand for Varuna, the Vedic god of law and order, "who after His decree o'er spread darkness with a robe of light." The stallion is first consecrated and tied to a post and then bathed in a stream. This is followed by the ritual killing of a dog by the son of a temple prostitute (who, it is taught, symbolizes the power of sex, and thus life over death). The horse is then released in the company of one hundred mares with the challenge: "Let Varuna advance against anyone who would presume to attack this steed." For one year the stallion runs at will followed by various ranks of soldiers. As he crosses the borders of neighboring kingdoms their regents are invited either to pay homage and tribute to his owner, the defender of moral order, or to take up arms and challenge the King's pretensions to rule the world. Refusal to pay tribute means holy war, a ritual reenactment of the cosmic struggle between the forces of order and the powers of darkness.[12]

All aspects of *dharma dig-vijaya* are governed by sacred law, from the collection and distribution of booty,[13] to the proper times for undertaking a march: "in the fine month of Maragarisha or towards the months of Phalunga and Kaitra," that is, during Spring or Autumn. These are times of harvest and plentiful water without the roads fouled with mud or the temperature too extreme.[14] Exceptions may be made in the case of neighbors suffering distress.

Here ancient law teaches that "when he has a certain prospect of victory or when a disaster has fallen his foe, he may advance to attack him."[15] Still, it is deemed crucial to consult astrologers (*naimittakas*) to determine the auspicious moment for departure of an expedition.[16]

Furthermore, before embarking upon a campaign the king is expected to engage in certain rites, both to insure that he does not accumulate unwanted karmic matter in the forthcoming slaughter and to guarantee that the enterprise will be successful. Both ends are served by first bathing in consecrated water ("It is ordained that kings at once become pure [by bathing] when they have done acts causing death.")[17] and then, after offering devotions to the relevant deities, bestowing precious baubles, cows, and other gifts upon the attendant *brahmana*. For it is also written that he who gives pleasure to the gods through sacrifice and to the "human gods" (the learned priests) with fees is rewarded with the beatitudes of heaven.[18]

Both the ritually correct manner of the *raja* moving his "fourfold army" (including elephants, horses, chariots, and infantry) and the proper manner of encampment (in the "lotus shape") are laid down in the law books.[19] Camp should be established in a place chosen only after consultation with auguries and only after care has been taken to "avoid cemeteries, temples, and compounds consecrated to the deities, asylums of sages, shrines, and other sacred spots."[20] Indeed, although we may be skeptical of adherence to this dictum, even the size of the righteous host was required to meet certain standards so as to give it an eye-pleasing symmetry, if not an outright sacred significance.[21] In addition, the *dharmashastras*, apparently owing to Persian influence, prescribed a particular manner of positioning one's troops for battle. In the midst of the vanguard "who are expert in sustaining a charge and in charging, fearless and loyal," sits the commander-in-chief on his elephant.[22] Protecting the van directly in the front is a legion of elephants especially trained to terrorize and trample the opposition. On either side are the infantry and chariot corps, and finally on the wings stand the cavalry.

We come, finally, to the obligations incumbent upon the individual combatants themselves. In essence, for large-scale engagements to comply with sacred law, they must consist of a series of chivalrous duels between knights of equal rank. The *kshatriya* is accordingly forbidden to strike a eunuch, anyone who has climbed upon an eminence, anyone who has joined the palms of his hands in supplication, someone who is fleeing the field with "flying hair," or one who has surrendered with the words, "I am thine."

Nor [can he attack] one who sleeps, . . . one who has lost his coat of mail, . . . one who is naked, . . . one who is disarmed, . . . one who looks on without taking part in the fight, . . . one who is fighting with another (foe), . . . one whose weapons are broken, . . . one afflicted (with sorrow), . . . one who has been grievously wounded, . . . one who is in fear, nor one who has turned to flight, (in all these cases let him remember the duty of honourable warriors).[23]

It is said in ancient scripture that he is no son of the Vrishni race who slays the foe fallen at his feet, for a wounded enemy must not be slain.[24] Rather, he should either be sent home or brought to the victor's camp and there cared for "by skillful surgeons" until that time when cured, he shall be set free. "This is eternal duty," say the Epics and the law books.[25] If by chance he dies while in captivity, he is to be properly buried.[26] An exception to these rules may be made in the case of an "assassin" who employs violence against one legally immune from harm, who fights without proper respect for feudal rank, or who uses unfair weapons.[27] However, it is preferred that "even he that is wicked should be subdued by fair means. It is better to lay down life itself in the observance of righteousness than to win victory by sinful means."[28]

As to the weapons that honorable *kshatriyas* can employ, *The Laws of Manu* are again clear: "When he fights with his foes in battle let him not strike with weapons concealed (in wood) nor with (such as are) barbed, poisoned or the points of which are blazing with fire."[29] Furthermore, he should warn the opponent before loosing an arrow or striking a blow with a call such as "Shoot, for I am shooting at thee,"[30] and he should avoid hitting below the belt. "No limb below the navel should be struck," admonishes Rama. "This is the precept laid down in treatises."[31]

This brings us to an important point. Although the Mahabharata is the source of authority for Hindu international law, it is by no means consistent in its teachings. While it does exalt conformity to the aforementioned restrictions, it also has savants speaking in favor of the lowest forms of deceit and the bloodiest weapons and tactics.[32] This apparent anomaly can be explained in part by noting that much of the dishonorable advice comes from the mouths of such Kuru counselors as Kanika.[33] The Kuru clan, it will be recalled, plays the role of the *asura*, the representative of cosmic evil, in the epic literature. Nonetheless, at least half the treachery in the Mahabharata is committed not by the Kurus but by the seeming defenders of morality, the Pandus. And most of the despicable acts are undertaken upon the recommendation of Lord Krishna himself, the incarnation of Vishnu.[34]

We have already examined the possible esoteric significance of this paradox. Here we need only note that Krishna resorts to highly gymnastic syllogistics to justify treachery on the part of the righteous. His argument is that insofar as "the gods themselves [most notably, Indra] in slaying the *asuras* [in particular, Vritra] have trod the same way, that way, therefore, . . . may be followed by all."[35] In other words, whereas at the beginning of time the Vedic storm god overcame Kali (the she-devil) and her serpent companion through deviousness, likewise in this last Great Battle between good and evil the Pandus may use unfair tactics to preserve the world from chaos. The Hindu legal principle states that in a situation of distress (*apattikala*) where "righteousness is transgressed by all," the *raja* may be permitted the use of any scheme or tack to defend the social order. Otherwise, he is required to fight with fair means.[36]

The holy war which ideally has been large, loud, and colorful, but generally bloodless, is over. And the losers have agreed to pay tribute to the king whose chosen stallion crossed their borders during the preliminary stages of the *asva-medha*. Sacred law holds that in truly righteous conquest, while the defeated regent must pay homage to the victor, he should be allowed to maintain his throne as the victor's vassal. Only demonic conquest, it is taught, entails the establishment of permanent political dominion over the territory that has been "conquered."[37] In this crucial respect the Hindu theory of the universal emperor, the *chakravarti-samrat*, is radically different from the Roman notion of a world monarch who rules all lands from a single throne and unites all peoples under a system of universal law. The *chakravartan* is required to protect the integrity of local customs and language and to promote local political autonomy. Although he is considered a savior of *dharma* and sustainer of the world, in fact he is a promoter of feudalism and of perpetual warfare between petty vassals.[38]

After a year, if all challenges to the chosen stallion, Varuna's representative and symbol of *dharma*, have been met successfully on the field of battle, the king is reaffirmed as *chakravartan* during the completion of the Horse Sacrifice. At this point the horse is killed, and the queen feigns ritual intercourse with the corpse to the accompaniment of explicitly erotic songs and verse.[39] Obviously, this is not a meaningless act of bestiality, for the horse has been transubstantiated into Varuna, or in another sense, into the king himself who, as *dharmaraja*, is sustainer of the cosmos. It is through the power of sex that life and energy are given, and the world itself is ultimately derived. This is the lesson retaught to the celebrants in the feigned act of intercourse. In this case, the stallion (the Law) whose virility has been tested in combat, injects its seed, its potency, into the divine mother (Earth) represented by the empress, resulting in the symbolic recreation of the world. Man is once again secured in the belief that anomie is held in abeyance.

THE PLACE OF RIGHTEOUS CONQUEST IN INDIAN HISTORY

We may justifiably question the degree to which this martial rite, particularly the niceties of chivalry so neatly pictured above, was observed. Historical documents confirm that after the fall of the Buddhist-inspired Mauryan empire in 184 B.C., and certainly by the time of the Gupta dynasty (est. A.D. 380) the *asva-medha* was celebrated widely throughout the Indian subcontinent. Literally scores of petty *rajas*, simultaneously in some cases, were anointed *chakravarti-samrat* (or assumed even more imposing titles such as *tratara* [savior], *rajatiraja* [king of kings], or *devaputra* [son of god]) during the Hindu Golden Age that lasted well into the period of the Arab conquests (ca. A.D. 1200). However, the paucity of reliable evidence makes it virtually impossible to say directly whether or not these reputed "saviors of the world" adhered to the precepts of *dharma dig-vijaya*. The statement by an obscure chronicler named Abhidharma Kosovyakhya—"Philosophers while destroying the opinion of their adversaries must carefully respect the principles of logic . . . just as kings, while destroying the soldiers of their enemies, respect the field labourer who is the common help of both armies"—can hardly be trusted. Philosophy and not accurate record-keeping has been the traditional preoccupation of Hindu cultural elites. Reports of the past have almost without exception been doctored irreparably in an attempt to lend support to the interests of different theological schools. Invariably, brahmanic accounts of wars have been colored in such a way as to demonstrate that observance of *dharma* never fails to be rewarded with victory, while disobedience universally reaps a harvest of military disaster.

There is, however, some consensus among Muslim, Greek, and Chinese travelers who were less likely to view Hindu warmaking in an uncritically favorable light, that *kshatriyas* did in fact fight chivalrously. Megasthenes, the Greek ambassador to the Mauryan empire (ca. 300 B.C.), wrote that "at the very time when a battle was going on, the neighboring cultivators might be seen quietly cultivating their work—perhaps ploughing, gathering in their crops, pruning trees, or reaping the harvest."[40] The Chinese Buddhist Hiuen Tsang writing about a thousand years later, concurred, significantly, because the area about which he was writing, the Deccan, was largely outside the territory of brahmanic influence.

When they have an injury to avenge they never fail to give warning to their enemy, after which each puts on his cuirass and grasps his spear in his hand. In battle they pursue the fugitives but do not slay them who give themselves up. When a general has lost a battle instead of punishing him corporally, they make him wear women's clothes and by that force him to sacrifice his own life.[41]

Admittedly, a handful of reports over many centuries is hardly sufficient to determine the actual conduct of Hindu military campaigns. We are therefore left to make indirect inferences on the basis of other historical facts. As mentioned at the beginning of the chapter, in the years following the Indo-Aryan invasions the *kshatriya* assemblies lost their preeminent positions to the *brahmin* courtiers of the various patrimonial rulers.[42] In reaction to this, disenfranchised knights residing primarily in the Ganges River basin began cultivating an interest in various heterodox confessions, most notably, Buddhism and Jainism. Gautama Siddhartha, reputed to have become the Buddha, was himself the son of a minor dispossessed *kshatriya* prince. The heterodox religions appealed to the disgruntled *kshatriyas* because they repudiated not only brahmanic claims to absolute authority, but also the idea that the Vedas are an infallible source of truth. They also criticized the theory of caste and the notions of kingship and warmaking as liturgical duties.[43]

The sectarians subsequently seized the thrones of several northeastern Indian states between 500 to 300 B.C. But Jainism and Hinayana Buddhism with their strict asceticism and unwillingness to compromise with the pastoral needs of the simple folk for an easily trod and highly objective path to salvation, never completely won the hearts of the Indian masses. Max Weber describes how over the decades unemployed brahmanic magis, confessors, and ecstatics were hired by Jainist and Buddhist monasteries to care for the popular cults of the laity living there as tenants. In time this resulted in the rise of a secular priesthood that eventually replaced monastic Buddhism altogether in India.[44]

As the brahmanic priesthood rose to prominence, a fascinatingly complex process occurred of syncretic adaptation of the Vedas to local cult practices. Vedic gods were mythically married to local fertility goddesses such as Lakshmi, Nila, Bhumi, and Radha. Popular phallic gods such as Shiva, the divine lingam, were elevated to a status superior to the ancient Vedic pantheon to teach and thus legitimize Vedic truths. Finally, local deities such as Narayana, Rama, and later even Buddha himself, were interpreted as avatars or incarnations of the Vedic god Vishnu.[45] The product of this unlikely conglomeration is known today as Hinduism. And it is depicted in all its color and richness in the epic literature from which the *dharmashastras* gain their authority. The eighteen-volume Mahabharata, the "Great Battle of the Bharatas," is the best known of the Epics. Originally a poetic rendition of a feud between two Aryan clans (the Kurus and the Pandus) sung by bards around campfires, it had at least by the time of Christ become overlaid with divine genealogies "proving" that the various "marriages" and incarnations just mentioned did really occur. These genealogies appear randomly intermixed with philosophical and ethical aphorisms and homilies concerning the necessity of obedience to *dharma*.[46]

The greatest book of this collection, a mere excerpt from the *Bhisma-parva*, is the Bhagavad-Gita, "The Song of the Lord," the earliest exposition of the Bhagavata cult which later evolved into a form of Vaishnavism. We shall spend some time with the Gita as it clearly illustrates, like no other document, precisely how, through a remarkable casuistry, the *brahmana* reintegrated warfare into the realm of the sacred, rendering military violence amenable to their control once again.

In the Gita, Vasudeva Krishna, who was originally the god of a powerful northeastern tribe of warriors which the *brahmana* apparently sought as allies, is identified as an avatar of Vishnu. Simultaneously, the violent life-style of Vasudeva Krishna's people is reinterpreted in the context of the esoteric brahmanic practice of *yoga*, becoming a type of *karma yoga*. Military violence, it is taught, if done in the proper frame of mind and with due care can be a means of attaining mystical union with God. (*Karma* action + *yoga* to yoke together one's consciousness with the divine = communion with God through activity.) The airy soteriology of the brahmanic intellectual contained in the Upanishads is thus integrated with the martial arts in just such a way that warriors, who would never countenance the idea of their being inferior to priests, could readily accept.[47] Krishna promises them that if they kill or die with enthusiasm but with no concern either for the fruits of victory or the rewards of heaven, fearless and desireless like the sage, recognizing that relative to God, this world even with its riches and sufferings is an illusion, then they too can obtain ultimate release (*moksha*) from the eternal wheel of reincarnation.

With its fundamental insistence on compassion and *ahimsa* (non-injury), and its belief in the superiority of the contemplative life over that of activity in the world, Buddhism's relationship with the *kshatriyas* was at best uneasy. (As we shall see in our study of Zen Buddhism and the Japanese samurai, however, it is far from impossible to forge an extremely intimate tie between the seemingly divergent demands of love and homicide. Throughout Buddhist history sympathetic prelates have been wonderfully adept at compromising "theological" principle to win more sheep to the fold.) But the Vedas with their blood-exalting hymns of praise to the war god Indra and their unstinting acknowledgment of the necessity of military force in human life seem to have offered fewer impediments for scholarly brahmanic *rishis* and this-worldly *kshatriyas* to reach an accommodation with which both could be happy.

All the same the Bhagavad-Gita is a very significant compromise on the part of the *brahmana* to political activism. It steers a narrow path between the total renunciation (*nivritti*) of the world *à la* monastic Buddhism, and *pravaritti*, mechanical adherence to Vedic ritual. Instead it promotes *sannyasa*, "actionless action," activity that has no end other than itself. "Having abandoned attachment to the fruit of works, ever content, without any kind of dependence, he does nothing though he is ever engaged in work," teaches Krishna (Bhagavad-Gita, 4:20).[48] Such a man is a *yogin*. But the *yogin* who renounces all ends apart from the faithful completion of his duty, who acts without concern for self, is in a strict sense *playing* not working. For play, as we have seen, is activity that is experienced by the actor as an end in itself. The significance of the Bhagavad-Gita and the Mahabharata in general is that, like no other holy book of the major world religions, it glorifies warfare as a form of gruesome play, even more, as a sacrificial banquet: "The flesh of foes constitutes its libations and blood is its liquid offering." Lances, spears, and arrows are the "ladles of the sacrificer," and bows "the large double-mouthed ladles." Swords are the *sphis* or the wooden sticks with which lines are drawn on the sacrificial platform. "Cut, pierce, and other such sounds that are heard in the front ranks of the array, constitute the *samans*" sung by the Vedic chanters "in the abode of death." "That warrior who in battle causes a river of blood to flow . . . the bones of heroes for its sands, blood and flesh for its mire, swords and shields for its rafts, the hair of slain warriors for its floating weeds and moss . . . is said to complete the sacrifice by performing the final ablutions." That warrior whose altar "is strewn with the severed heads of foes and steeds . . . obtains regions of felicity like" those of the gods. He should therefore join in battle "as he does with his wife, with joy." He "whose blood drenches the sacrificial altar already strewn with hair and flesh and bones, certainly succeeds in attaining a high end."[49]

By the time of the Gupta dynasty (A.D 330-445) the Hindu theory of war held sway over the subcontinent. Chandragupta II (A.D. 380-413) himself, the foremost Gupta king, was a devout practitioner of the Bhagavata cult as expounded upon in the Gita, and both he and his heirs assumed the title of *parama-Bhagavata* while claiming to be incarnations of Vishnu. Coins from this period show kings reclining beneath Hindu deities and beneath the White Umbrella, symbol of *dharma*, which they have sworn to uphold in both times of peace and war. In the Golden Age of India as it is now called by Hindu scholars, the Mahabharata and the Ramayana both reached their final form and the legal treatises of which *The Laws of Manu* is the most familiar, were committed to writing.[50]

CONCLUSION

India's capacity to resist foreign invasion decreased simultaneously as Hinduism evolved into the dominant Indian religion. Soon after the establishment of the Shunga dynasty based on Vedic law in 184 B.C., India experienced a series of military setbacks at the hands of the Scythians, Parthians, the Bactrian-Greeks, and the Yueh-chi Mongols, who set up a blur of tribal republics and monarchies from the Indus to the Ganges.[51] The Gupta dynasty offered only short respite from this process, itself overrun in A.D. 470 by Hunnish nomads. From A.D. 600-655 Harsha Siladitya founded another short-lived Hindu empire in Kanouj, but early in the eighth century the Arab adventurer Muhammed ibn-Kasim with 6,000 horses and the same number of camel riders together with 3,000 foot soldiers, plundered northern India. In the subsequent centuries, Islamized Turks and Afghans followed suit from October to February virtually every year, raiding successively each eastern Hindu kingdom, defeating its local *raja*, and either demanding tribute or enthroning a converted viceroy.[52] By 1200 purely Hindu military history had for all intents and purposes ended. Although it would go far beyond our present concerns to examine this phenomenon in any depth, let us conclude this chapter with a discussion of one possible reason for it.

The collective act of ordering existence, of creating reality where before there was nothing, and then maintaining it against chaos universally occupies a preeminent place in the world's great religious myths and rituals. The Babylonian New Year's festival, the Springtime celebration of Yom Kippur, the daily sacrifice in the Catholic mass, and the bloody fiesta of Huitzilopochtli all confirm this. For Hinduism it is also true.

In Hinduism the Bhagavad-Gita teaches that above all each individual must work (or more accurately play) at *lokosamgraha*, preserving this world from anarchy (Bhagavad-Gita, 3:20-24). Regardless of the caste into which a person is born, regardless of the onus of required duties, each person must adhere religiously to *dharma*, as this is what undergirds and sustains the universe (*dhr* = throne or support + *ma* = cosmos; literally, the cosmic illusion). Furthermore, it is taught that the final responsibility for sustaining the world falls upon the king's shoulders, on the back of the *dharmaraja*, the very person of *dharma* itself. Without the *raja's* use of "punishment," relates the lesson, without his embarkation on campaigns of righteous conquest first to establish and then to maintain sacred law, without his fighting justly against the enemies of order, then men would become corrupt. They would fall from the Way; caste lines would become confused; and the stronger would "roast the weak like fish on a spit." The horror of anomie, or to use the Sanskrit term *matsyanyaya*, "the way of the fishes," would replace the world of structure and psychological security.

Nor is this all. The phrase *Aum Tat Sat*, the Bhagavad-Gita continues, represents the three aspects of Atman (Self). *Aum* stands for the supremacy of Atman, *Tat* its universality, and *Sat* its reality. In its *sat* aspect, Atman symbolizes existence. But *sat* also refers to praiseworthy action, observance of *dharma*. Devotion to *dharma* thus implies union with reality. In a strict sense it means to exist

(Bhagavad-Gita 27:23-28). The feminine past participle of *sat* is *sati* (pronounced "suttee"). *Sati*, we may recall, refers to the ritual immolation of the faithful Hindu wife on her husband's funeral pyre. For a Hindu wife "to be," in the fullest sense, entailed paradoxically, among other things, that she annihilate her physical being at the required time.[53] Analogously, if the *kshatriya* (including the king) wished to obtain the status of *satyagrahi*, grasper of truth and of being, he had to fulfill selflessly the duties of his caste, risking his life in chivalrous combat.[54]

In the light of these considerations, religiously devoted kings like Harsha or Prthviraja and Jayacandra were faced with a dilemma as tragic as that experienced by the Mexicans during the Spanish conquest. (All three Indian kings died in battle, the last two around 1194, at Muslim hands.) They could attempt to defeat Allah's warriors by fighting as those warriors did, using any means including treachery. But this would mean not only ignoring the charge they had been given when crowned under the White Umbrella to uphold *dharma* at all costs. More importantly, it would mean excommunicating themselves de facto from the world of men by becoming beasts like their barbarian foe. This is why Megasthenes, the Greek ambassador to the Mauryan court, could say: "In the case of some arts, it is even accounted vicious to carry their study too far, the art of war, for instance."[55] On the other hand, if they chose to persist faithfully in their obedience to sacred law, fighting fearlessly, but honorably and courteously against an enemy who despised battlefield restraint as a form of idolatry, they might preserve the larger world from utter chaos, but at the expense of their own lives and patrimony. Therefore, the choice for Hindu kings when confronting a foreign invader was either to sacrifice themselves to Vishnu, the God who maintains the world, gaining heaven as a reward, as promised in the Gita, or to refuse to immolate themselves to God in order to preserve their own political power, but at the risk of knowing themselves to be less than manly.

Pandu Arjuna who symbolizes all faithful Hindu kings, is faced with the same terrible choice in the Bhagavad-Gita. At first he wavers, yearning, perhaps as all men naturally do, to avoid having to kill and be killed in war. Only after he experiences the horrifying vision of numberless *kshatriyas* on both sides willfully and joyfully dying for the sake of Vishnu and for the sake of *nomos*, does he realize, as did many *dharmarajas* later in turn, what he must do.

NOTES

1. The seminal work on Indian history is *History and Culture of the Indian People*, general editor R. C. Majumdar, 11 vols. (Bombay: Bharatiya Vidya Bhavan, 1951). For the history of the Vedic period, see the first volume of this collection, *The Vedic Age*. For a briefer but excellently written account of this period, see A. L. Basham, *The Wonder That Was India* (London: Sidgwick and Jackson, 1954), pp. 26-43. Max Weber's, *The Religion of India: The Sociology of Hinduism and Buddhism*, trans. and ed. by Hans H. Gerth and Don Martindale (Glencoe, Ill.: Free Press of Glencoe, 1956) is a classic and still very helpful.

2. Dumézil, *The Destiny of the Warrior* parallels in detail the myths of Indra, the Roman warrior-king Tullus Hostilius, Wodan or Odin, and the war gods of other Indo-Aryan peoples.

3. All three terms are derived from the Indo-Aryan *reg*, meaning tribal king.

4. Edward W. Hopkins, in his important study of the Mahabharata claims that *kshatriya* literally means "he who saves from destruction" (from *kshanitoh* = from hurt + *trayate* = saves life). See his *The Social and Military Position of the Ruling Caste in India* (Durga Kund, Varanasi: Bharat-Bharati, 1972 [1889]), p. 58.

5. For a recent thoroughgoing effort to explain this phenomenon, see Joan V. Bondurant, *The Conquest of Violence: The Gandhian Philosophy of Conflict*, rev. ed. (Berkeley: University of California Press, 1971).

6. *The Laws of Manu*, trans. by Georg Bühler (New York: Dover Books, 1969 [1886]), 7:98.

7. *Santi-parva*, lvii: 3. The complete parable reads: "Like a snake that swalloweth up frogs and other creatures living in holes, the earth swalloweth up a king that is peaceful. . . ." (*Sabha-parva*, lv).

8. *Adi-parva*, cxlii.

9. *Indian Antiquities*, X: 92, quoted in P.C. Chakravarti, *The Art of War in Ancient India* (Ramma, Dacca: University of Dacca, n.d.), pp. 183-84, see also pp. 181-82. For comparable admonitions from other holy books, see e.g. *The Laws of Manu*, 7:87-89, 94-95, 102-10, 158-65 and "Baudhayana's Dharmasastra," *Sacred Laws of the Aryas: Part 2 Vasishtha and Baudhyana*, trans. by Georg Bühler, (Delhi: Motilal Banarsidass, 1969 [1882]), *prasna* 1, *adhyana* 10, *kandika* 18, sec. 9.

10. *Santi-parva*, xcvii.

11. Ibid.

12. Campbell, *The Masks of God*, vol. 2, pp. 190-92. See also Vincent A. Smith, *History of India* (London: Grolier Society, Pub., 1906), vol. 2, pp. 182-83.

13. *The Laws of Manu*, 7:96-99.

14. Ibid., 7:182. See also Chakravarti, *The Art of War in Ancient India*, pp. 93-94.

15. *The Laws of Manu*, 7:183. I am unable to reconcile this bit of treacherous advice with the humane restrictions otherwise found in the *Manushastra*.

16. *Santi-parva*, c:26. For a fascinating account of signs of impending victory such as the presence in the field of battle of cranes and swans, fire smoke blowing directly south, rainbows and so on, see ibid., cii.

17. "Vasishtha's Dharmasastra," *Sacred Laws of the Aryas: Part 2 Vasishtha and Baudhyana*, trans. by Georg Bühler (Delhi: Motilal Banarsidass, 1969 [1882]), chapt. 19, sec. 47. See also *Santi-parva*, xcvii.

18. Chakravarti, *The Art of War in Ancient India*, pp. 96-97. See also *Santi-parva*, xcvii. In section cxlii the *kshatriyas* are admonished "to worship the *brahmana* as they are gods. . . . If gratified, the *brahmanas* become like nectar, if enraged they become like poison."

19. *The Laws of Manu*, 7:184-88.

20. *Udyoga-parva*, clii. See also Chakravarti, *The Art of War in Ancient India*, pp. 106-7 and W. S. Armour, "Customs of Warfare in Ancient India," *Transactions of the Grotius Society* 8 (1922): 71-88.

21. The basic combat unit is the *patti*, consisting of one chariot, one elephant, three horses, and five foot soldiers. Three *pattis* comprise a *senamukha*, three of these a *gulma*, three of these a *gana*, and so on through more inclusive units called, respectively, *vahini, prtana, camu,* and *anikini*. Finally, ten of these last make up a field army which includes 21,870 chariots, 21,870 elephants, 65,610 horses, and 109,350 infantry for a grand total of 218,700 (Bimal Kanti Majumdar, *The Military System in Ancient India*, 2nd rev. ed. [Calcutta: Firma K. L. Mukhopadhyay, 1960], p. 40). See p. 48 for estimated sizes of actual Indian hosts at famous battles.

Noting that $2 \times 218,700 = 437,400$, we find a number almost identical to the cosmic cycle of 432,000 years depicted in ancient Sumerian mythology: the period from the first descent of kingship upon the earth to the year of the Flood. And more remarkably still, that number is also congruent to the years of the last age of this world (the Kali Yuga) according to brahmanic calculations, which is exactly one-tenth of the 4,320,000 years of any complete Great Age (Campbell, *The Masks of God*, vol. 2, pp. 115-21).

Whether this is mere coincidence or the result of a conscious attempt by Hindu literati to fashion at least on paper a fighting force which replicates the movements of heavenly bodies awaits further investigation.

22. *The Laws of Manu*, 7:189-94.

23. Ibid., 7:91-93. The *Santi-parva* adds that a *kshatriya* should never attack

> "one that is walking (unprepared) along a road, . . . one engaged in drinking or eating, . . . one that is mad, . . . one that is insane, . . . one that has begun any task without having been able to complete it [particularly, a sacrifice], . . . one skilled in some especial art (as mining, &c), . . . one that is in grief, . . . one that goes out of the camp for procuring forage or fodder, . . . men who set up camps or are camp followers, . . . those that wait at the gates of a king or one of his ministers, . . . those that do menial services, . . . or those that are chiefs of such servants" (c).

For comparable lists, see Baudhayana, *Sacred Laws of the Aryas*, 1:10, 18, 11; *Santi-parva*, xlv, xcv-xcvi, xcviii-xcix, ci-ciii; *Bhishma-parva*, i:26-32, ci-iii:77-78; *Karna-parva*, lxix; *Adi-parva*, cliii, clv.

Many of these immunities are cited in Armour, "Customs of Warfare in Ancient India," pp. 73-76, Chakravarti, *The Art of War in Ancient India*, p. 185, and Majumdar, *The Military System in Ancient India*, pp. 40-42.

24. The *Santi-parva* even goes so far as to say that "an enemy should not be deceived by unfair means. Nor should he be wounded mortally. For if struck mortally, his very life may pass away" (xcv). The translator considers this "unintelligible."

25. Ibid.

26. Armour, "Customs of Warfare in Ancient India," pp. 75-77. The most complete analysis of the rules regarding captives can be found in Hopkins, *The Social and Military Position of the Ruling Caste in India*, pp. 51-52. It is based upon the injunctions reported in the *Vairata-parva*, lxiii, lxvi.

27. Baudhayana, *Sacred Laws of the Ancient Aryas*, 1:11, 18, 13 and Vasishtha, *Sacred Laws of the Ancient Aryas*, 3:15, 17, 18.

28. *Santi-parva*, xcv.

29. *The Laws of Manu*, 7:90. The prophet Baudhayana agrees: "Let him not strike with barbed or poisoned weapons" (*Sacred Laws of the Ancient Aryas*, 1:10, 18, 10). See also Majumdar, *The Military System in Ancient India*, p. 41 and Armour, "Customs of Warfare in Ancient India," p. 73.

30. *Santi-parva*, xcv.

31. *Salya-parva*, vi:6. See Armour, "Customs of Warfare in Ancient India," p. 73.

32. For the clearest examples of Machiavellian advice, see *Santi-parva*, lxix, cii-cv.

33. See, for example, *Adi-parva*, cxlii and *Sauptika-parva*, i-iv.

34. Pandu Arjuna is pursuing Kuru Karna in a chariot when Karna's wheels suddenly become lodged in the mud. He cries to his pursuer:

"Brave warriors that are observant of the practices of the righteous never shoot their weapons at persons with dishevelled hair, . . . at those that have turned their faces from battle, . . . at a brahmana, . . . at him who joins his palms, . . . at him who yields himself up or beggeth for quarter, . . . at one who has put up his weapon, . . . at one whose arrows are exhausted, . . . at one whose armour is displaced, . . . at one whose weapon has fallen off or been broken! Thou art the bravest of men in the world. . . . Thou art well acquainted with the rules of battle. For these reasons, excuse me for a moment, that is, till I extricate my wheel . . . from the Earth" (*Karna-parva*, xc-xci).

Arjuna turns to Krishna imploring him as to the proper course of action. Krishna replies, "Cut off with thy arrow the head of this enemy of thine . . . before he succeeds in getting upon his car." Arjuna dutifully obeys and another Kuru prince is destroyed through immoral means.

For other cases of outright Pandu treachery, see *Sabha-parva*, xx-xxiv; *Bhishma-parva*, cx-cxix; *Drona-parva*, cxlii-cxliii, cxlvi, cxc-cxcii and *Karna-parva*, lxxxiii.

35. *Salya-parva*, lxi.

36. *Santi-parva*, cxxx, xcl-xcli.

37. *The Laws of Manu*, 7:129-35, 201-3. See also Armour, "Customs of Warfare in Ancient India," p. 81 and Chakravarti, *The Art of War in Ancient India*, pp. 187-88.

38. *History and Culture of the Indian People*, vol. 3, pp. ix-x.

39. Campbell, *The Masks of God*, vol. 2, pp. 192-97.

40. The quotations from both Abhidharma and Megasthenes are found in Chakravarti, *The Art of War in Ancient India*, p. 188.

41. This is quoted in Majumdar, *The Military System in Ancient India*, pp. 95-96 presumably from the 1911 edition of *The Life of Hiuen Tsiang*, pp. 146-47. The translation in the 1973 edition reads: "The king is of the *kshatriya* caste, He is fond of military affairs and boasts of his arms. In this country, therefore, the troops and cavalry are carefully equipped and the rules of warfare carefully understood and observed. Whenever a general. . . ." (*The Life of Hiuen Tsiang*, trans. by Samuel Beal [Westport, Conn.: Hyperion Press, 1973 (1911)], pp. 146-47).

42. There are even records of attempts by kings such as Ajutashatru to

exterminate the remnants of the fast-disappearing warrior caste with the aid of vicious mercenaries recruited from wild tribes (*History and Culture of the Indian People*, vol. 2, pp. 32-33).

43. Ibid., pp. 360-62.

44. Weber, *The Religion of India*, pp. 291-93.

45. *History and Culture of the Indian People*, vol. 2, pp. 419-24, 431-41, 456-58, 469-71; vol. 3, pp. 293, 371, 424-25, 440-52. Cf. Weber, *The Religion of India*, pp. 293-328.

46. For an excellent analysis of the sources and significance of the Mahabharata, see B. A. Van Nooten, *The Mahabharata* (New York: Twayne Publishing, 1971), pp. 43-69. See also *History and Culture of the Indian People*, vol. 2, pp. 243-52.

47. Weber's analysis has yet to be superseded; see his *The Religion of India*, pp. 181-88.

48. Again: "He who in action sees inaction and action in inaction-he is wise among men, he is a *yogin*." See also Bhagavad-Gita, 3:1-16, 27-32; 4:14-34.

49. *Santi-parva*, xcviii.

50. For the best coverage of this period, see *History and Culture of the Indian People*, vol. 3, *The Classical Age*.

51. *History and Culture of the Indian People*, vol. 2, pp. 101-35.

52. Jadunath Sarkar, *Military History of India* (New Delhi: Orient Longmans, 1960), pp. 24-31. See also Majumdar, *The Military System in Ancient India*, pp. 100-126 and *History and Culture of the Indian People*, vol. 5, *The Struggle for Empire*.

53. Campbell, *The Masks of God*, vol. 2, pp. 62-67.

54. The tale used to be recited to *kshatriya* boys about a mother, Vidula, who threatened to disown her son because of his refusal to go to war: "Thou canst not be counted as a man. Thy features betray thee to be a eunuch!" she rebuked him. "Rise O coward! . . . Rather perish in plucking the fangs of a snake than die miserably like a dog." You are neither man nor woman, she continued, "But only your mother's excreta. O let no woman bring forth such a son (as thou)." Thus chastened, the scales fell from the youth's eyes and he understood what his destiny must be (*Udyoda-parva*, cxciv).

55. *The Geography of Strabo*, trans. by H. L. Jones, (Cambridge, Mass.: Harvard University Press, 1966 [1930]) vol. 7, chap. 1, sec. 34.

MARTIAL PLAY IN THE CHRISTIAN WORLD

5

In Christian orthodoxy, divinization of man's earthly enterprises is a sin. Daniel, Isaiah, and Ezekiel ridicule the sacred pretensions of the monarch, saying: ". . . [T]hine heart is lifted up, and thou hast said, I am a God, I sit in the seat of God. . . . Yet thou art a man, and not a God, though thou set thine heart as the heart of God" (Ezek. 28:1-9). They condemn him to "the death of the uncircumcised by the hands of strangers." Neither the Judaic nor the Christian king can be more than a temporary governor of worldly affairs, never a Vicar of God or His divine Deputy.[1]

But this is only theory. In fact, just as the heathen trappings of the Babylonian court influenced Judaic political workings, pagan rituals and Oriental administrative devices began informing the Christian world soon after A.D. 313 when Constantine declared Christianity to be the religion of the Roman Empire.[2] This chapter deals with one aspect of Christianity's accommodation to the material world, the evolution of the warrior-monk and the liturgy of martial play that became his religious vocation.

THE SOURCES AND MEANING OF THE CHRISTIAN NOTION OF HOLY WAR

We will not attempt to describe the origins of the Christian notion of holy war in exhaustive detail.[3] However, it is useful to note that the roots of the concept go back to the ancient rituals and myths of the Teutonic (including Frankish) warriors. In the German sagas those who die on the field of battle are promised eternal life in heaven, albeit, as we have seen, a heaven of a rather gruesome sort, involving perpetual battle and daily slaughter. As the sun sets, the resurrected hero drinks from fountains of mead, listens to lyric poetry, and later plays with the servant girls called Valkeries. The whole affair is supervised by Wodan, "the father of slaughter, God of desolation and fire; the active and roaring deity, he who giveth victory, and reviveth courage in the conflict, who nameth those who are slain."[4] Among the Vandals, Goths, and Alemanni, the sword was considered an instrument of the divine, horses were consecrated to the service of Wodan, and a type of formal initiation into the men's barracks was practiced, called "dubbing." ("Dub" derives from the Low German *dubben* meaning "to strike.")

With the development of class distinctions in the original *Hring* or assembly of freemen and the conversion of the Germans to Christianity, these notions became increasingly elaborate. Clovis, the Frankish chieftain, together with 3,000 followers were converted en masse on Christmas Day, A.D. 496. Thereafter, the Franks no longer fought merely for plunder or adventure, but for the elevated cause of a Christian god, under the banner of the red cross on a white field. Wodan was assimilated into the Christian pantheon as Michael the Archangel, whose ancient sanctuary at Monte Gargano evolved into a favorite shrine for Norman soldiers. The relics of Christian saints now accompanied the men into battle, before which the Christian mass was served.[5]

By the eleventh century the Frankish warriors were no longer merely "made" knights; instead, they were "ordained" as knights, and a body of them comprising an *ordo*, was a division of society established by God according to His divine plan. Although many dubbings still took place on the field of battle, by 1050 the Church virtually monopolized control over the knightly ordination, and in some regions the ceremony was called its "eighth sacrament." We know about the details of this "sacrament" primarily through the various pamphlets on chivalry written in the thirteenth and fourteenth centuries.

On the appropriate day, preferably Easter or Whitsunday, the candidate to knighthood would confess his sins to a priest, undergo a purificatory bath, and be dressed in white linen. Then there would be an "armed vigil" when his sword would be placed briefly upon the altar and the squire would be urged to meditate through the night on the vows he was about to take. The following morning a prayer similar to this one would be read by the presiding priest:

Hearken, we beseech Thee, O Lord, to our prayers, and deign to bless with the right hand of Thy majesty this sword with which Thy servant desires to be girded, that it may be the defense of churches, widows and all Thy servants against the scourge of the pagans, that it may be a terror and dread of other evil doers, and that it may be just both in attack and defence.[6]

The prayer was usually followed by a short homily on the code of chivalry, and while mass was celebrated each part of the initiate's armor and weaponry would be blessed, smeared with oil, and girded on. "As the hauberk safeguards the body," the priest might say, "so the knight defends the Church; as the helm defends the head so the knight protects the people; the two edges of the sword symbolize the knight's selfless devotion to both God and His people, and its point the community's obedience to him; his horse represents the people whom the knight must always lead but who in turn must support him." The ceremony was completed with a sharp blow to the cheek, the actual dubbing, which is analogous to that still given by a bishop to the clerk whom he invests as a priest. This blow, intended as the last strike the knight could take and not return, presumably was to remind him of the vows just taken. Finally, there was the customary benediction and a hearty "go forth," whereafter, in some cases, the newly dubbed knight mounted a steed and attacked a black dummy of an infidel with his lance.[7]

It is important to specify what canonical status the knightly "ordination" occupied in Church law, what the Church intended by having its clergy preside over it. In the first place, in light of its eschatological separation of the spiritual from the temporal life, the Church could never have countenanced the actual ordination of knights as priests, of giving them the power to transform bread and wine into the body and blood of Christ, to celebrate, that is to say, the Blessed Sacrament. Political authority, to use the language of the *magisterium*, although indeed ordained by God as are all things, is merely of the relatively natural order. It administers a fallen world. Were there no Original Sin, there would be no reason for political force. But the Church, through its sacramental devices, deals primarily with man's soul not with his body, mainly with the spirit not with matter; or better with the supernatural not the natural, let alone the "relatively" natural. The knight wields the sword and kills (*ad mortificandum*), whereas the priest saves and gives life (*ad vivificandum*). At best, then, from the Church's viewpoint, the dubbing ceremony could never be more than a highly stylized blessing confirming a secular legal status.[8]

Nevertheless, after the year 1000 the Gregorian (Cluniac) reformists clouded this picture for the average Christian confessor by asserting that henceforth Christ through His Church would rule the entire world.[9] The spiritual would command the temporal. All legitimate princes and vassals would be elected and then anointed by Christ through His Church, their fiefs made dependent upon their loyalty to His earthly Vicar, the Pope. Only he who received the chrism from a priest could rightfully claim the status of knight. And only that warrior anointed with oil might put his sword to the service of love and faith.[10] But in the eyes of the uneducated laity, including the knight himself in many cases, this had the effect of turning knighthood into a semidivine vocation, and the dubbing ceremony into a formal induction of the squire into the ministry of the Church.

The concept of knight-as-minister evolved over a period of centuries. Before Constantine (reigned A.D. 306-337), the confessor to the faith was absolutely forbidden to bear arms, even in defense of the Empire. By the time of Augustine (A.D. 354-430), however, the Church was permitting Christians to engage in "just" wars, those fought for the "right" cause as determined by "proper" authority. Later, this rather grudging admission was liberalized by the argument that participation in just war, as so defined and when so authorized by the Pope, could be an occasion for indulgence, a remission of time to be spent in purgatory after death. Pope Gregory VII, the first Cluniac reformer (reigned 1073-1085), went still further by explicitly proclaiming the concept of *militia Christi*, which secured complete *remissio peccatorum* (remission of sins) if a general absolution was declared by the Pope prior to battle.[11] Saint Bernard of Clairvaux completed the sacralization of combat by imposing monastic severities on the Knights of the Temple of Solomon, turning the vassals of Saint Peter into monks.

The Knights Templars were originally organized in 1118 as a police force to protect pilgrims traveling the perilous route from Constantinople to Jerusalem. Abbot Bernard of the Cistercian monastery of Clairvaux in France, intrigued by the possibility of harnessing the rude discipline and energetic life of the warrior for the purposes of Christianity, wrote a model Rule for the order after that of the Cistercians. It advised chastity, simplicity of barracks life, vows of silence, cropped hair with beard, a series of "pater nosters" repeated several times daily, absolute obedience to superiors, and for mealtime inspiration, reading from holy scripture, particularly the books of Joshua, Judges, and Maccabees.

Above all, wrote Bernard in his *De Laude Novae Militae*, a pamphlet used to attract new recruits, the Templars were to be *Dei ministere*, God's ministers of Christian justice in a heathen land. As such, they would be permitted to commit not *homicide*— Bernard did not think this term fitting enough to describe the calling of these trustees of violence—but *malecide*, the killing of evil. To this extent they would be technically free from the legal requirement of having the Pope authorize a crusade before they obtained remission from their sins. "The soldiers of Christ," says Bernard, "can fight the Lord's battles in all safety. For whether they kill the enemy or die themselves, they need fear nothing. To die for Christ and to kill his enemies, there is no crime in that, only glory."[12]

Soon after the dissemination of *De Laude Novae Militae*, the Templars were besieged with applicants from across Europe. The idea of the warrior-monk obviously had struck a responsive chord. After 1120 to meet this demand, a rival military order, the Hospitalers, was created, responsible not only for protecting but also caring for pilgrims.[13]

In our own time [reports Guibert de Nogent], God has instituted a holy manner of warfare, so that knights and the common people who, after the ancient manner of paganism, were aforetime immersed in internecine slaughter, have found a new way of winning salvation. They need no longer, as they did formerly, entirely abandon the world by entering a monastery or some other commitment. They can obtain God's grace in their accustomed manner and dress, and by their accustomed way of life.[14]

The term *militia Christi* was not coined by Pope Gregory. It had been widely employed centuries prior to the time of the Crusades, but previously had always referred to a form of spiritual combat conducted alone in the monastery. "The abbot is armed with spiritual weapons and supported by a troop of monks," recites a typical monastic charter of an early period. "They fight together in the strength of Christ with the sword of the spirit against the cunning of the invisible devils of the air."[15] But Pope Gregory altered this forever. As early as 1053, Pope Leo IX had negotiated to give "freedom from all sins" to soldiers promising to fight the Normans in southern Italy. Even earlier, in the eighth and ninth centuries Popes Leo IV and John VII had promised that all who defend the Church against either Arabs or Vikings will win eternal life.[16] But Gregory VII went much further, arguing that as the properly ordained knight is for that very reason Saint Peter's vassal, he deserves a spiritual benefice from his Lord, absolution. As for the argument against this idea, that Christ in the Garden of Gethsemane had ordered Peter to "put thy sword in its sheath," the Gregorian casuists maintained that this was not a command to fling the sword away altogether, but a suggestion to put it in its rightful place: in the hands of the Christian knight.[17]

THE GAME OF "CHRISTIAN" WARFARE

The Christian knight could legally participate in not just one, as is commonly thought, but two types of armed festival.[18] There was first and most notably what today we call the "crusade" (a term which was then unknown either in Latin or in the local vernacular), but which in those days was known as *bellum peregrini* or pilgrim's war.[19] Second, there was the just war against one's fellow Christians who were foreign invaders or disturbers of the public order as determined by proper authority. The latter will occupy our attention hereafter.

In just wars between Christians, the ideal was "fair play in fight," or to use the French phrase *sans peur et sans reproche* (without fear and without fault). Ideally, warfare was to take the form of a tournament of sorts in which soldiers would fight bitterly but in virtual safety. And indeed, although this was but the military *ethic*, not necessarily the actual behavior of the combatants, a close examination of the period makes it difficult to distinguish between mere armed sport and actual war.[20]

The original "tournament" was a wild clash ranging over several miles. The competitors, often representing feuding baronies, fought not as individuals but as teams. While in principle there were restrictions outlawing dangerous blows and weapons, originally there were no referees to enforce them. As a result, darts and crossbow bolts were not uncommon. In fact only after approximately 1250 did heralds staging the tourneys have effective control even over the division of prizes. It did not take on the pageantlike refinements familiar to the modern reader until the fifteenth and sixteenth centuries.[21]

Even as late as 1323-1357, a series of tourneys held in England would appear to the outsider to be a reenactment of an outright civil war in all but name. And as a consequence the Church was moved to forbid them once and for all. Those who were unfortunate enough to die in such violent sport, said the clergy, were to be given Extreme Unction but refused a Church burial.[22] This threat apparently meant little to the cavaliers, however, who continued the practice down through the Hundred Years' War (1337-1453). Then during the numerous truces, tournaments called *pas d'armes* were staged between knights of the opposing armies who, with time on their hands, needed a diversion. They would shatter lances until fatigued and scurry to safety behind their own lines. Misplays were possible, however. In 1351 when a joust to the death was arranged between thirty English and French knights in Brittany, fifteen knights met their deaths.[23]

Compare and contrast this with the practice of the martial arts during alleged "wars." The medieval armed force numbered any-

where from 1,000 to 10,000 men.[24] It would be unjustifiable in light
of what is known today to ignore mentioning the role of the foot-
man. But the fact remains that the cavalry was the main combat
force in Europe until the fourteenth century.[25] Furthermore, rarely
did full armies, whatever their supposed size, confront one another
in the field. Instead, twenty- to forty-man "battles" would skirmish.[26] But this is the decisive point: Casualty rates were rarely
greater in these "wars" than in the so-called "tournaments." For
example, at the Fair of Lincoln (1217), as it was revealingly called,
"vigorous jousting" and "hard blows" produced only one dead
knight. (The commentator adds as an aside: "Though many of the
foot soldiery on both sides and some citizens perished.")[27] Let us
look at this battle more closely.

The Earl of Gloucester had just captured King Stephan. And
although the latter was now at his mercy, the earl ordered him to be
treated with the utmost respect, "keeping him in safe but gentle
confinement." Why? Because in the first place, it was contrary to
les droits de guerre (the rights of war) for one to maltreat a noble
captive who had put up an honorable fight. And besides, earlier
that day Stephan himself had demonstrated his own chivalry by not
only refusing to imprison the enemy Empress Matilda, then besieged in Arundel castle, but by pledging her safe passage to Bristol
under an armed escort, the Earl of Millent. The empress's request
for passage, the commentator relates, "no true knight could ever
decline, even toward his greatest enemy."[28]

Approximately a century later during the battle for Navarre in
southwestern France, we are again at the scene of a capture. In this
case Bertrand du Guesclin, The Eagle of Brittany, is captured by
The Black Prince, the delight of English nobility, Edward, Prince
of Wales (1330-1376). Although the Frenchman, Guesclin, could in
principle be killed or enslaved by his captor, honorable custom
decreed that he be held only for ransom. As to its amount, this was
also, according to the rules of the game, to be negotiated in good
faith between captor and prisoner. Accordingly, Guesclin initiated
negotiations by proposing that his price be set at 100,000 florins. In
his courtliness the Black Prince refused to accept this as too large a
sum, for it seems that another rule of chivalry required that ran-

soms be reasonable and not bring financial ruin upon a knight. Henry V, in his articles of war published just prior to the invasion of the mainland in 1415, would establish the price as no more than one year's revenue of the captive's estate. But the Black Prince was fully aware that recently Guesclin had fallen into hard times and was, for all intents and purposes, impoverished. Guesclin then proposed a price of 70,000 florins and stubbornly insisted that he "would not abate a farthing." The Black Prince reluctantly agreed. Astonishingly, Guesclin was freed to fetch his own ransom, because still another chivalric norm of this impossibly wonderful game required that the captive give his word, if paroled to raise his own ransom, neither to fight nor escape, and to return to his prison cell within a year if his efforts to obtain the required sum failed. The word of honor not to escape was binding even when one's own captor was himself captured. Thus, when Redemen, an English knight, was captured by Lindefey, a Scottish nobleman, and then Lindefey himself collared, Redemen insisted on his word that he was still Lindefey's prisoner. They later agreed to be exchanged for one another. In another more notable case, when after no less than eight years of imprisonment the Lord of Barbason was freed from the dungeon in Chateau Gaillard by the French in 1430, he refused to leave his cell until his master, an English captain, formally released him from his obligations as a prisoner of war.

A man's word of honor given at a trying moment is, of course, often fickle. And many a knight deemed less trustworthy than the French gallant Guesclin was required to put his own family up as security against escape, once he had put his right hand in his captor's gauntlet and said, "I yield myself your prisoner." Indeed, when in 1359 the Duke of Anjou, son of King John of France broke his promise and failed to return to the Black Prince's court within the specified year, his own father, to wipe out the shame brought to his good name, put himself in the power of his son's captor. Although the Black Prince refused to honor John's request to be taken prisoner, he did die in London.

There was no standard sanction for one who broke his word as a Christian knight and was eventually recaptured. However, in several cases in the late Middle Ages the dishonorable man was tried by a tribunal of his peers and summarily excommunicated from his order. When Andrew de Harclay in 1323, or Ralph Grey in 1464, or Lord Audley in 1497 were convicted of "treason" to the vows of knighthood as defined by the English Court of Chivalry, their arms were taken from them and broken and their shields defaced by being dragged through the mud. In each case the priest officiating at the excommunication read a fitting Psalm (such as the 109th), and the knight's name was uttered three times, with the herald answering that it was no longer the name of the man who stood before them. The attendant then poured a basin of hot water over the villain (in contrast to the cool waters of Baptism) and a mock funeral was performed.[29]

In the case of Bertrand du Guesclin, no such precautions were necessary. He was given parole by the Black Prince with full confidence that he would return with the ransom of 70,000 florins. Why? Because—and here this true story approaches a fairy tale— Joan of Kent, his captor's very own wife (for reasons still somewhat obscure) gave the French knight 30,000 florins toward the sum. Furthermore, two other English cavaliers, Lord Chandos and Hugh de Calverly raised another 30,000. This same Lord Chandos had occasion to go to Guesclin's aid another time as well, at the battle of Auray in 1364 during the long war for Brittany. This time the Frenchman was surrounded by several English horsemen, when Chandos broke through the press and commanded that they leave him alone. Again we may ask, why such concern for the welfare of the enemy? And we discover that earlier in their careers all four men, the Black Prince, Chandos, Guesclin, and Calverly had sworn at a holy mass always to protect each another, share their ransoms, and help raise the ransoms of their brothers-in-arms.[30]

In 1370 when Chandos was dying of wounds on the field of another battle, his relatives vowed to kill all their prisoners in revenge. Yet this would have been contrary to the laws of war. In his last breath, at least according to his biographer, Chandos pleaded with his relatives not to commit such a crime. The captives, he said, in bringing him to this state had merely done their duty, and his death should not prevent him from doing justice to their valor.[31]

Such was the sport of war in the European Middle Ages, at least when played correctly (naturally it was not always) by the Christian knight. But let us not in our enthrallment with these examples forget the very real violence that these same warriors on horseback committed in the name of God. At the siege of Limoges (1370), the same Black Prince who demonstrated such courtesy to Bertrand du Guesclin ordered the extermination of 3,000 unarmed men, women, and children.[32] At the battles of Crecy (1346), Calais (1348), and Poitiers (1356), hundreds of French, according to English chroniclers, experienced violent deaths at the hands of his Welsh archers. Yet in each one of these cases, the Black Prince and his fellow warriors evinced a remarkable, in fact when compared to modern standards, unbelievable courtliness in the treatment of their noble adversaries.

At Crecy, for example, the Count of Luxembourg, otherwise known as King John of Bohemia, although blind in both eyes, insists on riding his horse into the melee to experience once more the thrill of swinging a sword in the company of his comrades against the English. Unfortunately, for all his fortitude, he suffers a mortal wound and "dies in glory." The Black Prince so struck by his gallantry, later adopts King John's insignia, three feathers underwritten by the phrase *Ich dien* (I serve), as his own.

Again at Calais, Edward III, father of the Black Prince, is beaten to the ground twice by Eustace de Ribeaumont. Later, the French knight himself is taken captive. That evening after a convincing victory, Edward entertains his prisoners at a dinner and presents Eustace with an honored chaplet, the prize of valor until now reserved exclusively for knights of his court, pronouncing him "the most valiant knight in Christendom." Thereupon he rewards him with complete liberty, free of ransom.

Following the French disaster at Poitiers, the scene is repeated when the Black Prince gives a sumptuous banquet in his pavilion in honor of his prisoner, the French King John and his son Philip, together with some other captive barons. The prince seats the King of France at an elevated table which he serves himself "with every mark of humility," disdaining even to sit with his company, "saying that he was not worthy of such an honor."

Customs such as these had the effect of turning the horror of war, at least for the nobility, into a magnificent and on the whole delightful ceremony.[33]

THE CHURCH AND THE RULES OF CHIVALRY

Within the fraternity of ordained knights, casualty rates in war were comparatively small for some 300 years after the beginning of the eleventh century when the Church came to control ordination into knighthood. Material factors contributed to this condition, most notably, the superiority of fortress architecture to the primitive science of siegecraft. Typically, from the year 1000 to about 1300, opponents sought refuge in castles instead of confrontation on the field.[34] In addition, the increasing weight and strength of armor rendered the man-at-arms virtually impervious to even the most energetic blow from mace, sword, or lance. So unwieldy had armor become by the Late Middle Ages that barons were dying of heart failure in battle, drowning in mud in frantic efforts to avoid capture, or becoming so fatigued that they were helpless victims to unencumbered footmen.[35] Yet alongside these elements stood another that would be equally unjustified to overlook, the place that Christian *fideles*, *honos*, and *justitia* occupied in the mind of the knight. It was not just the fact that the Christian warriors at Bremule, for example, "were clothed from head to foot in mail," that explains why so few met their deaths, says Ordericus Vitalis, the English historian; but also "because of fear of God and the fact that they were known to each other as old comrades, there was no slaughter."[36]

Over and above their fealty to warring lords, the knights constituted an invisible fraternity of arms, brothers of one blood, like the Black Prince, Guesclin, Chandos, and Calverly, symbolically confirmed by their drinking of the consecrated wine, the blood of Christ, at their ordination. In our earlier discussion of Aztec warfare, we spoke of how the captor and his prey ritually exchanged the words "father" and "son" to confirm the latter's spiritual adoption into the captor's family. Henceforth, the "father" would care for his "child," and the son would piously obey his patron even to the moment of his own sacrifice. Analogous rites are evident in the Chinese Spring and Autumn Period, in Hindu India, and in Tokugawa Japan. In all these cases the enemy is symbolically recognized as being in some essential sense identical to oneself. Although he may reside in a distant city and speak a foreign tongue, he is no longer viewed as a stranger or as a being with an alien nature, but rather as a brother. We do not need to describe in detail all the devices employed by Christian knights to reaffirm their kinship in God, the Father. However, the ceremonies included public swearing of their brotherhood at a mass (by the Black Prince, Chandos, Guesclin, and Calverly, among others); the exchange of locks of hair; the delivery of arms by an enemy "father" to his "adopted son"; the conferring of the right of an enemy "brother" to wear one's own heraldric regalia; or presenting him with a mail shirt, one's own "persona" to don in battle, perhaps against oneself.[37] The point is that even in war, enemies so confirmed in their kinship were not only justified, but positively motivated to practice merciful restraint and fair dealing with each other.

This is perhaps why after the year 1000 it became a general practice to give the enemy three days notice before initiating an attack; why the heralds of battle were not only protected from harm, but in some cases lavished with gifts from the opponent to whom they gave the unpleasant tidings; why the declarations themselves were executed meticulously in accordance with the seventeenth chapter of the *Golden Bull*; why the armies would agree to meet in battle at a time and place generally dictated by the party challenged; why the besieged would agree, under the custom known as *appointment*, to surrender within a stipulated length of time if the castle was not relieved, if the besiegers promised to withhold their forays until then; and why the besieged troops would be granted the "right of ingress and egress" from the castle during such truces.[38] (There is a favorite story that was once widely told about one of Bertrand du Guesclin's brothers who, taking advantage of such a truce, was accosted by Thomas of Canterbury while exercising his horse outside the castle walls. The French knight appealed to the duke in command on the grounds that Thomas had dishonorably broken the *appointement*. The duke, at first unsure what to make of the situation, finally ordered a joust between the two to determine who was in the right. Only after Guesclin had unseated Thomas from his charger was he set free. In this contest, by the way, Lord Chandos, the same knight who helped raise Bertrand du Guesclin's ransom, loaned Guesclin his own arms and horse, although they were to be used against one of his own party.)[39]

One may be somewhat reticent about attributing to a religious institution the power to enforce conformity to any set of standards whatsoever, much less norms limiting the harshness of war. Most authorities concur, however, that indirectly Christianity mitigated the violence of medieval war in three distinct ways: by laying the foundations for the system of ransom by its criticism of slavery; by establishing various truces and peaces of God; and by restricting the use of weapons to those innocuous to anyone encapsulated in iron.

Both Greco-Roman and ancient Germanic law held that captives in war, if not killed, were automatically the slaves of their captors. The Church fathers, while acknowledging the "inevitability" of slavery, accepted it at best as a "relatively natural" institution. The Church always held that in his natural condition man was free and equal to his brothers in Christ. This position was used in several ways to attack the enslavement of Christians by their fellow confessors.[40] First, it refuted the dual standard of justice heretofore regulating affairs between slaves and Roman freemen. The Code of Justinian (A.D. 533) directs that the rape of a slave woman, for example, be punishable by death. Second, it proposed that slaves be permitted to marry free persons and to pass on their legacy in property to their heirs. Third, the Church viewed the emancipation of slaves as an act of particular piety. As an example to his people, Pope Gregory I freed two of his slaves while proclaiming the liberty of all men (although he continued to employ slaves to work on papal lands). Finally, at the Third Lateran Council held in 1179 under Pope Alexander III, the Church expressly outlawed slavery for Christians.[41] As slavery evolved into a spiritual liability, war captives were viewed increasingly as vehicles of immediate financial gain. Out of this idea grew the intricate ransoming rituals just recounted. Negatively viewed, of course, this meant that the captor had perhaps even less reason to spare the life of a soldier without means than he had previously.

The medieval peace movement owed its legendary inspiration to an angel appearing at the Council of Charroux to the Bishop of Aquitaine in 989, ordering the laying aside of weapons in remembrance of the passion and resurrection of the Lord. Impressed, the bishops in attendance agreed to a number of edicts extending immunity from the ravages of war to specific persons and things: unarmed clerics and merchants, church buildings, mills, vines, and those coming either to or from worship. Subsequent synods at Narbonne (990), Limoges (994), and Poitiers (1011) were even more ambitious. Finally, at a synod conducted in 1054 at Narbonne, the clergy, in what came to be known as the *treuga Dei*, sought to proscribe armed violence on specified days, not only on the major feast days and Sundays, but in addition the three days of each week preceding Sunday during which preparations were presumably made for mass. Thursday was given to remembrance of the Last Supper, Friday to meditation on the Crucifixion, Saturday to Christ's burial, and Sunday to the celebration of the Resurrection.

Truce, itself the public peace and Religion, through the teaching of the Church, two companions, one with the Fathers and Clerics and a quorum of nobility and not a small number of holy commoners, will be renovated, extended and strictly observed of the *Treugi* [Treuga] *Domini*; besides which all hostilities having their occasion on the four feast days [i.e., Thursday through Sunday] shall be strictly prohibited.[42]

In 1059, by decree of Pope Nicholas II, infractions of the Truce of God and its associated immunities were declared punishable by excommunication. In this way, as canon law, these restrictions eventually found their way into the fifteenth-century compendium of Christian martial law, *The Tree of Battles*, written by the Benedictine monk, Honoré Bonet. They are to be excommunicated, says Bonet, who harm clerks, hermits or monks (4:97), old people, children, women, or the infirm (4:70, 92-94) during times of war. Oxherds, husbandmen, ploughmen (4:100), the insane (4:91-92, 95), ambassadors and pilgrims (4:96-99), and even foreign students and their relatives (4:86-90) are also to be protected.[43]

These truces and immunities reflected the desires of the Church to regulate warfare more than they ever did the actual conduct of the nobility. (Although legend has it that on the "Day of Indulgence" at Constance in 1043, Henry III, Holy Roman Emperor, offered to pardon all who had injured him, and exhorted his subjects to renounce all vengeance. For a decade he and his barons cooperated with the *treuga Dei*.)[44] But there were attempts to enforce the Peace of God through more than just psychological threats. In 990, Bishop Guy of LePuy compelled the neighborhood *chevaliers* to swear to uphold the *pax Dei* at the point of a sword held by an armed consociation of commoners.[45] In time tournaments were held on Mondays, so that they could be completed by Thursdays, the first day of that week's *treuga Dei*.[46] In more than one instance, those who either failed to profess Christianity, or were known to have committed treason, perjury, "slaughter in cool blood," sacrilege, or violation of women were banned from participating in the frivolities.[47]

At the Lateran Council of Pope Innocent II in 1139, the use of bows and crossbows was outlawed in these words: "The deadly art, hated of God, of crossbow-men and archers against Christians and Catholics is prohibited on pain of anathema."[48] In 1215, the English barons following suit, forced the king under the threat of death to agree in section 51 of the Magna Carta to disband his crossbow corps.[49] The Christian combat arm par excellence had become the lance and stirrup which the Church, in the celebration of the "eighth sacrament," now blessed as part of the divinely appointed order.

What makes this development significant is the fact that originally the Franks were infantrymen; the lance, stirrup, and heavy armor were not even introduced in western Europe until the time of Charles Martel (689-741). Within less than three centuries, however, the ancient German tradition of foot soldiery had been superseded by the mounted warrior, who came to epitomize honorable military tactics. "Chivalry" as well as "cavalier" both come from the French *chevalier*, meaning "horse soldier." The French term is in turn a corruption of the Spanish *caballero*, which is derived from the Latin *caballus* (pack horse).[50]

Even more than he sought heavenly salvation, perhaps, the European knight like his Teutonic ancestors, sought to be recognized as a hero. But he knew that winning this acknowledgment was predicated upon his acting virtuously, in accordance with the standards of true manliness: justly, moderately, and above all courageously in the face of death. The armed contests of the Middle Ages, more than anything else, were stages for the public exhibition of these virtues. By acting in conformity with the popularly held myth of Christian virility, the knight could identify himself as the embodiment of that myth. This myth held that one is truly courageous only if he fights his opponent directly and fairly, in the "chivalric" manner, the manner of the lance-armed horseman. The knightly objection to the bow weapons was not, as we noted earlier, that they were inefficient, but rather, too efficient. They could be effectively employed by those of little strength who were afraid of battle. "Such arms," to quote Lykus in *Herakles Distracted*, "afford no proof of courage."

CONCLUSION

The Middle Ages were a time of religious hysteria: itinerant preaching, dance epidemics, swarms of naked flagellants, and the invention of legitimate (the Franciscans) and illegitimate (the Free Spirits) extremist movements. People migrated by the thousands to monasteries and convents, endowed them with their worldly riches, or underwent arduous pilgrimages. A "fourth path" offered by the Church, the way of the sword, was greeted with an equally enthusiastic reception. By following this way, so it was taught, one could act consistently with the four cardinal virtues: prudently (in conformity with the dicates of the clergy), justly (in defense of churches, widows, orphans, and law), courageously (that is, chivalrously), and with temperance. In other words, one could not only help save the world from chaos, but in doing so demonstrate one's own manliness. In this regard the military symbolism of the Christian Middle Ages was identical to that of Nahuatl Mexico and classical Hinduism. It was also analogous to that of Confucianism.

NOTES

1. Werner Stark, *The Sociology of Religion*, vol. 3, *Universal Church* (New York: Fordham University Press, 1967), pp. 31-37.

2. Campbell, *The Masks of God*, vol. 4, *Creative Mythology*, pp. 95-171.

3. The modern discussion of the concept of Christian holy war begins with the classic history of Carl Erdmann, *Die Entstehung des Kreuzzugsgedankes* (Stuttgart: W. Kohlhammer, 1935). The interested reader will also want to consult the seminal work of Marc Bloch, *Feudal Society*, trans. by L. A. Manyon, 2 vols. (Chicago: University of Chicago Press, 1970).

4. Cf. the excellent description and analysis by Campbell, *The Masks of God*, vol. 3, pp. 473-90.

5. For the role of the Christian clergy in the Carolingian conquests, see Erdmann, *Kreuzzugsgedankes*, pp. 86-106. For typical banners and pre-battle prayers, see pp. 39-50. Cf. Bloch, *Feudal Society*, vol. 2, pp. 312-14.

6. Michel Andrieu, *Le Pontifical in au Moyen-Age*, vol. 3, *Le Pontifical de Guillaume Durand* (Studie e Test 88: Citta del Vaticano, 1940, p. 448, quoted in Richard Barber, *The Knight and Chivalry* (New York: Charles Scribner's Sons, 1970), p. 26. Cf. Erdmann, *Kreuzzugsgedankes*, pp. 24-26, 40, 71-78, 326-35.

7. Robert W. Ackerman, "The Knighting Ceremonies in Middle English Romances," *Speculum* 19 (July 1944): 290, 309-11. Barber, *The Knight and Chivalry*, pp. 25-36. Laffont, *The Ancient Art of Warfare*, vol. 1, pp. 356-58.

8. For a careful statement of the exact meaning of such ceremonies in the Catholic world, see Stark, *The Sociology of Religion*, vol. 3, pp. 60-68. His analysis is based in large measure upon Bloch, *Feudal Society*, vol. 2, pp. 379-83.

9. For the classic sociology of the idea of the universal church, see Ernst Troeltsch, *The Social Teachings of the Christian Churches*, trans. by Olive Wyon, intro. by Richard Niebuhr (New York: Harper & Row, 1960 [1911]), vol. 1, pp. 201-327.

10. For the concept of the universal church as it applied to knighthood, see ibid., pp. 253-56.

11. There is a plethora of recent literature on *militia Christi*, all of which is based on Erdmann. For example, see I. S. Robinson, "Gregory VII and the Soldiers of Christ," *History* 58 (1973): 169-92; E. O. Blake, "The Formation of the 'Crusade Idea'," *Journal of Ecclesiastical History* 21 (1970): 11-31; H. E. J. Cowdrey, "The Genesis of the Crusades: The Springs of Western Ideas of Holy War," in *The Holy War*, ed. by Thomas Patrick Murphy (Columbus: Ohio State University Press, 1976), pp. 9-32; James

A. Brundage, "Holy War and the Medieval Lawyers," *The Holy War*, pp. 99-140.

12. Bernard de Clairvaux, *De Laude Novae Militae*, cap. 1, quoted in Laffont, *The Ancient Art of Warfare*, vol. 1, p. 356. Cf. Cowdrey's translation of this same line in "The Genesis of the Crusades," pp. 23-24.

13. For the standard history of the military religious orders, see Desmond Seward, *The Monks of War* (London: Archon Books, 1972).

14. Quoted in Cowdrey, "The Genesis of the Crusades," p. 23.

15. *Liber Vitae. Register and Martyrology of New Minister and Hyde Abbey, Winchester*, ed. by W. de Gray Birch (n.p., Hampshire Record Society, 1892), pp. 232-46, quoted in Robinson, "Gregory VII and the Soldiers of Christ," p. 178. Cf. Paul: "No man that warreth for God entangleth himself with affairs of this world" (2 Tim. 2:3-4) and Saint Martin of Tours (d. 397): "I am a soldier of Christ: I am not permitted to fight."

16. For representative statements, see Erdmann, *Kreuzzugsgedankes*, pp. 267-69, 272, 300-1, 313.

17. Cf. Robinson, "Gregory VII and the Soldiers of Christ," pp. 185-92.

18. This very important point is made by M. H. Keen, "Chivalry, Nobility, and the Man-At-Arms," in *War, Literature and Politics in the Late Middle Ages*, ed. by C. T. Allmand (Liverpool University Press, 1976), pp. 35-36. See also Brundage, "Holy War and the Medieval Lawyers," pp. 116-17. For a careful analysis of the conditions under which violence done to fellow Christians could be considered just, see M. H. Keen, *The Laws of War in the Late Middle Ages* (London: Routledge & Kegan Paul, 1965), pp. 63-118.

19. Cowdrey, "The Genesis of the Crusades," p. 26.

20. J. F. Verbrugen, "La Tactique Militaire des Armées de Chevaliers," *Revue du Nord* 29 (1947): 161-80.

21. Barber, *The Knight and Chivalry*, pp. 155-77.

22. Ibid., pp. 184-88.

23. Ibid., pp. 173-75, 184-85, 198-99.

24. For a careful study of the sizes of typical armed forces in the Late Middle Ages, see Postan, "The Costs of the Hundred Years' War," pp. 34-55.

25. For a list of famous battles fought with little or absolutely no reliance upon infantry, see Charles Oman's classic work, *The Art of War in the Middle Ages* (New York: Burt Franklin, 1969 [1924]) vol. 1, p. 357.

26. Barber, *The Knight and Chivalry*, pp. 190-92.

27. At Tenchebrai (1106), a day-long battle resulted in but 2 English knights killed and 400 Normans captured but not otherwise harmed. At Bremule (1119), 140 horsemen were captured and only one slain. At Ther-

oulde (1124), there were absolutely no fatalities. At Lewes (1264), the number of deaths was exceptionally high for this period, but this apparently was due to the fact that insults had been heaped upon the king's wife the previous year. All these engagements took place in England and are vividly described in Oman, *The Art of War in the Middle Ages*, vol. 1, pp. 380-441. For a detailed study of comparable cases in France around the same time, see pp. 442-526.

28. Robert Ward, *An Enquiry into the Foundation and History of the Law of Nations in Europe from the Time of the Greeks and Romans to the Age of Grotius*, intro. by Carlisle Spivey (New York: Garland Pub. Inc., 1973 [1795]), vol. 2, p. 164. This work will hereafter be cited as *Law of Nations*.

29. Ibid., vol. 1, pp. 298-320; vol. 2, pp. 166-67, 175-88, 203-4. See Keen, *The Laws of War in the Late Middle Ages*, pp. 156-83 for a detailed description of the law of ransom.

30. See M. H. Keen, "The Brotherhood in Arms," *History* 47 (February 1962): 9-11.

31. Ward, *Law of Nations*, vol. 2, pp. 168-69.

32. It was standard military practice that a town refusing the invitation to surrender be shown no quarter when its walls were breached. Women could be raped legally and men and children killed out of hand. Lives were spared only through the clemency of the victorious captain and not as the result of any law of chivalry (Keen, *The Laws of War in the Late Middle Ages*, pp. 120-24). For atrocities, see Bloch, *Feudal Society*, vol. 2, pp. 297-98 and Ward, *Law of Nations*, vol. 1, pp. 248-66.

33. Thomas Bulfinch, *Bulfinch's Mythology* (New York: Random House, n.d.) is a rich source of legends concerning medieval chivalry.

34. Oman, *The Art of War in the Middle Ages*, vol. 1, pp. 126-48; vol. 2, pp. 10-42.

35. Ibid., vol. 1, pp. 377-93.

36. Ibid., p. 418.

37. For the steps in the ceremony conferring the relationship of "brother" upon two or more knights, see Keen, "The Brotherhood in Arms," pp. 3-4. For various means used to communicate "brotherhood," see Ward, *Law of Nations*, vol. 2, pp. 189-99.

38. Keen, *The Law of War in Middle Ages*, pp. 103, 119-20, 194-96. See also Ward, *Law of Nations*, vol. 1, pp. 289-92; vol. 2, pp. 168, 215-16.

39. Ward, *Law of Nations*, vol. 2, p. 168.

40. The Church also recognized that because of Adam's sin, man was no longer in his natural state. Slavery, she argued, has been ordained by God both as a punishment for the sins of some and a preparation for the recep-

tion of grace by still others. This caveat permitted the Church to laud the sale of Muslims to Christians and to justify the use of Muslim slaves on its estates. For these points, see Troeltsch, *The Social Teachings of the Christian Churches*, vol. 1, pp. 132-33.

41. For an excellent history of slavery during the Middle Ages, see Bloch, *Feudal Society*, vol. 1, pp. 255-74. See also Will Durant, *The Age of Faith*, vol. 4, *The Story of Civilization* (New York: Simon & Schuster, 1950), pp. 77, 112-13, 553-54.

42. Quoted from Ward, *Law of Nations*, vol. 2, pp. 22-23, my translation. For a history of the peace movement, see H. E. J. Cowdrey, "The Peace and the Truce of God of the Eleventh Century," *Past and Present* 46 (February 1970): 42-67. See also Bloch, *Feudal Society*, vol. 2, pp. 412-20.

43. Honoré Bonet, *The Tree of Battles*, trans. and ed. by G. W. Coopland (Liverpool: Liverpool University Press, 1949). Cf. N. A. R. Wright, "The Tree of Battles of Honoré Bonet and the Laws of War," in *War, Literature and Politics in the Late Middle Ages*, pp. 12-30.

44. Durant, *The Age of Faith*, pp. 513.

45. See Bloch, *Feudal Society*, vol. 2, pp. 414-20 for the largely futile attempts to declare "war on war."

46. Barber, *The Knight and Chivalry*, p. 171.

47. Ward, *The Law of Nations*, vol. 2, p. 161.

48. Quoted by Hatto, "Archery and Chivalry," p. 44. For an analysis of comparable attitudes taken toward gunpowder, see M. G. A. Vale, "New Techniques and Old Ideals: The Impact of Artillery on War and Chivalry at the End of the Hundred Years' War," in *War, Literature and Politics in the Late Middle Ages*, pp. 57-72.

49. Oman, *The Art of War in the Middle Ages*, vol. 2, p. 58.

50. For a history of cavalry in Europe, see ibid., vol. 1, pp. 1-170.

THE GENTLEMAN WARRIOR: RITUAL WARFARE IN ANCIENT CHINA

6

THE RUDIMENTS OF CONFUCIANISM

A religious mythology embodies in a highly abstract and elaborate form, the taken-for-granted truisms comprising a people's cognitive reality. As we have seen among the Aztecs and the Indo-Aryans, a war god, whether Huitzilopochtli, Wodan, Zeus, or Indra, coerces light, law, and life from the powers of darkness. The truth apparently conveyed in this act of mythic violence is that ultimately cosmic order and personal sanity rest upon force. In Confucianism, however, a radically different story is related and an altogether different lesson instilled.

Huang Ti, the legendary Yellow Emperor and reputed ancestor of the Chou dynasty, the historical paradigm of concord and civilization, is said to have brought harmony from chaos, tamed the barbarians and wild beasts, cleared the forests and marshes, and invented the "five harmonious sounds," not through an act of epic bloodshed, but through his superior virtue, by adapting and yielding to "natural conditions" and to the Will of Heaven. Confucianism henceforth repudiates as unworkable the idea of military solutions to human problems.

Huang Ti's most notable heir, we are told, was Ti Yao, a gentleman who "naturally and without effort," embraced reverence, courteousness, and intelligence. Nevertheless, during his reign, the Deluge, mythology's universal symbol of anomie, threatened to inundate the land. Thus it fell upon him to appoint a successor to preserve the order his father, Huang Ti, had instituted. In perfect Confucian manner, over the protests of his own son, Ti Yao chose the most qualified man for the job, the venerable Shun, who had in various tests already demonstrated a capacity to harmonize human affairs through righteousness. "The farmers of the Li-shan encroached upon each other's boundaries. Shun went there and farmed and after a year the boundaries were correct. The fishermen on the Ho bank quarreled about the shallows. Shun went there and fished and after a year they gave way to their elders."[1]

Shun in turn selected Yü the Sage to engineer an end to the flood. Because Yü refused wine and always acted appropriately, moving with and not resisting nature, the Way of Heaven (*T'ien Tao*) was revealed to him. He subsequently harnessed the river waters not by fighting against them with a dam, but by yielding to them and clearing for them a wider channel within which to run. Were it not for Yü, so the story goes, who herein personified the wisdom of both Confucius and Lao-tzu, the Taoist prophet, we would all be fish.[2]

While this is highly controversial, some scholars argue that climatic forces partially account for the differences in outlook between Confucianism and other world religions. In the Ganges River valley, for example, there is rarely a shortage of rain, rice being easily cultivated several times yearly. Furthermore, as the monsoon normally announces its coming unambiguously, there is little danger of planting either prematurely or too late. The indifference to time and historiography allegedly characteristic of all the major Ganges River cults, it has been suggested, may be due to this meteorological fact. But in the Middle East and China, lack of concern about the passage of time would eventuate in agricultural disaster. The scarcity of rainfall and erratic Spring and Autumn showers place a premium on the exact determination of seasonal changes, and on the farmer adjusting his planting accordingly. Inspired by the world view of Chinese agrarianism, Confucian heroes, without exception, assiduously accommodate their affairs to the Way of Heaven, instead of attempting to force fate to do their bidding.

Confucianism criticizes the use of violence[3] and speaks nostalgically of the age when complete concord presumably prevailed, during the epoch of the Chou dynasty when the government was staffed by true gentlemen (*chün tzu*) who were both morally righteous (*yi*) and meticulously devoted to *li* (ritual propriety). Because *li* is considered the mother, so to speak, of all Confucian virtue, it will be well worth our while to examine its sources and meaning in some depth.

Li is "the map of *tao*," the written objectification of the divine will. Its character consists of two elements, one representing "spirit," the other "sacrificial offering" or "worship." This seems to indicate that in its earliest meaning *li* signified religious ritual exclusively.[4] However, over the centuries, particularly as a result of the teachings of the Confucian prophet Hsün Tzu and the collation of ancient court practices, *li* became generalized to cover the standard of conduct required in all spheres of social life. In the end, theoretically at least, the complete life of the aristocrat came to be understood as a gigantic religionlike ritual. The "secular," or what moderns take to be secular, had become transposed into the sacred. "Human life in its entirety finally appear[ed] as one vast spontaneous and holy Rite; the community of man."[5]

Beautiful and effective ceremony, as *li* was intended to be, requires personal presence to be fused with learned ceremonial skill, reverence and attentiveness to the task coupled with exact performance of its liturgy.[6] This is why Confucius could say, "merely to feed one's parents well" is not true filial piety, for "even dogs and horses are fed." But to feed them properly with sincere devotion to the task: This is how one communicates both his respect for them and his attainment of manhood, his "*jen*-ness," to use the Confucian term. To serve tea and to eat with full attention and ritual propriety: This alone transforms mere biological sustenance into a ceremony and allows one to recognize, to re-know the ultimate beauty and harmony of human society, the sacred dignity of social intercourse, the dimension of the holy in man's existence.[7]

LI AND THE MARTIAL ARTS

Notwithstanding its genuine dislike for armed combat, Confucianism was intimately acquainted with holy war. "The Great Affairs of the state," says the *Tso Chuan*, the massive commentaries to the *Spring and Autumn Annals*, "are sacrifice and war. At sacrifices [in the ancestral temple], the officers receive the roasted

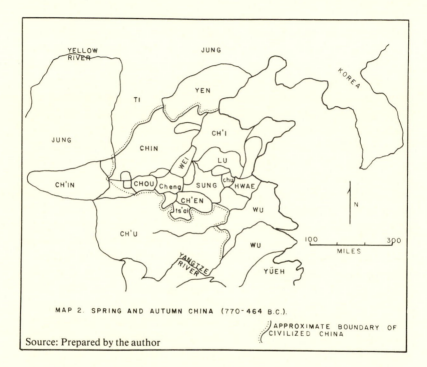

MAP 2. SPRING AND AUTUMN CHINA (770-464 B.C.).

APPROXIMATE BOUNDARY OF CIVILIZED CHINA

Source: Prepared by the author

flesh; in war they receive that offered at the altar of the land. These are the great ceremonies in worshipping the spirits."[8]

Because the killing of man in combat can so easily degenerate into bestial slaughter, Confucian literati considered the battlefield a good (if not the best) setting for determining who among the warriors is a truly self-possessed man, an aristocrat. In this regard, the Confucian ideal of *jen*-ness, the quality said to characterize the *chün tzu*, is almost identical in meaning to the Greco-Roman notion of manhood or *virtus* (*aretē* Greek). In both, manhood is

conceived as a habit, a practiced state of being in constant possession of one's innate human potentiality. ("Habit" derives from the
Latin *habitus*, the past participle of *habere*, meaning "to have or to
own.") The *jen* man, as opposed to the mere brute, is one who consciously "owns" his humanness because of his dignity, sincerity,
tranquility, compassion, and above all, ritual propriety, even in
moments of great duress as when confronting death at the hands of
the enemy.[9] The exchange of compliments and gifts prior to battle,
an ancient Chinese ceremonial custom, affords an excellent example of this. In a celebrated battle between the Chin and the Ch'u,
in the course of the preliminary skirmishes preceding the onslaught,
a Ch'u charioteer shot a stag. He politely turned to the pursuing
Chin chariot and said: "It is not the season of the year for such a
thing, the time for presenting animals has not arrived, but I venture
to offer this feast to your followers." The Chin warrior replied to
his driver, "He on the left shoots well, he on the right speaks well—
they are superior men [*chün tzu*]." Later that day after another
skirmish, the Chin returned the favor: "Amid the business of the
army, your hunters may have failed to supply you with fresh meat,
and I venture to present this to your followers."[10] In this encounter
both sides were able publicly to demonstrate and have confirmed
their self-control and liberality. In addition, they were given the
opportunity to recognize the basic harmony underlying all dualities,
integrating even warring parties in a unified cosmic whole.

In the Confucian world virtuous warfare conformed to two types
of ritual prescriptions, which correspond roughly to the Roman
distinction between *jus ad bellum*, the occasions for just war, and
jus in bello, the tactics and weapons allowable in just war. Let us
examine each of these requirements separately.

"*She ch'u yin ming*," admonishes the Confucian edict: "For war
you must have a cause." Without a just cause the solidarity of the
army will be compromised and the probability of its defeat increased. "Soldiers are weak in a bad cause, but strong in a good
one. Thrice armed is he who hath his quarrel just."[11] Among other
things, the Confucian mind considered any refusal of proper courtesies to diplomatic missions an occasion for just war. Emissaries
from enemy states were to be immune not only from physical harm,

but also from psychological embarrassment.[12] This was complicated by the fact that each diplomat assumed the rank of his sovereign and there were five feudal ranks with detailed sumptuary rites
associated with each. The Prince of "Chi" once insulted four
envoys by making fun of a deformity of each. One was blind in one
eye, a second bald, a third lame, and the last a dwarf. The prince
provided to each an attendant similarly deformed and then berated
the pairs for the ridiculous sight. The next Spring found the dis-
courteous grandee faced with an allied force of four armies who
withdrew only after he had made "humiliating concessions" to
them.[13]

Ironically, apart from the fact that courtesy communicates the
host's virtue, one reason for the impeccable treatment of foreign
emissaries was that they commonly functioned as spies.[14] The
guarantee of their immunity allowed them to examine the positions,
sizes, and strengths of the host's various armed forces, without fear
of harassment, and to estimate their powers of resistance. It is a
well-known sociological proposition that if two parties in conflict
can accurately assess one another's power before fighting, the
probability of violence between them decreases. This is because the
weaker of the two will realize the futility of resisting certain demands, while the stronger will understand the rationality of limiting
its demands to those that will be met given the power of the
weaker.[15] Appreciative of the fact that the minimization of international violence entailed the promotion of international espionage,
Confucian literati considered breaches of diplomatic immunity a
crime serious enough to justify war.

But even justified incursions had to adhere to standards of gallantry that virtually eliminated the likelihood of bloodshed.
Roswell Britton in his study of a twenty-year period in the *Spring
and Autumn Annals* shows that in the more than forty battles
fought there were but two reported casualties. A nobleman is killed
accidently by an arrow from one of his own men, and the King of
Chou is injured in a duel by the Earl of Cheng, who later apologizes
for the misfortune and sends condolences.[16]

If the *Tso Chuan* is even partially reliable as a report of contemporary events, chivalry during the Spring and Autumn Period (770-

464 B.C.) approached what from a practical standpoint, can only be considered absurd lengths. The states of Ch'u and Sung were in the throes of war in 638 B.C., begins one classic tale. The Ch'u army was halfway across the Hung River when the Sung minister urged his commander-in-chief, Duke Hsiang, to attack. But the duke refused, arguing that a *chün tzu* should never attack one who is unprepared. When the army had at last crossed but was not yet in battle array, the minister again admonished the duke to strike. Hsiang rebuked him: "The superior man does not inflict a second wound, and does not take prisoner any one of gray hair. When the ancients had their armies in the field, they would not attack an enemy when he was in a defile; and though I am but the poor representative of a fallen dynasty, I would not sound my drums to attack an unformed host." The minister was furious. "Your grace does not know the rules of fighting," he said:

Given a strong enemy, in a defile or with his troops not drawn up, it is Heaven assisting us. Is it not proper for us to advance upon him so impeded with our drums beating, even then afraid we may not get the victory? . . . If our antagonist is not wounded mortally, why should we not repeat the blow? If we grudge a second wound, it would be better not to wound him at all. If we should spare the gray haired, we had better submit at once to the enemy. In an army, what are used are sharp weapons. . . . The sharp weapons may be used against foes entangled in a defile.[17]

The duke listened politely but then ignored the advice of his Machiavellian counselor. In the ensuing clash he was severely wounded and his army scattered. (While he could certainly approve of Duke Hsiang's chivalry, the Confucian could also forecast his "disgraceful defeat" but for an altogether different reason. The house of Sung observed the much-hated Shang court ritual, refusing to conform to Chou ceremonials, the presumed norm of civilized courtliness.) In any case, courteousness, and by implication being known to his peers for his manliness, meant more to the Duke of Sung than military victory, a fact which, as our studies of Aztec Mexico, Hinduism, and medieval Christianity all have shown, was not peculiar to the ancient Chinese gentleman.

Confucian *jus in bello* consisted of three major proscriptions. In the first place, the superior man should never attack another without warning and then not until the latter is fully prepared for combat. Indeed, perhaps he should not strike the enemy at any weak spots whatsoever. An allied army composed of the states of Chin and Cheng made a sudden incursion into the country of Sung via the kingdom of Wei. Seeing that the citizenry of Wei had taken no precautions to prevent an assault, the ministers attending the allied force advised their generals to attack: "Although we may not be able to enter it [i.e., the Wei capital] yet we shall bring back many prisoners, and our offence will not be deemed a mortal one." But the Chin commander, a celebrated "superior man" in Confucian annals, replied to the contrary: "Wei is trusting Tsin [Chin] and therefore, though our army is in the outskirts of the city, it has made no preparations against an attack. If we make a dash upon it, we abandon our good faith. Though we should take many prisoners, yet having lost our faith, how could Tsin seek the leading of the states?" How, in other words, if international political influence rests not upon force but virtue, could the house of Chin presume to be a Great Power in the Chinese world? Knowing this to be impossible, the allied army retreated without a battle.[18]

In the second place, the superior man should not loose an arrow toward one of greater virtue than himself, or if he contemplates doing so, he should allow the other the opportunity to shoot first. There is no explicit formulation of this rule in the statute books; instead, instances of similar behavior are lauded in the *Tso Chuan* by Confucian commentators. There is an armed encounter between the Ch'i and an allied force of Chin and Sung described in one report. After the preliminary exchanges of gifts and haughty compliments together with individual duels, the charioteers fall upon one another en masse. Han Keueh, marshall of the allied army, riding in one of the carts, comes within range of Ch'i arrows. Ping Hea, chariot driver for the Marquis of Ch'i advises the marquis to "shoot the driver, he is a superior man." The marquis solemnly replies, "Since you call him a superior man, it would be contrary to rule to shoot him." Thus speaking, he shoots instead those to the driver's left and right. What determines the appellation "superior man," is revealed in a later incident. Attempting to save the Marquis of Chin from capture, Han Keueh sets up a charade and is himself made prisoner. When he is threatened with decapitation for his dishonesty, the Marquis of Ch'i again comes to his enemy's defense saying, "this man did not shrink from the risk of death to secure the life of his ruler. If I execute him, it would be inauspicious. I will forgive him as an encouragement to those who wish to serve their ruler."[19]

In rare cases *chün tzu* are permitted to shoot at others of the same status in the *Tso Chuan*, but only after tolerating them to fire first. When a royal allied army came to the aid of Sung, then under siege by the Hwae and the Wu, the commanders of the opposing forces came upon each other. Hwa P'aou of the investing army notched an arrow, shot first and missed. He was preparing to fire again, when Kun-tsze Shing, his foeman pleaded, "if you don't let me return your shot it will be mean." P'aou relented, and Shing aimed carefully and killed him, another case of gallantry being rewarded with disaster.[20]

According to the third proscription, in warfare there should be a minimum of violence. Furthermore, the vanquished should not suffer needlessly nor should they be pursued to such a degree that they lose face. A celebrated example of adherence to this admonition occurred during an encounter involving a royal alliance sent to punish the Earl of Cheng for his failure to pay tribute to Chou. The Cheng footmen and chariots put the police force to flight and in doing so wounded the emperor himself in the shoulder. The Cheng minister requested that his ruler follow up their victory and humiliate their foe. The Earl of Cheng, however, resisted the temptation saying, "a superior man does not wish to be always showing superiority to others; much less dare he to insult the Son of Heaven!" That evening the earl sent a messenger with gifts to comfort the emperor and to inquire into the welfare of his troops.[21]

During the course of another battle decades later, Keoh Che, a noted sage-warrior from Chin was faced with a similar choice, acted in the same manner as the Earl of Cheng, and justified his action with these words: "I ought not a second time to disgrace the ruler of a state." Earlier that day, Keoh Che had personally confronted his enemy, the Viscount of Ch'u, no less than three times. But instead of taking up bow and arrow, each time he bowed courteously to him and passed. For all his gallantry, Keoh was murdered by jealous court officials. To the end he was a *chün tzu*; out of fidelity to the king he refused to revolt, even while knowing beforehand of the plot against his life.[22]

The intention not to disgrace one's bested opponent sometimes went so far as to restore him to his throne. Through this, a person could demonstrate both his liberality and also his fearlessness of future insurrection. When the Earl of Ch'in defeated the Marquis of Chin, he reestablished him as a vassal. The *Tso Chuan* commented: "To take him prisoner because of his doubleness, and to let him go on his real submission: What virtue could be greater than this? What punishment more awing? Those who submit to Ts'in [Ch'in] will cherish virtue, those who are disaffected will dread the punishment: The presidency of Ts'in over the states may be secured by its conduct in this one case."[23]

WARS, EXPEDITIONS, AND DRIVES

Before moving to a discussion of the alleged power that virtue confers upon the Confucian gentleman, it is important to emphasize that not all ancient Chinese military engagements followed the colorful idealization just presented. Ignoring the obvious discrepancies that arise between any ethic and the actual conduct of men in battle, the commentaries to the *Spring and Autumn Annals* distinguish between three types of armed strife: expeditions, wars, and drives. Only the Son of Heaven, the regent of the Chou dynasty, it is taught, or representatives directly delegated by him, can embark upon expeditions, an "expedition" being the use of military force by a superior to compel the obedience of the inferior. But feudal lords are equals. Thus, while they are permitted to address the emperor as "father" or "parent," they may use only the appellation "brother" in salutations to each other. Brothers, it is said, "war" among themselves but not with those outside the "family" (*lieh-kuo*) of neighboring lords.[24] Armed engagements against these others, the barbarians with names such as I, Ti, Jung, and Man, are called "drives." Drives are analogous to hunting expeditions for wild animals.[25]

The upshot of this is that while expeditions of the father-emperor against an impious "son," or wars between "brothers," were ideally bound by the rules of war just enumerated, in drives against barbarians "there was neither right nor wrong." Thus, while it was considered dishonorable for a Chinese lord to attack his "brother" before both warning him and providing him an opportunity to deploy his army, all manner of subterfuge and ambush were permitted in his dealings with foreigners. The Marquis of Chin sent some officials with a military escort to make a sacrifice at the Loh River. The local Jung tribe, suspecting nothing, was surprised in its camp and "extinguished."[26] Again, in 714 B.C., when a body of Jung raided Cheng, the Earl of Cheng took the suggestion of his son to have a few men "who are brave, but not persistent," pretend to fall upon the brigands and then to feign retreat. Meanwhile, he went on, put men in ambush to await their pursuers. The plan worked perfectly. The Jung, seeing they were trapped, fled in disorder and were annihilated.[27]

In the Catholic Middle Ages, as we have seen, kinship metaphors were also used to convey the idea of the unity of all Christian knights under "God the Father," while those of an alien confession, either heretics or Saracens, were treated savagely in warfare. Similarly in the *Spring and Autumn Annals*, while the ideal in "war" with one's "brothers" was to limit the amount of spilled blood, with "animal-barbarians" the preferred course of action was complete extermination. The Chou commander, Yü, campaigned in "demon territory." Returning victoriously he presented three chieftains and 5049 *kuo* (heads) to the emperor at the ancestral temple. The chieftains were beheaded and the *kuo* offered as burnt sacrifices to the Chou spirits.[28] Authorities have long noted the absence of chivalry in combat in the Western Chou Period (1122-771 B.C.), which preceded that of the Spring and Autumn Period. Perhaps, a major cause was that apart from police actions against rebels in the opening years of the dynasty, the vast majority of armed confrontations of this time were against so-called barbarians.[29]

Who then were the members of the Chinese "family," and how were they distinguished from the foreigner? In the Spring and Autumn Period, membership in the family of civilized or "flowery states" was determined not so much by racial as by behavioral traits. Specifically, to be a Chinese state, its sovereign must be invested officially with a feudal rank (*chiao*) by the Chou dynasty and must observe Chou protocol in his dealings with his "brothers."[30] This also required that he be a gentleman during times of "war." A major rationalization for the virulent hatred of the barbarian by the Chinese was exactly this: They employ surprise in their wars and, when faced with danger, cowardly flee to the security of the wilderness.[31]

In addition to the "Chinese" and the barbarians, there were "transitional peoples," who, while feeling no great compulsion to adhere to *li*, were too formidable militarily for the general states to ignore. Among these were counted the houses of Ch'in, Ch'u, Yen, Wu, and Yüeh.[32] These states seem to have followed *li* in their conflicts with the flowery states only when this supported their claims to rule the world. Indeed, it may well have been their freedom from ritual constraints that enabled the transitional peoples to develop into military greatness during the Spring and Autumn Period. Centuries earlier Chou had conquered Shang in part because the latter had militarily "sunk" (or risen, as the case may be) to using courtesies like those of the Duke of Sung, whose demise was just recounted. In the Spring and Autumn Period and especially in the Era of Warring Principalities (beginning in 463 B.C.), the "flowery states" including a now decadent Chou, stood graciously but helplessly by as Ch'in, Wu, and Ch'u began undermining through treachery the mutual trust upon which chivalrous restraint in war depended. Stories are told of rivers being poisoned, of incursions on neighbors without warning, and of the breaking of reputedly sacred compacts.[33] As Tsze-fan of Ch'u, who led an invasion of Chin only a year after signing a peace treaty with them said, "When we can gain an advantage over our enemies, we must advance, without consideration of covenants."[34] Generals began pursuing war with little thought of the costs to their men. Thus, when Wu invaded Yüeh, the Viscount of Yüeh forced three ranks of criminals to slit their throats and so communicate to the enemy the willingness of the Yüeh army to fight to the death.[35] So sanguine had wars become by 546 B.C. (when Confucius was a child of six) that Heang Seuh of Sung presided at history's first attempt to outlaw war at an international conference. Popular opinion of the day rebuked him for his "delusions."[36]

THE TÊ (POWER) OF VIRTUE

This important point aside, let us return to our discussion of military etiquette. In the *Spring and Autumn Annals*, the gentleman warrior typically enjoys mastery over his foes by means of his superior virtue rather than through the employment of violence per se. He reigns over his enemies because, unlike them, he acts in accordance with the Way of Heaven in general and the *tao* of war in particular.[37] Observing *li*, the map of *tao*, and acting appropriately given the circumstances, he shares in the divine force, *ch'i* (Sanskrit *prana*) undergirding the universe. Self-disciplined, humble, courteous, turning to *li* whenever possible, acting prudently elsewhere, "everyone under Heaven . . . respond[s] to his goodness [*jen*-ness]." Thus Shun, the mythical sage-ruler introduced at the beginning of this chapter, "merely placed himself gravely and reverently with his face due South [the ruler's ritual posture]; that was all." Which is to say, all the affairs of the empire proceeded without flaw.[38]

The word *tê*, charisma, the social influence presumably issuing from a leader's access to grace, is more than fitting in this context.[39] The gentleman-warrior's power (*tê*) is ultimately said to arise not so much from his weaponry nor numbers of troops, but from the charisma of his example.[40] His *tê* is irresistible. "The character of a noble man [*chün tzu*] is like the wind, that of ordinary men like grass, when the wind blows the grass must bend."[41] For him, other things being equal, defeat is theoretically impossible, and victory can be earned without the use of "naked blades." The classic example of this, the model which all Confucian generals sought to emulate, was Earl Wen and his son Wu, the founders of the Chou dynasty. The *Shu Ching* relates that at the time of their rise to prominence, the Shang dynasty had become dissolute. "Injurious and tyrannical to the multitudes of the people," they collected around them "beasts of the prairie." In the west, however, lived a paragon of virtue, the Earl of Chou, named Wen. Out of fear and jealousy of his increasing popularity, the Shang had him imprisoned. He died soon after he was ransomed, but his son Wu vowed to continue his work to seize the Mandate of Heaven and liberate the masses.[42] At the time "but a little child," Wu together with but 50,000 trusted men defeated the "700,000" soldiers of Shang at the battle of Mu.[43] Accounts of the victory vary. Orthodox literati prefer the following, that of Ssu-ma Chi'en: Wu ordered his general Shang-fu with only a hundred of his most daring warriors to dash forward at the head of a large body of foot soldiers. The opposing army, knowing full well the Shang dynasty's lack of virtue and thus the inevitability of its own defeat, inverted its lances and surrendered without suffering a casualty.[44]

The *Shu Ching*, however, describes the confrontation this way: After the Shang troops had inverted their lances, Shang-fu "attacked those behind them, till they fled, and the blood flowed till it floated the pestles about."[45]

Mencius, one of the great Confucian minds, takes issue with the latter rendition, arguing that it is self-contradictory and thus logically impossible. "When the prince [Wu] the most benevolent was engaged against him who was the opposite, how could such a thing happen?" he asks. Given Wu's access to heavenly *ch'i*, his *tê* would have made it superfluous and stupid for him to have drawn so much blood.[46] As the *Tao Tê Ching* teaches: "The best fighters do not make displays of wrath. . . . This is called the power [*tê*] that comes of not contending. . . ."[47]

SUN TZU AND THE CONFUCIAN TRADITION

Sun Tzu (lived ca. 400-320 B.C.) was the "divine doctor" of Confucian military thought. Emperor Sheng-tsung (reigned A.D. 1065-1085) of the orthodox Sung dynasty, as part of his program to expand and democratize the examination system, issued an imperial decree designating the "Seven Martial Classics" to be obligatory study for all aspirants to military commissions. Preeminent among these classics was Sun Tzu's *Art of War*.[48] Until 1912 cadets were required to memorize and transcribe 100 characters from the *Art of War* in competitive exams.[49]

At first glance it appears that Sun Tzu's Machiavellianism contradicts Confucianism, debunking as it does battlefield ceremony, courtesy, and chivalry. "An army," he says, "cannot be run according to rules of etiquette." "As far as propriety, laws and decrees are concerned," agrees Tu Mu, a T'ang commentator, "the army has its own code. . . ."[50] "The most cynical, the very worst passages in the notorious eighteenth chapter of 'The Prince'," says one critic, "pale before the naked and full-bodied depravity of . . . Sun Tzu's lore on espionage."[51]

But first appearances can be misleading. It is important to understand that the Confucian sage was above all a practical man. And while it is accurate to say that he hated military force, he abhorred even more disorder and rebellion. "Rather be a dog and live in peace," directs a popular Confucian proverb, "than a man and live in anarchy."[52] Hsün Tzu, the foremost promulgator of the theory of *li*, when asked to choose between war and civil unrest, advocated military force "for the purpose of stopping tyranny and getting rid of injury."[53] When his home country of Lu was attacked by the state of Ch'i, Jen Yu, one of Confucius's disciples, led a revolutionary army to resist the incursion. Confucius said that this was an example of "righteous courage."[54] Wang Mang, the Confucian revolutionary who usurped the Han throne and sought to institute a *jen* regime from A.D. 9 to 22, was also an outstanding general who used violence without qualm to quell the enemies of virtue.[55] Ts'ao Ts'ao (A.D. 155-220) "mowed down numerous scoundrels . . . in his military operations" and spread peace throughout the land by following "in the main the tactics laid down in the Sun Tzu and Wu Tzu." For this he was canonized as "Martial Emperor" by Confucian historians.[56]

And yet fundamentally pacifist, Confucianism preferred that victory be obtained with a minimal expenditure of life and treasure, "committing no excess, inflicting no injury."[57] An imperial decree of 1731, verbalizing this preference, provided death by decapitation for forty different military crimes. The felons included those "who oppress the people, native or foreign, on a line of march, by forcing them to buy or sell, plundering, destroying buildings, or violating women."[58] One struck by the seeming radical novelty of Mao Tsetung's "Three Main Rules of Discipline and Eight Points for Attention" need look no further than to Manchu law as precedent.[59] In 1748 and 1784 additional sections were added to the military code. They condemn to "instant death" any general convicted of either "trifling and willfully protracting war by his want of energy or misrepresentation of facts" or "of throwing his own work on another with a view to injure him out of jealousy, thereby delaying the close of the war and causing wasteful expense."[60]

Sun Tzu would have applauded these edicts. Even with its Machiavellianism his strategy of war is calculated to minimize the harm done to the combatants.

Victory is the main object in war. If this is long delayed, weapons are blunted and morale depressed. When troops attack cities, their strength will be exhausted. When the army engages in protracted campaigns the resources of the state will not suffice. . . . Thus while we have heard of blundering swiftness in war, we have not yet seen a clever operation that was prolonged. For there has never been a protracted war from which a country has benefited.[61]

One should never declare war, says Sun Tzu, unless he is virtually certain that the rewards of victory will be substantially greater than the costs to be expended. To this end, he recommends that the regent's advisors carefully weigh and compare their kingdom's military strength with that of their neighbors on the basis of five factors.[62] Let us ignore the first two considerations of terrain and administration and deal with the remaining three.

The *jen*-ness of the sovereign must be greater than that of his antagonists. As in any human enterprise, success in war depends upon good "human relations." In Confucianism, however, the kingdom's social harmony is said to be a direct function of the degree to which the king himself is observant of *tao*. He who acts consistently with *li* and adheres to *yi* will be a good example to others who will follow his ways. Such a ruler can become the emperor of "all under Heaven," never to be defeated by an unrighteous foe. The king who terrorizes his people only increases his enemies, as did King Hsuan of Ch'i, who once pleaded with Mencius, "The princes have formed plans to attack me—how shall I prepare myself for them?" Mencius brusquely answered him by citing the example of the benevolent and unconquerable King T'ang.[63]

The "will of *T'ien*," the circumstances of the Heavens, must be properly discerned. For Sun Tzu, the character "*t'ien*" was used in the sense of "weather" only, and in several places he and his commentators explicitly caution against astrological divination. "Exterminate superstitions," says Ssu-ma Ch'ien, Sun Tzu's biographer.[64] Typically, however, the recommendation to "estimate *t'ien*" regressed to the practice of hiring a *tao-shih* with *I-Ching* in hand to determine the auspicious moment for an attack. This is how Wu Ch'i in his "Art of War" interprets Sun Tzu's insistence.[65]

The commanding general must be a superior man. As it is this factor that most clearly demonstrates the continuity between Sun Tzu's strategy and Confucian orthodoxy, let us examine it in some detail.

The general should use all manner of ruses, lures, feigns, and surprises in order to concentrate superior force at the enemy's weak points. "There can never be too much deceit in war," Sun Tzu declares. Accordingly, when in close proximity to the enemy, he should pretend he is distant; when far away, that he is near. He should employ the major part of his force (*cheng*) merely to fix the enemy's attention; his extraordinary force (*ch'i*, literally "divine force") to strike at unanticipated places. Not knowing exactly where the foe is going to attack, the enemy will eventually be driven to distraction. Frantic, seeking to prepare everywhere, he will prepare adequately nowhere.[66]

Admittedly, this advice does seem inconsistent with Confucian doctrine, but a closer analysis shows that this is not the case. The commander, it is true, should capitalize on the weaknesses of the opposing leader. If he is vain, the commander should flatter him; if lustful, he should send concubines to entice him and render him less wary; if cruel to his men, he should promise them leniency for surrendering; and if overly compassionate, he should continually harass his troops. If the man is cowardly, he should provoke his fears; if quick to anger, he should frustrate him.[67] By the same token, the master general will take care not to be seduced, provoked, or misled himself. "Do not gobble proferred baits," warns Sun Tzu, be not like the fish whose blind greed determines its disastrous fate.[68] Be cautious, but not timorous; discipline your troops to be sure, but do so justly; be neither reckless nor inhibited; in short, emulate the *chün tzu*, the superior man, in whom "there are no stirrings of pleasure, anger, sorrow, or joy."[69]

"It is the business of the general," says Sun Tzu, "to be serene and inscrutable, unfathomable, if upright, not improper; if self-controlled, not confused."[70] But such a state of simultaneous imperturbable equanimity and cleverness is possible only for one who clings assiduously to the Middle Way, the Way of Heaven. He who fails to follow the Way experiences *yu*: fear, anxiety, trouble, and confusion (perhaps in our vocabulary he would be called "insane"). In any case, he is the opposite of *jen*, closer to a beast than a man. On the other hand, he who attends to the Middle Way is not only fully human, he has access to the mysterious power (*ch'i*) of the universe. As a result, his defeats will be few: "Those skilled in war cultivate *tao* and preserve the laws, and are therefore able to formulate victorious policies." Tu Mu agrees: "The *tao* is the way of humanity and justice. . . . Those who excel in war first cultivate their own humanity [their own *jen*-ness]. . . . By [this] means they make their governments invincible."[71]

The sage-general in his oneness with *tao* is insubstantial, inaudible, "divinely mysterious."[72] As such he is like water, the outward sign and preeminent medium of the wisdom and power of Heaven. But who applauds pent-up water when, suddenly released, it fills the lowlands? Who cheers the boulder when it rolls inexorably down hill? So it is with the truly artful general: He whose victories "leave no tracks behind," to use the Taoist phrase, in this case blood-soaked tracks, is a great general. But for that very reason, his successes will go unnoticed by the public. "A victory gained before the situation has crystallized is one the common man does not comprehend. Thus its author gains no reputation for sagacity.

Before he has bloodied his blade the enemy has already submitted.''[73]

We arrive, finally, at the heart of Sun Tzu's art of war and observe that it is identical to the ancient Confucian ideal expressed in the *Tso Chuan:* "The best-won victory is that obtained without the shedding of blood. . . . To win one hundred victories in one hundred battles is not the acme of skill," says Sun Tzu, "to subdue the enemy without fighting is the acme of skill. . . . He who achieves victory without bloodshed is the talented commander.''[74] Through intricate preparation, the calculated use of deception, and swift troop deployment, the sage-general demonstrates to his opponent his insurmountable *tê*, and the futility of further resistance. If the opponent is rational he will surrender without a struggle.

Ironically, then, in order to decrease the costs of war, Confucianism became inextricably welded to a perfidious Machiavellianism, just as for the same reason it promoted the practice of international espionage. Confucian historiography hails countless military engagements won "without the effusion of blood." One legendary encounter, that between Chu-ko Liang and Ssu-ma I, has even provided the plot for a modern Chinese opera: Chu-ko Liang, the story relates, was left holding a strategically important city with only a small detachment. Ssu-ma I, hearing of Chu-ko's situation, prepared a surprise attack. But he approached warily, as he had already been taken in before by Chu-ko's wiles. Reaching the city walls he found Chu-ko playing his flute and his troops in high spirits sweeping and sprinkling the streets. Concluding erroneously that Chu-ko was attempting to lure him into a trap, Ssu-ma quickly retreated, turning a strategic opportunity for himself into a bloodless victory for his protagonist.[75]

CONCLUSION

Sun Tzu's influence was not limited to orthodox Confucianism. His *Thirteen Chapters* was introduced into Japan as early as the eighth century A.D., dominating that country's military thinking down through the Second World War. Furthermore, it inspired the Oriental art of guerrilla war; Mao Tse-tung acknowledges Sun Tzu's authority countless times in his selected military writings:

TABLE 5: Chronology of Chinese Military History from the Legendary Past to the Sung Dynasty, Showing Important Events in the Formation and Use of the Confucian Military Ethic Discussed in This Chapter.

1. Legendary Past. Yü the Sage defeats the flood waters of Chaos not by resisting them, but by yielding to them.

2. Shang Dynasty (1765-1123 B.C.). House of Shang rules China and falls into dissolution.

3. Western Chou Period (1122-771 B.C.). Prince Wen of Chou "but a little child" with a few men, defeats the "700,000" Shang soldiers because of his superior virtue, establishing the reign of Chou (1122 B.C.). Military "drives" during this period are primarily against barbarians and are characterized by brutality. This is called "Western Chou" because the Chou capital is located in the "West."

4. Spring and Autumn Period (770-464 B.C.). So named after the *Spring and Autumn Annals* compiled by the state of Lu for these years. An estimated one-hundred and seventy states are under Chou control at the beginning of this period. At the end there are only eight. During this period, according to the *Annals*, "wars" are fought chivalrously, the victors having superior virtue to the defeated. Confucius, born in 551 B.C. in Lu, will base his ethical-religious doctrines on the stories and commentaries found in the *Annals*.

5. Period of Warring Principalities (463-221 B.C.). Chou rule disintegrates, chivalry being replaced by military anarchy and savagery. Sun Tzu is born around 400 B.C. His Machiavellian *Art of War* gains a wide audience.

6. Ch'in Dynasty (221-207 B.C.). Out of the wars, the state of Ch'in emerges as the dominant Chinese power and establishes military-totalitarian rule. The literary classics, including Confucius' works are burned.

7. Han Dynasty (206 B.C.-A.D. 220). Literati overthrow Ch'in rule and Confucian doctrine wins favor at court. All basic Confucian holy books, including the *I-Li* and the *Chou-Li* assume their final form. Confucian military heroes Wang Mang and Ts'ao Ts'ao employ Sun Tzu's tactics in victorious wars.

8. T'ang Dynasty (A.D. 618-879). First hard evidence of both Sun Tzu and Confucian archery ritual in Japan.

9. Sung Dynasty (A.D. 960-1275). Sun Tzu's doctrines of bloodless victory and overcoming the enemy by yielding to him found compatible with orthodox Confucianism. His *Art of War* becomes required reading for all aspirants to military office.

When the enemy advances, we retreat.
When the enemy halts, we harass.
When the enemy tires, we attack.
When the enemy retreats, we pursue.[76]

This sixteen-character formula virtually paraphrases Sun Tzu's repeated cant to avoid the enemy when he is strong and strike when he withdraws.[77] As twentieth-century neocolonial powers have learned to their misfortune, this ancient lesson is still practiced in Asia.

Mao's belief that victory ultimately depends upon having more wisdom than one's adversary—"know your enemy and yourself and you can fight a hundred battles with no danger of defeat"—is lifted directly from Sun Tzu's treatise.[78] And his infamous quote—"We are not Duke Hsiang [whose exploits are recorded in the second section of this chapter] and have no use for his asinine tactics"—is based upon Sun Tzu's teaching that "all warfare is based on deception."[79] And even the examples Mao uses to color his tactical theorizing—"make a feint to the east but attack in the west" and "relieve the state of Chao by besieging the state of Wei," and "make every bush and tree on Mount Pakung as an enemy soldier" —are jingles and aphorisms such as Sun Tzu employed.[80]

Thus, it is clear, that an understanding of Confucian military doctrine is not simply an exercise in empty historical exegesis. On the contrary, such understanding is essential in deciphering the contemporary Oriental military mind. Moreover, Confucianism, and Sun Tzu in particular, influenced Oriental thought in an even more intriguing way. We refer to the esoteric mystical meaning that came to be given to the ideal of bloodless victory. During the Tokugawa period in Japan, combat without "naked blades" came to be reinterpreted as identical to the individual ascetic's passionate struggle for enlightenment and release from the eternal wheel of reincarnation. Such a concept may be considered the ultimate elaboration of the cosmological symbolism of warfare.

NOTES

1. *Han Fei Tzu*, nan I, quoted in Campbell, *The Masks of God*, vol. 2, p. 388.

2. For an abridged version of the Epic of the Ten Kings, see ibid., pp. 382-92. The story from Yao Ti onward is contained in the *Shoo King* (*Shu Ching*) or *Book of Historical Documents*, trans., intro., and interp. by James Legge, *The Chinese Classics*, vol. 3 (Hong Kong: Hong Kong University Press, 1970 [1865]).

3. "The people may be made well affected by virtue, [but] . . . not . . . so by violence. To use violence with that view is like trying to put silk in order and only raveling it" (*Ch'un Ts'ew with the Tso Chuen* [*Ch'un Ch'iu with Tso Chuan*] or *Spring and Autumn Annals with Commentaries by Tso Chuan*, trans., intro., with notes by James Legge, *The Chinese Classics*, vol. 5 [Hong Kong: Hong Kong University Press, 1970 (1872)], I, iv, 4. "Military weapons are like fire; if you don't lay fire aside it will burn yourself" (ibid.).

For discussions of Confucian pacifism, see Herrlee G. Creel, *The Origins of Statecraft in China*, vol. 1, *The Western Chou* (Chicago: University of Chicago Press, 1970), pp. 242-56; René Grousset, *The Rise and Splendour of the Chinese Empire*, trans. by Anthony Watson-Gandy and Terence Gordon (Berkeley: University of California Press, 1958), pp. 161-63; and finally John Fairbank, "Varieties of the Chinese Military Experience," in *Chinese Ways of Warfare*, ed. by Frank A. Kierman Jr. and John K. Fairbank (Cambridge, Mass.: Harvard University Press, 1974), pp. 1-26.

4. Creel, *The Origins of Statecraft in China*, vol. 1, pp. 335-36.

5. Herbert Fingarette, *Confucius: The Secular as Sacred* (New York: Harper & Row, 1972), p. 17.

6. Ibid., pp. 8, 76.

7. Ibid., p. 16.

8. *Ch'un Ch'iu with Tso Chuan*, VIII, xiii, 2.

9. Fêng Yu-lan, *A History of Chinese Philosophy*, trans. with notes by Derk Bodde (Princeton, New Jersey: Princeton University Press, 1952), vol. 1, p. 69. See also Max Hamburger, "Aristotle and Confucius: A Study in Comparative Philosophy," *Philosophy* 21 (1956): 324-57.

10. *Ch'un Ch'iu with Tso Chuan*, VII, xii, 3; V, xxvi, 3; X, xxiv, 6. See also Frank A. Kierman Jr., "Phases and Modes of Combat in Early China," in *Chinese Ways of Warfare*, pp. 36-38.

11. Quoted from W. A. P. Martin, "Traces of International Law in Ancient China," *International Review* 14 (1883): 75. Cf. *Ch'iu Ch'iu with Tso Chuan*, V, xxviii, 209.

12. *Ch'un Ch'iu with Tso Chuan*, VIII, ix, 8; VIII, xvi, 6. For a concise description of the courtesies accorded visiting dignitaries, see Roswell S. Britton, "Chinese Interstate Intercourse Before 700 B.C.," *American Journal of International Law* 24 (1935): 615-35.

13. Martin, "Traces of International Law in Ancient China," p. 72, related without a source. Although Martin speaks here of a state of Chi, as far as I know there is no such state by that name during this period of Chinese history. "Chi" is the surname for members of the Chou family. The author is apparently referring to Ch'i.

14. *Ch'un Ch'iu with Tso Chuan*, X, v, 6.

15. See Lewis Coser, "The Dysfunctions of Military Secrecy," in Lewis Coser, *Continuities in the Study of Social Conflict* (New York: Free Press, 1970), pp. 246-64.

16. Britton, "Chinese Interstate Intercourse Before 700 B.C.," p. 619. For an example of one of the bloodless battles, see *Ch'un Ch'iu with Tso Chuan*, II, xi, 4.

For analyses of chivalry during the Spring and Autumn Period, see Creel, *Origins of Statecraft in China*, vol. 1, pp. 256-61; Sun Tzu, *Art of War*, trans. by Samuel Griffith (New York: Oxford University Press, 1963), pp. 30-33; and Grousset, *The Rise and Splendour of the Chinese Empire*, pp. 24-27.

17. *Ch'un Ch'iu with Tso Chuan*, V, xxii, 4.

18. Ibid., VIII, vi, 3; IX, xiii, 13; II, ix, 3; V, xiii, 13; VI, xii, 7. See also Martin, "Traces of International Law in Ancient China," pp. 74-75.

Corollary to the edict not to attack one who is unprepared is that proscribing attacks on another during the year of mourning required for a deceased ruler. We learn of this primarily through military actions that breached this proscription and were deplored accordingly as being "contrary to rule" (*Ch'un Ch'iu with Tso Chuan*, IX, ii, 5; IX, iii, 5; X, xvii, 2).

19. *Ch'un Ch'iu with Tso Chuan*, VIII, ii, 3.

20. Ibid., I, xxi, 5.

21. Ibid., II, vi, 6.

22. Ibid., VIII, xvi, 6 and 13.

23. Ibid., V, xv, 13. See also Martin, "Traces of International Law in Ancient China," pp. 75-76.

24. Says Mencius: "The Son of Heaven had only expeditions and no wars; the feudal lords had only wars and no expeditions" (*Works* [Shanghai, 1934], XII: 40, quoted in Shih-tsai Chen, "The Equality of States in Ancient China," *American Journal of International Law* 35 [1941]: 648). The Legge translation of this same line reads: "'Correction' is when the supreme authority punishes its subjects by force of arms. Hostile states do not correct one another." (*The Works of Mencius*, trans., intro. with notes by James Legge, *The Chinese Classics*, vol. 2 [Hong Kong: Hong Kong University Press, 1970 (1895)], VII, ii, 2).

25. Thus, in referring to armed conflict between Ch'i and the Shang-

jung in 646 B.C., Ku-liang's commentary to the *Ch'un Ch'iu* asks: "This was practically a war. Why was it not called a war? In *Ch'un-Ts'ew* (the armed strife between) equals were called wars. (The armed strife between) Huang-kung (of Ch'i) and the barbarians was simply a drive." (*Ku-liang*, III: 30, quoted in Shih-Tsai Chen, "The Equality of States in Ancient China," p. 649).

26. *Ch'un Ch'iu with Tso Chuan*, X, xvii, 4. See also ibid., X, xxii, 6.

27. Ibid., I, ix, 6. Cf. II, xii, 9; VIII, xii, 3; VI, xvi, 6.

28. Creel, *Origins of Statecraft in China*, vol. 1, p. 233.

29. Ibid., pp. 260-61.

30. For a clear delineation of these criteria, see ibid., pp. 196-204.

31. *Ch'un Ch'iu with Tso Chuan*, I, ix, 6; IV, ii, 7. Desmond Martin, *The Rise of Ghingis Khan and His Conquest of North China* (Baltimore, Md.: Johns Hopkins University Press, 1950) contains many examples of the ingenius treachery used by "barbarians" against the Chinese. See pp. 37-41, 143-45, 205, 207-9.

32. The Ch'in, it was long maintained, could trace their ancestry back to the Western Jung (Creel, *Origins of Statecraft in China*, vol. 1, pp. 59-60). The Ch'u were said to have descended from the Eastern I (Ibid., p. 218). The Wu and the Yüeh were reputed to have been raised by "tiger suckled peoples," the Man, from the south (Ibid., pp. 224-25).

33. *Ch'un Ch'iu with Tso Chuan*, IX, xiv, 3; XII, xviii, 2; X, xviii, 3; IX, xxiii, 13.

34. Ibid., VIII, xv, 7. Cf. VII, xi, 2.

35. Ibid., XI, xvi, 5-6.

36. Ibid., IX, xvii, 2-5.

37. Weber concurs with this. See his *The Religion of China: Confucianism and Taoism*, trans. by Hans H. Gerth, intro. by C.K. Yang (New York: Macmillan, 1964), p. 113.

38. *The Analects of Confucius*, trans. and annotated by Arthur Waley (New York: Random House, 1938), XV: 4. Cf. XIII: 6. See also Fingarette, *The Secular as Sacred*, pp. 1-7.

39. For a discussion of the meaning of *tê*, see Holmes Welch, *Taoism: The Parting of the Way* (Boston: Beacon Press, 1966), pp. 22, 78-79, 83-86.

40. Weber, *The Religion of China*, pp. 30, 119, 164, 190. Creel supports this contention, see *The Origins of Statecraft in China*, vol. 1, pp. 65-66.

41. *The Analects of Confucius*, XII: 19.

42. *Shu Ching*, V, i.

43. Ibid., V, iii, 9.

44. Ibid., commentary.

45. Ibid.

46. *The Works of Mencius*, VII, ii, 3.

47. *The Way and Its Power: A Study of the Tao Tê Ching and Its Place in Chinese Thought*, trans., intro. with notes by Arthur Waley (New York: Grove Press, 1958), poem 68.

48. Sun Tzu, *Art of War*, p. 18. See also pp. 16-19.

49. Weber, *The Religion of China*, p. 281, n. 18.

50. Sun Tzu, *Art of War*, 3:21.

51. James H. Murdoch, *A History of Japan*, (London: Kegan Paul, 1910), vol. 1, p. 631. Espionage agents, says Sun Tzu, are the "treasure of the sovereign." He speaks of their use as "living agents," native spies, double agents, and "expendable agents" who are given fabricated information and then executed as being responsible for tactical miscalculations (Sun Tzu, *Art of War*, 13:6-18).

52. Weber, *The Religion of China*, pp. 169-70.

53. *Hsün Tze: The Moulder of Ancient Confucianism*, trans. by Homer H. Dubs (London: Probsthain, 1927), p. 161.

54. *Ch'un Ch'iu with Tso Chuan*, XII, xi, 1.

55. Grousset, *The Rise and Splendour of the Chinese Empire*, pp. 64-66.

56. Sun Tzu, *Art of War*, pp. 184-85.

57. *Ch'un Ch'iu with Tso Chuan*, IX, ix, 5.

58. T. F. Wade, "The Army of the Chinese Empire." *Chinese Repository* 20 (1851): 400-1.

59. See Mao Tse-tung, *Selected Military Writings* (Peking: Foreign Languages Press, 1967), p. 343.

60. Wade, "The Army of the Chinese Empire," p. 402.

61. Sun Tzu, *Art of War*, 2:3-7, 9-14, 19-21; 3:1-2, 7, 11; 13:2.

62. See ibid., 1 for this list. These factors and their prioritizing are identical to that contained in *The Works of Mencius*, II, ii, 1. Legge is of the opinion that Sun Tzu's list was lifted directly from *Works*. Tu Mu, a commentator to Sun Tzu, explicitly quotes this chapter of Mencius.

63. *The Works of Mencius*, II, ii, 11.

64. Sun Tzu, *Art of War*, 11:44; 13:4.

65. See Wade, "The Army of the Chinese Empire," p. 400 for relatively recent attempts to outlaw divination in military affairs. See, however, "Wu Ch'i's Art of War," II, iii, 3 which is also contained in Sun Tzu, *Art of War*.

66. Sun Tzu, *Art of War*, 1:17-26; 5:3-18; 6:13-17, 20.

67. Ibid., 8:17-24; 3:19. See also *Ch'un Ch'iu with Tso Chuan*, VI, xii, 7.

68. Sun Tzu, *Art of War*, 7:27-29.

69. *Doctrine of the Mean*, trans., intro. with notes by James Legge, *The*

Chinese Classics, vol. 1 (Hong Kong: Hong Kong University Press, 1970 [1892]), I:4; II:1-2; X:5; XIV:4.

70. Sun Tzu, *Art of War*, 11:42.

71. Ibid., 4:15.

72. Ibid., 5:9. Cf. *Doctrine of the Mean*, XI:3; XII:1; XXXIII:1, 6.

73. Sun Tzu, *Art of War*, 4:11.

74. Ibid., 3:2-3, 6, 10; 4:9.

75. For scores of other legendary examples of bloodless victory, see Dennis and Ching Ping Bloodworth, *The Chinese Machiavelli: 3000 Years of Chinese Statecraft* (New York: Farrar, Straus & Giroux, 1976). This book, although well-written, suffers from a paucity of documentation.

76. Mao, *Selected Military Writings*, pp. 72, 115. For Sun Tzu's influence on this modern revolutionary, see *Art of War*, pp. 45-56.

77. Sun Tzu, *Art of War*, 1:21; 3:16; 6:6. See also "Wu Ch'i's Art of War," in Sun Tzu, II, iii, 2.

78. Mao, *Selected Military Writings*, pp. 88, 238. Cf. Sun Tzu, *Art of War*, 3:31; 3:32-33; 10:26.

79. Mao, *Selected Military Writings*, p. 239. Cf. Sun Tzu, *Art of War*, 1:17; 7:12.

80. The sources of these three teachings and the historical events to which they refer are, in order (1) Mao, *Selected Military Writings*, pp. 116, 239, 254. He refers to the occasion when the armies of Yüeh and Wu were encamped on opposite sides of the marsh of Leih. The army of Yüeh made "noises first to the right, and then to the left." As a result the Wu army split its forces and the Viscount of Yüeh stole directly across the marsh into the center of the Wu camp to defeat it (*Ch'un Ch'iu with Tso Chuan*, XII, xvii, 2). Cf. Sun Tzu, *Art of War*, 3:13. (2) *Selected Military Writings*, p. 178. In 353 B.C. Wei besieged the capital of Chao. The king of Ch'i, an ally of the latter, ordered his generals to attack Wei's capital. The Wei troops withdrew from Chao to defend their homeland, and when exhausted after a hurried march were defeated by the Ch'i. (3) *Selected Military Writings*, p. 239. In A.D. 383, according to Mao, the ruler of Chin, mistaking the woods and bushes on Mount Pakung as Tsin soldiers, retreated without a fight from the Chin capital. It is unclear to this author exactly what historical states Mao is referring to in this example.

MYSTICISM AND THE MARTIAL ARTS: THE MEANING OF *BUSHIDŌ* IN TOKUGAWA JAPAN

In Japan, even to this day in some places, there is "*-dō*," a proper Way to accomplish every significant act.[1] There is the *-dō* of flower arranging (*kado*), of tea serving (*chadō*), the way of the literati (*judō*), of the king (*o-dō*), indeed even of Buddha Himself (*butsudō*) or of the lesser domestic Japanese numina (*shintō*). Finally, there is the path of righteousness to be traveled by the *bushi* or warrior, *bushidō*. It is the source and religious significance of *bushidō* that we will deal with in this chapter.

A BRIEF HISTORY OF BUSHIDŌ

The idea of a distinct Way to be followed by the samurai goes back at least to the time of Minamoto Yoritomo (1148-1199), founder of the first shogunate at Kamakura.[2] Either as a result of his authentic devotion to Buddha or in an attempt to foster effective social control over his unruly vassals, Yoritomo ingeniously welded together the Buddhist notion of release from the eternal wheel of reincarnation with the dirty work common to soldiering.[3] The vocabulary for his synthesis of sacred and profane came in part from a Buddhist sect which had just recently been introduced into the islands, called Zen (a Japanese rendition of the Mandarin Chinese *Ch'an* [from Pali *jhana* and the Sanskrit *dhyana* meaning meditation]). Zen had several characteristics that appealed to those living a barracks life at Kamakura, and at the same time it avoided the pretentious verbiage and effete ritual of other Buddhist cults. Zen was explicitly anti-intellectual and world-affirming. Neither through passive contemplation nor withdrawal from one's social duties, it taught, does one come to repossess his "soul," but only through attentive action in the world. In addition, Zen demanded stoic resignation in the face of suffering and death, encouraged a self-mortifying discipline, and, perhaps above all, was adamantly authoritarian—the person of the master becomes the embodiment of Truth—a fact which was not lost on Yoritomo. It was exactly these elements which evolved into the rudiments of *bushidō*. First, absolute loyalty to one's superior: "Wherever we may be, deep in mountain recesses or buried underground, anytime or anywhere, our duty is to guard the interest of our Lord. . . . This is the backbone of our faith, unchanging and eternally true." Next, renunciation of reason: "When you are on the field of battle, close your minds to reasoning; for once you begin to reason, you are lost. Reasoning robs you of that force with which alone you can carve your goal." Finally, friendliness with death: "A man once asked: 'What is the meaning of the way of death?' The answer was given in the form of a short-syllable poem which ran as follows: 'When all things in life are false, there is only one thing true, death.'"[4]

Throughout the Japanese feudal age, the relationship between Zen monasteries and feudal magnates grew increasingly intimate.[5] The Ashikaga shoguns (1336-1467) built scores of Zen altars and gave munificent support to monasteries, levying heavy taxes to do so. Legend has Ashikaga Takauji ordering 60,000 images of the Bodhisattva Jizo struck to commemorate each soldier for whose death he was responsible in the wars of 1331-1336.[6] By the same token, Zen prelates assumed influential roles in the shogunate, becoming in some cases personal advisors to the shogun himself. However, as a general rule, the influence seems to have flowed in the other direction, religious values being adapted to political-military demands.[7]

The precedent for this had been long established in the islands. Neither Shintoism nor Buddhism developed ecclesiastical structures independent of the state or the clan. On the contrary, in both cases those who belonged to a particular liturgical community did so because of their clan and locale. In ancient times, each clan had its own divine patron, called a *kami*-spirit, and the clan patriarch was the head priest (*uji-no-kami*) for the family cult. Customarily, clan patriarchs delegated ritual responsibilities to designated family members, one becoming the supplicator, another the ablutioner, and another, perhaps, the master of worship. When around A.D. 300 the Yamato clan assumed paternal rule over the whole of the Japanese family, its clan totem or *kami* naturally became that of all the subjects as well. And the traditional manner of appointing priestly authority by the patriarch was simply imperialized. Shintoism, and later Buddhism, evolved into departments of the imperial government; henceforth, the relationship between church and state would consist of privileges in exchange for divine legitimization and implementation of state policy.[8]

The subordination of sacred matters to reasons of state had at least an indirect bearing on a number of political and cultural developments in the islands. In the first place, Shinto and Buddhist priests tended to be corrupted by their association with worldly power. Gambling by clerics, notorious abuses of vows of chastity, financial extortion of the laity, and even armed combat between monasteries are common to Japanese religious history.[9] In the second place, Japanese warmaking as a rule was much freer from ethical and ritual constraints than was the case particularly in China. Whether or not this was encouraged by the theoretical Buddhist indifference to the world, the fact is that it was the most religiously zealous Zen generals, Yoshimitsu, Takauji, Yoritomo, Kusunoki Masashige, and "Archbishop" Takeda Shingen, who were the most murderous in war. Takeda Shingen (d. 1573), for example, a renowned Zen scholar and Oda Nobunaga's major antagonist in the last years of the Era of Warring Principalities (1478-1600), included in his camp three large kettles in which to boil criminals.[10] In the third place, and most importantly for our purposes, Shintoism and Buddhism could, at the convenience of the shogun, be used to domesticate the samurai, turning their interests from bloody skirmishes to spiritual enlightenment. This is precisely what occurred during the Tokugawa period (1600-1867) when a series of *Rules for Military Households* (*Buke Sho Hatto*) were enforced eventuating in the pacification of the islands after several centuries of virtually constant warfare. It was at this time that *bushidō* was converted from a form of military discipline into a means of personal contemplation—a type of esoteric combat in which the warrior no longer fought primarily with another, but with himself.

In its subsequent editions, the *Buke Sho Hatto* insisted that the samurai turn their attention more and more from military to civil, literary, and other-worldly pursuits, until finally they were admonished to ignore martial arts (*bujutsu*) altogether. In the first edition, rendered by Tokugawa Ieyusa in 1615, the violent role of the samurai was still emphasized: "Literary arts and weapons including *kyujutsu* (archery) and *bajutsu* (horsemanship) are to be the regular and favorite pursuits. . . . Weapons are ill-omened words to utter; the use of them, however, is an unavoidable necessity. In times of peace and good order we must not forget that disturbances may arise. Dare we omit the practice of our martial arts?" But in the second edition in 1635 by Tokugawa Iyemitsu, the precedence of martial over literary arts had been subtly reversed. The way of literature, *bundō*, assumed superiority to *bujutsu*. In 1685 the fifth shogun, Tsunayoshi, virtually ignored the practice of the martial arts altogether. "Literature and weapons, loyalty, and filial piety should be earnestly cultivated, and ceremonial decorum and rectitude be correctly observed."[11] As the samurai lost their military functions, the nagging question arose of how to legitimize their existence. Forbidden by law to farm, labor, or trade, and with the number of appropriate government openings always limited, they would have been considered even more parasitical by the masses had it not been for the invention by Hayashi Razan (1583-1657) and his student Yamaga Soko (1622-1685) of the concept *bushidō*.[12]

Like the *dharma* of the *kshatriya*, the *-dō* of the *bushi* was not viewed by Hayashi and Yamaga as simply a list of ethical imperatives. Rather, it was conceived as a spiritual practice, wherein reverent devotion to the correct manner of acting could become an occasion for profound insight (*satori*) into That Which Is.[13] Through loyalty to one's master, simplicity, austerity, and courage, they taught that the soldier could, like the gods themselves, attain *seishi no choetsu*, a state transcending both life and death. This, then, was to be the role of the samurai in a peaceful Japan: to be exemplars of frugality, correctness, fortitude, and subserviency, and through their charisma, inspire in others the same qualities.

In the Tokugawa period several practices emblematic of egoless fealty to authority reached their final form: *kataki-uchi*, the obligation to avenge violently an insult to one's superior, *seppuku* or "hara kiri," and the obligation to immolate oneself upon the death of his master, called *junshi*. These liturgies have been dealt with elsewhere more than adequately.[14] We wish to focus our attention upon an aspect of *bushidō* which until recently had been completely overlooked by American social scientists, the ritualization of combat itself into various *-dō* forms: *kenjutsu* (swordfighting) into *kendō* (the way of the sword), *kyujutsu* (archery) into *kyudō* (the way of the bow), *jujutsu* (wrestling) into *judō* (the way of yielding), *karate* (pugilism) into *karate-dō* (the way of the "empty hand").

MYSTICISM AND THE MARTIAL ARTS

Legend tells of the Buddhist monk Bodhidharma (Bodai-Daruma in Japanese) who undertook a mission to China from India in A.D. 525. Arriving at the famed Shaolin monastery, he noticed the inability of the Chinese monks to sustain what he believed was a reasonably long period of silent meditation. To provide them the discipline necessary for the attainment of bliss, he introduced them to a type of combatlike calisthenics employing the upper torso, together with yoga breathing exercises. Authorities believe that these drills contain not only the roots of *Ch'an* (Zen) Buddhism, but also constitute the basis for what is variously known as *ch'uan fa* (law of the fist), or by its more popular names *kung fu* or *karate* (*kara* China + *te* hand).[15]

Exactly where Bodhidharma obtained the rudiments of *kung fu* is a matter of considerable debate, perhaps in his native country, for in India the original adherents of Buddhism were *kshatriya* knights. And Buddhist documents contain references to an unarmed combat style, *vajramushti* ("the clenched fist as weapon") that may have been used in the training of the military caste.[16] (Cf. Indra's magical *vajra*, the bolt with which he destroys Vritra.) After the demise of the Mauryan empire around 184 B.C., India entered a time period similar in many respects to the European Dark Ages. It is not farfetched to suggest that traveling Buddhist mendicants, such as Bodhidharma himself, disdaining the use of weapons as contrary to *ahimsa*, but still in need of a means of self-defense, may have found in the *vajramushti* taught to them as *kshatriya* youth a convenient way to fend off highway robbers. In any case, *kung fu* was brought to Japan by Buddhist missionaries, and *kempō* (the Japanese version of the term) became a part of the regimen at Kamakura, to be learned along with horsemanship, fencing, and archery primarily for military ends.[17]

The precise truth of these conjectures is irrelevant in regard to the point to be made here; namely, during the Tokugawa period these boxing techniques lost their military significance and began reassuming the status of spiritual disciplines. They became, to use the Chinese term, *nei-chia*, internal arts of boxing, where the opponent no longer resides outside the self, but within. It would be incorrect to suggest that this notion was totally unknown in Japan until the Tokugawa period. By the twelfth century, to cite just one instance, Minamoto Yoshimitsu (d. 1112) was advocating the use of fencing, together with macrobiotics and meditation to tap *ki* (Chinese *ch'i*, Sanskrit *prana*), the cosmic energy presumed to underlie all power and serenity and thus to guarantee victory against the foe.[18] During the height of the civil wars, Tsukahara Bokuden (1490-1571) was experimenting with *kenjutsu* as a Zen form of active contemplation.

But it was not until the time of enforced peace under the Tokugawa shoguns that these anticipations were brought to their final conclusion by a monk-warrior named Takuan (1573-1646). "When your attention is engaged and arrested by the striking sword of the enemy," he would tell his pupils, "you lose the first opportunity of making the next move by yourself. You tarry, you think, and while deliberation goes on, your opponent is ready to strike you down. The thing is not to give him a chance."[19] Only through daily practice in the *-dō* of the sword, he continued, can one overcome this impediment to success. For then one will begin to respond to each thrust and parry of the opponent reflexively, habitually, literally without thinking. But to act immediately, without the mediation, the meddling of conscious thought, is action in a state of egolessness or "no-mind" (*muga*). And this is precisely the "goal," as it were, of Zen in the first place.[20]

Immediate action in this sense is, of course, not truly action in the literal sense of the word. It is not, in other words, behavior consciously directed toward the achievement of a goal apart from itself. It is more correctly *wu-wei*, nonaction, or to use the paradoxical language of Zen, "actionless action."[21] But whether it is action or not, once one has attained the state of "no-mind," boxing, fencing, and fighting in general become effortless. The combatant resists not, so the theory goes, but flows flexibly (*ju*) with the situation. He becomes like water: of all things least resistant, but that which in the end overcomes all. He becomes tranquilly resilient, not straining against the foe, but yielding to the passionately delivered attack, and in doing so turns the opponent's strength against himself. This is called attaining victory by cultivating *wa* (accord) or *ai* (harmony) with the enemy. In this you "do not recklessly resist your opponent's physical strength," but rather "imitate the action of a boat adrift upon the surface of the ocean." You "pull when pushed—and push when pulled," blending with the opponent, thus allowing him to be self-eliminating.[22] Let us examine this strategic doctrine in the context of a single martial art —archery.

"ZEN IN THE ART OF ARCHERY"

Archery (*kyujutsu* in Japanese) was adopted by the Chinese peasantry from their nomadic neighbors, and during the Era of Warring Principalities (463-221 B.C.) came to provide the basis of military machines the fire power of which was not matched in Europe until around 1620. But during the tranquility of the Han dynasty (206 B.C. - A.D. 220), it evolved into a court ritual, the performance of which was claimed to bring harmony to the empire and peace of mind to its participants. In Confucianism, archery occupies a status second only to daily court ceremonies and music (and ahead of both writing and arithmetic) in cultivating gentlemanly virtue. And the *Li Chi* speaks of promotions to and demotions from office based on the degree of skill with which the candidate wields the bow. For "in this way (from their archery) their characters could be seen."[23]

The archery meeting was incredibly complex. Every act down to the seating of the guests (facing east, graded from the north), the offering of the wine (by the host descending the eastern steps of the great hall, facing west, laying the cup down after sitting, and then rising and excusing himself), and finally the guests refusing and then accepting invitations to eat, was circumscribed by *li*.[24] Only after thirteen distinct ceremonies, including the eating and drinking of consecrated meats and wine, the entry of musicians, the pledging of all celebrants, and the appointment of an overseer of the tournament itself, was the first invitation to shoot given, politely refused, insistently repeated, and then graciously accepted.

Three pairs of contestants, standing to the west of the west hall, facing south, prepared to shoot in the first round of competitions. All were expected to take painstaking care to follow the *tao* of shooting. In the initial contest, "though a hit is made, no tally is laid down," signifying that this was primarily a game of form and style; not of accuracy or strength.[25] For as Confucius taught: "In archery it is not going through the leather which is the principal thing; because people's strength is not equal. This is the old way."[26] In the *Chou Li*, still another court missal, the goal of the first competition, *chu p'i*, is translated by Arthur Waley as "hitting the mark."[27] However James Legge points out that the phrase "hitting the mark" is really a pun or play on words. Accurately construed, he says, *chu p'i* means "to achieve one's ideal," specifically, the ideal of complete manhood. Those who "hit the mark" in this regard, are by definition superior men (*chün tzu*).[28]

The proper form of archery involved first of all standing correctly; left side turned toward the target which was located to the north, after first bending to the right and adjusting the right foot. The archer then firmly grasped the bow in outstretched arms and held the arrow with proper reverence. Finally, he "effortlessly" drew the bow taut and released the arrow without jerking.[29]

During the second competition, the archers were to be scored on their capacity to pierce the target, and the last contest once again reverted to the issue of style. Specifically, "whoever does not shoot in time with the drums will not have his shot counted."[30] Thus, the bandmaster would strike up *Tsou-yu*, and the pairs would shoot to its accompaniment. That person judged victorious was the one with the rhythm of *tao*. For such a person was, at least so the theory went, truly human:

How difficult it is to shoot! How difficult it is to listen (to the music)! To shoot exactly in harmony with the note (given) by the music; and to shoot without missing the bull's eye on the target—it is only the archer of superior virtue who can do this! How shall a man of inferior character be able to hit the mark.[31]

Exactly when a facsimile of this ceremony found its way to Japan (probably as early as the sixth century A.D.) is a question that can be ignored at this time. It is sufficient to note that during the Tokugawa period it was simplified and converted into a Zen ritual called *kyudō*.

Kyudō was not a skill to be learned in a few months. It took Eugen Herrigel, a recipient of a master's degree in the art, the better part of one year just to acquire the ability to draw the bow back without straining. Even then he was warned in all seriousness by his Zen master that whoever makes such swift progress would surely be fated to shipwreck later.[32] This portent proved true for Herrigel who was attempting to master the task of smoothly loosing the arrow at the moment of highest tension. For three years he sought conscientiously without success to emulate the technique of his master, thinking in a typically Western manner that, after all, there must be a secret knack to the effort. He finally did discover what he thought the trick was: cautiously easing the pressure of the fingers on the thumb until it is torn out of position by the power of the bow string. But he was shocked when instead of applauding his achievement, his master frowned, turned his back, and walked out of the *dōjō*, refusing to speak to him for several weeks. It is considered a mistake to confuse *kyudō*, or for that matter any *-dō* form, with mere technical accomplishment, where the performer is fully conscious of his actions, and his mind still mediates on the act. The ultimate goal in *"dō-ism"* is to attain a state of no-mind.

"Only he whose soul is bewildered by the self sense thinks, 'I am the doer'," says Krishna in the Bhagavad-Gita (3:27). The practice of the *-dō* of archery results presumably in the annihilation of this "self-sense." Thus it follows that the truly accomplished archer will have done away with the "illusion" that he has loosed the arrow. Rather, he will appreciate that "soul" or "God" has acted through him. Of course in the literature of Buddhist mysticism, neither soul nor God is really a particular *thing*. That is to say, *It* is not like other phenomena and cannot be objectified: It has neither time, place, nor gender. It is Nothing (*Wu-I-Wu*), the Unspeakable, whereof those who truly know remain silent.[33] Thus during the excruciating period when he was learning to allow the arrow to "release itself," Herrigel pointedly asked his master: "How can the shot be loosed if 'I' do not do it?" "'It' shoots," he replied. "I have heard you say that several times before, so let me put it another way: How can I wait self-obliviously for the shot if 'I' am no longer there?" "'It' waits at the highest tension." "And who or what is this 'It'?" "Once you have understood that, you will have no further need of me."[34]

We might well ask at this point: Seriously, how does one come to realize that it is not I that shoots, but *It* that shoots the arrow? Or to recall Paul's paradoxical aphorism, how can it be that "I live, yet not me but Christ in me"? The assertion which appears just prior to this utterance in Galatians—"I have been crucified with Christ" (Gal. 2:19-20 JB)—reveals the path to this profound realization which is found in all mystical doctrines, whether East or West. The fact is that more than anything else, all the combat *-dō* forms are systematic schools of "crucifixion," or more correctly self-mortification.[35] The task of the Zen master is to destroy the ego of even the most proud samurai warrior by showing day after day the futility of consciously willing "actionless action," of consciously choosing that the sword "move itself" or the arrow "loose itself." Humiliated, close to despair, abandoning forever the elusive goal of achieving union with *michi* (the Way) he renounces his will and surrenders his pride—and precisely at this moment, at least in theory, he attains *satori*. (In Christian mystical literature, the state analogous to the "Great Doubt" or *tai-gi*, is called "the Dark Night of the Soul.")

CONCLUSION

Before their assimilation into Western civilization, the Japanese resided in a sacred life-world. The holy was believed to permeate the whole of things from eating and sleeping to sex and defecation. Naturally, they were often "forgetful" of the truth of this notion, just as people everywhere are plagued with what might be called "mythical amnesia." The genius of the Japanese mind, with ample help from Chinese missionaries, thus created a number of mimetic devices, tools to help them recall the plausibility of the mythos of divine immanence. Among these were the *-dō* forms of Zen and neo-Confucianism, the most influential of which was *bushidō*. Through the absolutely correct, reverent, and self-consciousless performance of boxing, fencing, or archery, ordinary acts—or more accurately acts that are often "misunderstood" as ordinary— were seen "as they truly are," as extraordinary events, imbued with the holy. Even the accomplished performer of *bushidō* himself could be literally transubstantiated into a god, or to use Japanese terminology, into a *kami* or *bodhisattva*. This is not to make a theological claim, but an empirically testable assertion that such an artist could be recognized by believers as manifesting divine charisma. Thus, when in 1912 General Nogi, the hero of Port Arthur, ritually disemboweled himself as required by the ritual of *junshi* upon the death of the emperor, a newspaper editor commenting upon the lurid spectacle felt compelled to say: "Falsely, I thought him / An old soldier: / Today, I confess him / God incarnate."[36]

It is important to clarify exactly what is being said here. Our phrase "recognized as a god" is carefully chosen, because "recognition" implies knowing *again* what was always the case, but what had perhaps been overlooked or forgotten. For the fact is that according to Zen doctrine, General Nogi was always a *bodhisattva*. Only our ignorance and preoccupations prevented us from realizing this earlier.

Let us return to Herrigel's tribulations with the bow and arrow which thus appear in a startling new light. What he, like any other devoted practitioner of a combat -*dō* form, came to realize in the course of his baffling endeavor to achieve union with the divine, was that it is impossible: Buddhahood is not something that can be achieved. However, this is not the case because the Buddha is a Person residing in a heaven and radically estranged from man. That very supposition is precisely the fundamental error or illusion, says the Zennist, which is the source of all human pathos. On the contrary, Buddhahood cannot be obtained, earned, or achieved for the simple reason that we are already the Buddha. The divine is already freely given as a "gift of grace," to employ the language of Christian eschatology. "Not knowing how near the Truth is, people seek it far away: what a pity!" says Master Hakuin. "This very earth is the Lotus Land of Purity, and this body is the body of the Buddha."[37]

It is not only superfluous but a serious misconception to manufacture esoteric techniques to acquire Buddhahood. Japanese Zen has historically taken a stance against becoming preoccupied with *dhyana yoga*—the tranquilizing, quietistic, self-absorbing withdrawal from the world—for its very use implies separation from God. It has urged instead participation in life—"Zen is life itself" —which was why it appealed to the men in the military camp at Kamakura in the first place. But such involvement should be correct participation: One should live attentively and "undualistically," viewing one's work not merely as a means to an end higher than itself, but as an end in itself. "*This* is it!" proclaims the title of a popular Zen pamphlet. However, one's "work" is no longer work; in the classical sense it is play. One's life, if seen correctly, is no longer a burden but a celebration; one's fate is no longer suffered silently, but enthusiastically affirmed.[38] The esoteric combat of the Orient banishes sin, the individual's estrangement from the divine. It does this not through a ritual extermination of an objective enemy "out there," but rather through the sudden symbolic, painful and humiliating wound of *satori*, which shatters the delusions upon which this alienated consciousness rests.

NOTES

1. A corruption of the Chinese *tao*, -*dō* is used only as a suffix in Japanese. The independent Japanese equivalent to the Way is *michi*.

2. The term *bushidō*, however, apparently was not introduced until the Tokugawa period (1600-1867). The term was apparently introduced into Occidental literature only at the end of the nineteenth century by a Captain F. Brinkley in his travelogue *China and Japan*. It is a revealing comment on the relative scarcity of the term's use that the English scholar J. C. Hall could even deny its existence as late as 1915. See his "Teijo's Family Instruction: A Samurai's Ethical Bequest to His Posterity (1763)," *Japan Society Transactions and Proceedings* 14 (1915): 150-55.

3. Minoru Hashimoto, "The Keystone of Medieval Bushido," *Cultural Nippon* 4 (1936): 263-72; Masaharu Anesaki, *History of Japanese Religion* (Tokyo: Charles Tuttle, 1963 [1930]), pp. 210-14; George Sansom, *A History of Japan*, vol. 1 *To 1334* (Stanford, Calif.: Stanford University Press, 1958), pp. 429-31.

4. "'Hagakure Bushido' (Book of the Warrior)," trans., intro., and ed. by Z. Tamotsu Iwado, *Cultural Nippon* 7 (1937): 37-39. This book is attributed to Yamamoto-Tsunetomo, a samurai who served under the second master of the House of Nabeshima in the last quarter of the seventeenth century. It is perhaps the most significant original document on the nature of *bushidō* available in English.

5. The best characterization of this relationship is found in Sansom, *A History of Japan*, vol. 2, *From 1334-1615*, pp. 151-53, 156-66, 410-11.

6. Ibid., pp. 100-1.

7. Says Joseph Kitigawa: "The state functioned not as patron (*schutzpatronat*) [as in German Lutheranism] but as the religious police (*religiös-Polizei*) of Buddhism" (*Religion in Japanese History* [New York: Columbia University Press, 1966], p. 34. Cf. pp. 110-11).

8. Ibid., pp. 30-45, 122-30, 163-64.

9. For an interesting account of the fate of the armed monasteries, see Sansom, *A History of Japan*, vol. 2, pp. 134-35, 287-88, 309-10.

10. Sun Tzu, *Art of War*, p. 173. The "Seven Martial Classics," containing the unrestrained Machiavellianism of Sun Tzu, were read in Japan as early as A.D. 760 and probably two centuries earlier. Indications are that while the Chinese Confucians treated Sun Tzu's *wu-ching* with cautious circumspection, the samurai embraced it enthusiastically. By A.D. 891 Fujiwara-no-Sukeyo in the *Nihon Genzaisho Mokoroku* (*A Catalogue of Books Existing in Japan*) listed no less than six editions of the *Art of War* published in the Japanese vernacular (ibid., pp. 169-78).

The Gempei military romances (1180-1185) report practices alien to anything known in feudal Europe, including sophisticated ruses, feigns, night attacks, and encircling movements of thousands of troops (although we may justifiably view with considerable skepticism the extravagant totals reported in these documents) (Sansom, *A History of Japan*, vol. 1, pp. 289-316; vol. 2, pp. 70-71). After the 1300s, any semblance of chivalry in military engagements was gone. Already by 1333, Takauji had organized a host which Sansom estimates at 100,000 to suppress a rebellion. (The size of the Protestant force at Austerlitz during the seventeenth century was 80,000.) And a new type of soldier, the *ashigaru*, had been introduced to meet the needs of street fighting. Lightly armed, acting alone with little control by his superiors, he engaged in acts of terrorism, arson, assassination, and looting. During the Period of Warring States (1478-1600) the *ashigaru* were arranged in ranks, dressed in uniforms, armed with matchlocks, and supported by large bore artillery. They were systematically employed in pursuit of the strategic doctrine *yami yami tani tani* (search out and exterminate). It was not until the Thirty Years' War that Gustavus Adolphus's Swedish army duplicated these accomplishments and European warmaking assumed a comparable level of rationality (Sansom, *A History of Japan*, vol. 2, pp. 14, 251-60, 309-10).

11. Donn F. Draeger, *The Martial Arts and Ways of Japan*, vol. 2, *Classical Budo* (New York: Weatherhill, 1973), pp. 20-21.

12. For excerpts from the writings of these two scholars, see Hayashi Razan, "On Mastery of the Arts of Peace and War," pp. 355-56 and Yamaga Soko, "Way of the Samurai," pp. 398-400, both in *Sources of Japanese Tradition*, ed. by William Theodore de Bary (New York: Columbia University Press, 1958).

13. Oscar Ratti and Adele Westbrook, *Secrets of the Samurai: A Survey of Feudal Japan* (Tokyo: Charles Tuttle, 1973), pp. 445-59.

14. The interested reader may wish to consult Jack Seward, *Hara Kiri: Japanese Ritual Suicide* (Tokyo: Charles Tuttle, 1968) and J. Dautremer, "The Vendetta or Legal Revenge in Japan," *Asiatic Society of Japan Transactions* 13 (1885): 82-90.

15. For this legend, see Bruce A. Haines, *Karate's History and Traditions* (Tokyo: Charles Tuttle, 1968), pp. 100-103. In 1937 the term *kara* lost its Chinese association for political reasons and was given a Buddhist ideogram "empty," rendering *karate* into "empty hand." See ibid., pp. 14-16, 95-96, 105.

16. Ibid., pp. 18-20.

17. Ibid., pp. 126-31. During the decline of the Han dynasty (ca A.D. 184) peasant rebels led by Taoist monks are said to have employed techniques similar to those of *kung fu* and *t'ai chi chuan* to drive off the imperial armies. If true, this would set the invention of unarmed combat forms and

their association with Oriental mysticism back at least 300 years before Bodhidharma's mission. See Ratti and Westbrook, *Secrets of the Samurai*, p. 365.

18. Ibid., pp. 376-423. In classic Oriental military doctrine it is taught that an individual or an army that has direct access to *ch'i* or *ki* will always be victorious over one that resorts exclusively to muscular or armed force. Thus, says Sun Tzu, use ordinary force (*cheng*), including large numbers of troops and sophisticated weaponry only to distract the opponent. But employ "extraordinary force" (*ch'i*) to defeat him (Sun Tzu, *Art of War*, 3:2-3, 6, 9; 4:10).

19. D. T. Suzuki, *Zen Buddhism*, ed. by William Barrett (Garden City, N.Y.: Doubleday & Co., 1956), p. 291. Cf. Eugen Herrigel, *Zen in the Art of Archery*, trans. by R. F. C. Hull (New York: Vintage Books, 1971), pp. 94-109.

20. The Zen concept of *muga* was employed not only to promote spiritual values, but also mindless fanaticism in war. Iyemitsu, the third Tokugawa shogun, summoned two barons, Sukekuro and Nabeshima-Motoshige, to reveal to him the secrets of war, according to a favorite tale. Sukekuro wrote his doctrines on three large pieces of paper. However Motoshige on a single page wrote, "It will never do to think which is wrong and which is right. Nor will it do to think what is good and what is not. To be asking what is wrong is just as bad as to be asking what is good. The point is that one should never try to think." The following lesson repeats the same point:

"Calculation means weighing in the balance what might be lost and what might be gained. The minds that calculate can never rise above the thought of gain or loss. And what is death but loss? What is life but gain? He that calculates means to gain. When and where he works for gain he must shun death. Hence his cowardice." ("Hagakure Bushidō," pp. 38-41).

21. Suzuki, *Zen Buddhism*, pp. 17, 281-82, 290.

22. These are quotations of Master Kano, the nineteenth-century founder of judo, and Master Uyeshiba, the inventor of modern *aikidō*.

23. *Li Chi: Book of Rites. An Encyclopedia of Ancient Ceremonial Usages*, vol. 2, trans. by James Legge, edited with an introduction and study guide by Ch'u Chai and Winberg Chai (New Hyde Park, N. Y.: University Books, 1967 [1885]), xliii, 46:2. See also sections 4-6.

24. *The I-Li or Book of Etiquette and Ceremonial*. trans. and intro. by John Steele (London: Probsthain & Co., 1917), pp. 74-83.

The actual steps in the meetings varied depending upon the "level" or feudal rank of the celebrants. Our description refers only to the simplest of four ceremonies, the district archery tournament, which was performed by officers of the local district courts.

25. Ibid., p. 89.

26. *The Analects of Confucius*, trans., intro., with notes by James Legge, *The Chinese Classics*, vol. 1, (Hong Kong: Hong Kong University Press, 1970 [1892]), III:16. "The Master angled—but did not use a net. He shot—but not at birds perching" (VII:26).

27. *The Analects of Confucius*, trans. and intro. by Arthur Waley (New York: Random House, 1938), III:16, note 3.

28. *Li Chi*, vol. 2, xliii, 46:9.

29. *The I-Li*, pp. 84-89.

30. Ibid., p. 105.

31. *Li Chi*, vol. 2, xliii, 46:9. Cf. *Shi Ching*, II, viii, 6, stanza 1.

32. Herrigel, *Zen in the Art of Archery*, pp. 60-61.

33. Suzuki, *Zen Buddhism*, pp. 157-70, 187-94.

34. Herrigel, *Zen in the Art of Archery*, p. 76.

35. Significantly, Suzuki uses quotations from both Saint Francis of Assisi and Saint Ignatius of Loyola to show the similarity of Christian mortification to the method of Zen (*Zen Buddhism*, pp. 197-200). For a valuable discussion of further parallels between Christian and Zen mysticism, see Thomas Merton, *Zen and the Birds of Appetite* (New York: New Directions Books, 1968).

36. Campbell, *The Masks of God*, vol. 2, pp. 500.

37. D. T. Suzuki, *Manual of Zen Buddhism* (London: Rider & Co., 1935), pp. 151-52.

38. Suzuki, *Zen Buddhism*, pp. 104-5, 113, 156-63, 169-70, 175-77, 181-85, 194-97, 201-2.

PART II

THE TRANSCENDENT-HISTORICAL SYMBOLISM OF WAR

THE TRANSCENDENT-
HISTORICAL WAR MYTH
AND MILITARY ETHIC

8

INTRODUCTION

The war camp was the cradle of ancient Hebraism, its oldest sanctuary; "Israel" the name given Jacob's descendants after his combat with God's angel in the wilderness (Gen. 32:26-32). ("Israel" [*Yisra'el* in Hebraic] means literally "God fights"; *sarah* "contends" + *el* "god.")

The historical books of the Old Testament are a military history, little being known of an Israel at peace. In the frenzy of battle, Yahweh's presence in His people's midst is truly felt and known.[1] Likewise, in the confessions most indelibly imprinted with the Hebraic outlook—Islam and Reformation Protestantism—the military significance of the cult will be recalled during times of religious fervor. Thus, from the seventh to the tenth centuries (the period of the Great Conquests) the *jihad*, the holy war, became a sacred duty incumbent upon each free, healthy, adult, male Muslim. "It is incumbent upon you (now) to fight however much you may be disinclined to it; for it is possible that things which ye abhor are good for you, while things you are inclined to are bad for you. Allah knoweth; ye, ye do not know!" (Qur'an 2:216).[2] The world was divided into two domains: *dar al-Islam* (the territory subservient to Allah's revelation), and *dar al-harb* (the territory of the enemy). Each year, it was taught, every Muslim prince must campaign at least once in *dar al-harb* to force its population into submission to God's law.[3] And "if ye are slain in the way of Allah or, if ye die with His mercy and forgiveness, that is far better than all they could amass! No matter if ye die or ye are slain, [in either case] unto Allah you must wake" (Qur'an 3:157-58).

The dramatic scene of Jacob's struggle with the angel at Peniel and the military histories of the Pentateuch have inspired not just literal, exoteric understandings of holy war in Occidental religion. The original rendering of "holy war" in Christianity was esoteric.[4] Origen (ca. A.D. 183-253), Augustine (354-430), and Jerome (ca. 340-420) all viewed the real enemy in Christian warfare as residing within the soul of each confessor, and the fight itself as a psychological struggle against worldly temptation. Even as late as the fourteenth century, the mystic Heinrich Suso was employing military symbolism to describe his own mystical journey to the unitive life. Meditating one evening on Job's words—"The life of man upon the earth is like unto that of a knight" (Job 7:2 Vulg.)— he had a vision of a young soldier offering him spurs and knightly apparel. A pacifist, Suso was horrified at the thought of what God was ordering him to do, when the visitor laughed and said: "He who would play a valiant part in the spiritual chivalry of God must endure more numerous and dreadful combats than any which were encountered by the proud heroes of ancient days."[5] The combats to which the visitor was referring are technically known as the Dark Night of the Soul (cf. the Zen *tai-gi*, the "Great Doubt"), the final purgative step in the attainment of illumination in Christian mysticism.[6] It is the point at which the devotee is forced to fight with all his strength against despair, against creeping doubts concerning the meaningfulness of his past life and previous sacrifices.

Viewed esoterically, the Battle of the Apocalypse (Rev. 19:11-21, 20:7-10) *is* the Dark Night of the Soul: the Word of God confronting the Beast for the final time to determine who is to rule the mystic's soul. And the New Jerusalem, described in the concluding chapter of the Bible, is the vision promised to the faithful and true, who throws his own beast of seven heads and ten horns into the fiery lake of sulphur.[7]

THE WAR MYTH

In ancient Judaism, Islam, and Protestantism, a male god who is himself unborn, alone manufactures the world from nothing. Unlike the goddess whose holiness nourishes and sustains the cosmic order and who, behind the veil of appearances, is the world, this god totally transcends creation.[8] He has a relationship with the world, but like that between any producer and his product, it is "artificial" rather than organic.[9] He does not give birth to the world but rather accomplishes creation through command: "And God said, 'let there be light,' and there was light."

The alienation of God from the world is symbolized in several ways in the Old Testament: First, by his very nature, man is fallen, not holy. This fact is represented by Adam's sin in the Garden of Eden, but in another way as well. Although man is made "in the image and likeness of God," he is produced from a substance different from God's; namely, matter, with its associated images of darkness, earth, and the still waters. The Hebrew word for man, *adam*, means "of the soil" (*adamah*).[10] In the second place, *eloah*, the Hebrew term for spirit or ghost, is also a favored designation for God in the Old Testament. But since God alone is spiritual, and man is of the soil, there can be no concept of a spiritual life after death in ancient Judaism. Death is final. It can only mean return to the dust and ashes from whence man came. "For dust you are and to dust you shall return" (Gen. 3:19).[11] In the third place, Yahweh refuses to be objectified by ritual, subordinated to any eternal law, or bound inexorably to any bargain. He is beyond magical manipulation, not even revealing his name to Moses (Exod. 4: 13-15). To the end he remains a mystery to his people. Furthermore, he is a mobile god with a movable ark. He is the god of a nomadic folk who, to find him, must exile themselves, literally and symbolically, from the security of the Egyptian, Mesopotamian, and Philistine cosmic worlds and wander in solitude struggling against despair in the desert, the place of abandonment and lifelessness.

Freed from the fetters of the cosmic world, the transcendent god is absolutely free to act according to his own will and intellect. Judaism, Islam, and Protestantism will, as a consequence, be *historical* rather than cosmological symbolizations of reality. Instead of interpreting public and private experiences as phases of a never-ending cosmic cycle, these religions view them as theophanies outwardly manifesting God's intentions, placing them on a unilinear, one-directional continuum having its beginning and end in God.[12] The historical narratives of all three religions open with the act of creation and man's exile from God. All subsequent events are elaborations of three fundamental motifs: (1) God's love and mercy, signified preeminently by the act of creation itself followed by God's repeated attempts to reestablish a faithful relationship with his creatures through covenant, prophecy, word, sacrament, and book. (2) Mankind's free responses to these revelations, both individually and collectively. (3) God's justice, his repayment to each man as his works deserve.

It is in the context of these three motifs that the myth of the holy war can be understood. (A) The holy war is a sign of God's wrath, symbolically reestablishing God's justice in history while preserving a sense of the orderliness of human existence despite its suffering. (B) Thus, the holy war is an act of rebellion against injustice. (C) Accordingly, the holy war is always fought between absolute good and evil. Let us examine each of these themes in order.

(A) The holy war is conducted in God's behalf, by a specifically delegated people, a faithful "remnant," to punish the sinful—heretics, blasphemers, and apostates—thus restoring God's kingship on earth. However much it may vary in detail as a result of local custom, sin is infidelity to divine revelation, a lack of trust in God's love and mercy. Sin is demonstrated in two ways: through the refusal, upon invitation, to live voluntarily in accordance with a particular revelation, or by breaking a vow to do so.

The specific contents of the revelations naturally vary from sect to sect, but they all call man to have faith and hope in God the Father, and to act righteously, to love and care for one's neighbors. Sin always finds outward expression in some form of injustice in man's dealings, in his not giving to others their rightful due. The holy war scourges the wicked and rewards the righteous. Through it a sense of justice, of the "all-rightness-of-things-in-the-world," is accomplished collectively and psychologically. Human experience is reordered ("re-nomized"), and the historical world is preserved from meaninglessness.

Hindu, Aztec, and Far Eastern mythologies have concepts analogous to justice, but it is not considered the highest virtue as it is in ancient Judaism, Reformation Protestantism, and Islam. In Confucianism, as we have seen, *li* (ritual correctness) is the sine qua non of gentility. But *li* is neither *yi* (moral rightness, the most important aspect of which is filial piety), nor *fa* (legal justice). In the *Analects*, the Duke of She praises the "Upright Kung" for testifying against his father in a case of theft. But Confucius disagrees, saying that in his country the virtuous son will at all costs "screen" even his criminal father, and likewise the father his delinquent son.[13] This concept is alien to the spirit of the Old Testament. In the book of Deuteronomy, partiality in the administration of justice is condemned: "Thou shalt not respect persons. . . . That which is altogether just shall follow" (Deut. 16:18-19; cf. Qur'an 4:135).

To be sure, in the paradigmatic holy war between the houses of Shang and Chou, reported in the *Book of Historical Documents,* Prince Wen indicts the Shang for their "tyranny."[14] However, their most serious offenses, outside of "blindly throwing away [their] . . . relatives," involve "neglecting sacrifices" and "discontinuance of the offerings."[15] In Chinese mythology, the holy war to preserve the cosmos is not motivated to secure congruence between man's affairs and a transcendent, universal, ethical maxim.

In contrast, while ritual propriety and sincerity were well known to Judaism, the prophets of the holy war relegate these virtues to a status far inferior to justice. "What are your endless sacrifices to me?" asks Yahweh through Isaiah, "I am sick of holocausts of rams and the fat of calves. The blood of bulls and of goats revolts me. . . . Bring me your worthless offerings no more, the smoke of them fills me with disgust. New Moons, sabbaths, assemblies—I can not endure festival and solemnity. Your New Moons and pilgrimages I hate with all my soul." Instead, God admonishes his nation to "cease to do evil. Learn to do good, search for justice, help the oppressed, be just to the orphan, plead for the widow" (Isa. 1:11-17 JB).[16]

(B) Justice is continually problematic in Occidental religion; the suffering of the innocent and the happiness of the wicked being, on the face of it, is inconsistent with the absolute power and goodness of God. In Hinduism and Buddhism the world is *ipso facto* just; each act contrary to the Way eventuates necessarily in a particular type of suffering either in this world or the next rebirth. But Judaism, Islam, and Christianity have nothing equivalent to *karma-samsara*, the law of automatic compensation. Consequently, theodicy or the justification to man of God's allowing evil to exist, becomes a major pastoral preoccupation.[17]

Several distinct solutions to the problem of injustice have appeared in Occidental religion, although they have rarely appeared separately in any instance:

1. Final submission to God's inscrutable designs (the answer given by Job, Sufism, and Calvinism); 2. Compulsive conformity to the Law (the answer of the Pharisees, the Shiite Muslims, and Christian fundamentalists); 3. Transference of the yearning for just compensation to one's descendants or to a Last Day of Judgment (millennarianism, as practiced by Jewish, Muslim, or Christian believers); 4. The participation of the innocent God himself in the world's evil, through his own incarnation as man and unjust crucifixion (Christology);[18] 5. *Ressentiment*, the striking out against injustice either literally in political-military action, or figuratively in violent poetic and pictorial imagery. Only this last theodicy need concern us here.

Rage often accompanies the frustration of man's sense of justice when no alternative vehicle, intellectual or political, exists to redress the wrong against him. The experience of powerlessness and injustice, and the act of violence, as Nietzsche has pointed out, are directly correlated. The man of *ressentiment* is a rebel. He emphatically says "no" to undeserved suffering and by implication "yes" to the possibility of rightness in human affairs. His violence is an assertion of faith, hope, and love in the face of death, hopelessness, and absurdity.[19] The highest expressions of Jewish passion, found in the Psalms and the prophets, are, in the main, expressions of *ressentiment*—pleas for revenge against injustice.[20] And their refrains echo through the centuries of Occidental history, sacred and secular, to this day.

> Oh let the wickedness of the wicked
> come to an end; but establish the just; for
> the righteous God trieth the hearts and reins.
> . . . .
> God judgeth the righteous, and God is
> angry with the wicked every day.
> If he turn not, he will whet his sword;
> he hath bent his bow, and made it ready.
> He hath also prepared for him the
> instruments of death; he ordaineth his arrows
> against the persecutors (Ps. 7:9-13).

(C) There is a significant difference between the *causes* of an act and the *responsibility* for it, between the conditions that "produce" injustice, for example, and the individual or group that is called to "respond" to it or to repent for it. In the transcendent-historical myth of holy war the crucial question is invariably "who shall *answer* for injustice," not "who *caused* it." (Normally a person is not held accountable for sin unless he is believed to have been one of its perpetrators, but by no means is this the case universally. At most, causality is a necessary but insufficient condition for responsibility. And during times of severe social crises and rampant paranoia, it is not even necessary.) Rarely is divine punishment employed merely as a utilitarian deterrent to stop further injustice. Instead it is a form of retribution, cancelling out a debt allegedly incurred against God.[21]

As a rule, in Judaism, Islam, and Protestantism, responsibility for the world's sin is projected onto minority populations, strangers, and foreigners; those with tongues, customs, and pantheons alien to God's faithful. In collectively objectifying evil and positing it upon this external enemy, a sense of the cleanliness of His "remnant" is created symbolically. Analogous to the Levitical rite of the scapegoat (Lev. 16:20-23), the projectors can "escape" from acknowledging the possibility of their own blemish. "Imagine 'the enemy' as conceived by the man of *ressentiment*—and here precisely is his deed, his creation: he has conceived 'the evil enemy,' '*the evil one*'—and indeed as the fundamental concept from which he then derives, as an afterimage and counter-instance, a 'good one'— himself."[22]

Thus mythologically, the holy war will be fought between the absolutely righteous and the equally absolute incarnation of Evil. Insofar as it exorcises the objectified evil, the ferocity of the violence in the war must reflect the enormity of the crime against God and man. But the debt of the evil one to his Maker is necessarily fathomless, his sin immeasurable. Therefore, in principle, no limit is placed upon the violence done to him in recompense for his sins. The Hebraic, Muslim, and Christian holy wars, both in myth and enactment, are among the most ruthless in human experience:

> Now will I shortly pour out my fury upon
> thee, O thou that dwellest in the land: the time is

come, the day of trouble is near, and not the
sounding again of the mountains.
  Now will I shortly pour out my fury upon
thee, and accomplish mine anger upon thee: and
I will judge thee according to thy ways, and will
recompense thee for all thine abominations.
  And mine eye shall not spare, neither will
I have pity: I will recompense thee according
to thy ways and thine abominations that are in
the midst of thee; and ye shall know that I am
the Lord that smiteth (Ezek. 7:7-9).

Exoterically, the cosmological holy war is also fought between diametrically opposed principles. But esoterically, this opposition is understood as more apparent than real. Ideally, the conflict is transcended by a vision of the fundamental unity of all dualities in the cosmic whole, for example, *yin* and *yang* in *Tao*. The offspring of Aphrodite (Beauty) and Ares (War), as Greek mythology teaches, are Eros and Harmonia. But in Judaism, Islam, and Protestantism, good and bad are not simply illusions. They are the ultimate categories of reality—*A* and *not A*; and no thing, as the law of identity proves, can be simultaneously *A* and *not A*.

We are not suggesting that in the Occidental religions there are no incidents comparable to the psychic wound experienced by Osiris during his epic combat with Seth, for example, or by the Pandus in theirs with the Kurus, which shocks them into recognizing both their own tainted state and the essential goodness of the foe. Comparative religionists have not fully appreciated that the circumstances surrounding the fight to which Israel owes its name —that between Jacob and the angel of God—bear remarkable parallels to the circumstances of Hinduism's Great Battle.[23]

Jacob wrestles with the angel on the evening before the confrontation with his archrival Essau, patriarch of the Edomites, one of the God-displeasing nations upon whom Yahweh will later place the ban (Isa. 34:1-17). But Essau is Jacob's half-brother, through whose veins runs the same lifeblood as his own. And Jacob, we read, has obtained Isaac's blessing, Essau's legal birthright, through malicious cunning (Gen. 27:1-40). Israel's very origin thus rests upon a crime of epic proportions committed by its first son.

This fact is explicitly acknowledged by the prophets, thus, Jeremiah's warning: "Let each be on his guard against his friend, be mistrustful of your brother, for every brother is a Jacob" (Jer. 9:4 JB).[24]

Esoterically, the injury suffered by Jacob, probably to his sciatic nerve, during his fight with the angel—no doubt an electriclike jolt such as one experiences whenever a nerve is hurt—may be understood as the pain experienced when the warrior sees the evil against which he struggles so furiously as indivisible from himself. Jacob's hip nerve is incapacitated (*sciatica* [*passio*], medieval Latin meaning "[suffering] in the hip") precisely at that moment when perhaps for the first time, he confronts his own shadow.[25]

Recall too the battle in Exodus 4:24-26 wherein Yahweh attempts to kill Moses. Only after Zipporah symbolically circumcises Moses by touching his genitals with her son's severed foreskin, does Yahweh spare his prey. Circumcision is conventionally viewed as a sign of God's covenant with Israel (Gen. 17:9-14). But Jewish prophecy always understood circumcision as more than just a physical operation. Esoterically, it is a psychological wound analogous to that of Jacob's; a painful and humiliating admission of one's own sin. "Circumcise yourselves to the Lord, and take away the foreskin of your heart," admonishes Jeremiah (Jer. 4:4; cf. Ezek. 44:7-9, Rom. 2:28-29).

Be this as it may, *exoterically* the transcendent-historical myth of holy war has little patience with such vagaries. The enraged revolt against injustice blinds the victim (now become the executioner) to everything but white (us) and black (them). "We are at one neither in our thoughts nor in our commands, understandings, nor beliefs, deeds, consciences, nor souls," says Ahura Mazda, the Zoroastrian god of light, in comparing himself to his antagonist Angra Mainyu.[26] Accordingly, Jewish prophecy—which after 600 B.C. was indelibly etched with the myth of Zoroastrian apocalypse—even while acknowledging Israel's sin, posited the existence of a "remnant," a promising shoot of the root of Jesse, who on the Last Day, would inherit the earth. It is a rare Jewish, Muslim, or Christian sect that has not identified itself with this sacred nation, as the sons of light, the One True Church, relative to which the rest of the world is a *massa perditionis*.

THE MILITARY ETHIC

The Occidental holy war symbolically functions thus to cleanse the world of an alien darkness, not to reconcile man to the inevitability of darkness, particularly in himself. It is a world-reforming, revolutionary act of violence, not a sacrificial rite rebalancing good and evil in a vision beyond ethics. An acceptable motive for fighting, a preferred attitude to be assumed toward war, and an ideal way of engaging the enemy, are all implied in this myth. Let us examine each of these components of the military ethic separately.

The Motives for War

Preferably, the holy war is motivated to redeem the historical world, to repay through vengeance the debt accumulated by sinners against revelation. Naturally, considerable controversy centers around the question of whether alleged holy wars in the West have actually been motivated by this idea or by some other less commendable purpose, such as land hunger. Authorities have argued, for example, that the original Islamic conquests were "in fact" motivated less by the spirit of *jihad* than by Bedouin migrations stimulated by several years of drought in the Arabian desert.[27] By the "motives" of holy war, however, as has already been mentioned, we are referring not necessarily to its actual causes (if indeed these can ever be determined accurately), but only to the meanings collectively attributed to it by the combatants; how they themselves are expected to understand their acts of violence. In this regard it is important to keep in mind two facts:

In the first place, it is erroneous to think that what economists call "booty capitalism," the manner in which, perhaps, both the original tribes of Israel and Muhammad's marauding bands from Medina supported themselves, is as such devoid of religious meaning. In Bedouin ethics, the *ghazw* (hence, *razzia*), the caravan or oasis raid, is considered one of the few god-pleasing and manly occupations: "Our business is to make raids on the enemy, on our neighbor and on our own brother, in case we can find none to raid but our brother," reads a line from an ancient Arabian poem. The obligations of the Sabbatical and Jubilee years (Lev. 25:1-19), whereby the fields are to lie fallow and all are to return to their ancestral homes, each to his own clan, are in part ritual recognitions of this original, more holy economic condition. The early Islamic caliphs sought, without great success, to forbid Arab soldiers from partaking in either agriculture or commerce, physically segregating them from tributary populations for fear that they would become corrupted by the sedentary life just as Israel had been centuries before.

In the second place, both the Torah and the Qur'an forbid the soldier to engage in a campaign for worldly motives, although land, slaves, and booty could certainly be enjoyed as gifts after battle. Deuteronomy 20:5-8 lists four criteria to be used for screening out those who might have on their minds thoughts other than Yahweh's glory during the engagement: A man can fight in Yahweh's wars only if he has dedicated his house, consummated his marriage, harvested the crop from his vineyard, and is not "fearful and faint-hearted." Muslim law is just as explicit: Allah's warrior must be an adult male or otherwise have his parent's permission, be of sound mind, and above all be financially independent. Some schools of Muslim law further argue that he must also be a Muslim. However, the more liberal Hanafi school maintains that as Muhammad himself had Jewish and Christian aid in Medina, a sovereign can employ nonbelievers in his own armies.[28]

Although it does not strictly prove anything, the following exchange may be instructive. It took place between Sa'd ibn Abi Waqqas, the Islamic field commander, and Rustim, the marshal of the Persian army, soon after the latter had been extended an "invitation" to join Islam (ca. A.D. 639):

> RUSTIM: I understand that the motive of your coming here is the poverty of your country, and under such cirumstances, I shall be willing to order a suit of clothing, a mule, and one thousand *dinars* for your commander, and a *waqr* of dates for each warrior . . . as I have no desire to kill you or imprison you.
> WAQQAS: . . . [W]hat you have said about our poverty is clear to us and we do not ignore that. . . . But the conclusion you reached as to the motive of our coming here is not correct. . . . For Allah has sent us a prophet and we are united and honored by him.[29]

The Attitude toward War

The enhancement of the spiritual in the cult of the transcendent god and the relative devaluation of the material world lends plausibility to the separation of absolute ends from material means, of the telic and ethical from the practical and utilitarian aspects of economics, politics, and war. It makes credible the experience of military violence as work, servicing an end apart from and higher than itself. In *bushidō* the way of war is simultaneously the end sought by the practitioner. Any idea of an ultimate Truth transcending the present combat is an illusion to be shattered by the insight of *satori*. Ideally, Zen combat is a performance signifying in its meticulously correct, imaginatively colorful, and playfully self-consciousless enactment, the omnipresence of That Which Is in ordinary affairs. But in ancient Judaism, Islam, and Protestantism, what makes warfare holy (when it is so), is the manifestation of God's awesome historical justice in a fallen world. The weapons and tactics employed in this theophany are just that. The exact manner in which God's hosts go about subduing the world is relatively unimportant, as long as it is done with sufficient ferocity to effectively communicate the immensity of His rage.

That a military ethic's preferred attitude toward war is one of work instead of play is indicated outwardly by two things: skepticism about militarism and deglorification of death in battle.

The first consideration is an insistence that "militarism"—extravagant uniforms and accoutrements, useless spangles, feathers, jewelry, flags, and armory, as well as prebattle gift exchanges, personal contact between foemen, and honorable restraint—be replaced by the "military way." By this is meant the selection of costume, baggage, weaponry, and tactics exclusively on the basis of cost-accounting techniques relative to the overall goal of the state to augment its power at minimal expense.[30] "Militarism" is the very thing that demonstrates to the participant-observer that warfare is indeed an end in itself. But the "military way" systematically demystifies warfare by destroying the romantic props, masks, scenery, and roles. It lifts the veil of appearances and reveals warfare in its essence as collective killing, raping, burning, and looting.

By 1513, in Niccolo Machiavelli's *Il Principe*, medieval militarism had come under bitter attack as a form of elevated vanity cultivated by the cynical flattery of courtiers. Under the sponsorship of the *condottieri*, the Italian mercenary captains, military encounters had evolved into picnics, parades, and largely harmless tilting matches between heavily armored horsemen using brittle wooden lances. In Machiavelli's judgment, "Italy was brought to shame and slavery by this system."[31] At Fornovo in 1495, when the *condottieri* faced the coordinated handgun and artillery fire of Charles VIII's French army, they suffered an estimated 3,500 casualties in fifteen minutes. In response to this and the subsequent disasters at Bologna, Capua, Alessandria, Taro, and Genoa, Machiavelli composed *L'Arte della Guerra* (1520). Its celebration of the discipline of the Roman legion and rebuke of the mounted knight found an immediate and enthusiastic reception in the courts of Protestant Europe, becoming a major inspiration of the military revolution that shook the continent in the next century.[32]

The second attitude reveals that a work-oriented military ethic, far from gruesomely reveling in death and battle for their own sakes, ideally views them as liabilities to be avoided if the same goal can be achieved in any other less costly way. Again, Machiavelli typifies the attitude that became predominant in Protestant Europe after 1600. "Better one hundred years of war than one day of battle," he says, "good generals never fight battles unless necessity forces them or opportunity calls them."[33] Machiavelli rebukes the kind of bloodthirstiness glorified in the Mahabharata, expounding upon the utilitarian necessity of sobriety and impersonality in combat, "Discipline does more in war than enthusiasm." Only when order is preserved can the optimum power of attack be realized at minimal cost.[34]

As we shall see later, both Muslim and Protestant generals acknowledged the importance of religious sentiment in battle. (Even Machiavelli lauds Alexander of Macedon and the ancient Roman field marshals for their demagoguery.) Singing, preaching from a holy Book, collective prayer, hypnotic drum cadences, and in the case of Islam, dancing dervishes all were systematically employed to induce mass assurance of the presence of the Holy One in the field. These techniques, however, were not intended to create orgiastic frenzies; on the contrary, their object was to instill level-headed serenity in the face of danger. Accordingly, the use of chemical intoxicants, homo- or heterosexual stimulation, and the consumption of blood and raw flesh, any of which might result in uncontrollable irrational seizures, were absolutely forbidden both in Allah's and in Christ's camps. In the Turkish and in the Swedish armies the suicidal berserker corps were relegated to the largely subsidiary tasks of prebattle harassment and demoralization of the enemy host. As terrifying as the Arabic and Turkish *ghazi* horse-man or Gustavus Adolphus's Finnish cavalry appeared, the final responsibility for engaging the enemy in actual battle always resided with the closed phalanx, "the lines of which," to quote ibn-Khaldun, "are orderly and evenly arranged like arrows or rows of worshippers at prayer." For as Muhammad says: "God loves those who fight in His behalf in a line, as if they were a strongly constructed building."[35] Both Protestant and Muslim military thought adhered closely to Roman teachings which held that the *ekstasis* of the heroic Greek hoplite was a liability, a form of *superstitio* that could upset the discipline of the legion and endanger the campaign.

War as Science

In a world where means are separate from ends, the relative ethicality of the means depends upon their utility to the end. In the context of the holy war this means that might, or to use Machiavelli's term *virtù*, becomes the basis of right.

The introduction of *virtù* into common parlance and its equivalents—the Elizabethan "policie," the French *raison d'état*, or the German *Realpolitik*—during the sixteenth and seventeenth centuries represented a far-reaching alteration in European moral thought. The word *virtus* (manhood), with which *virtù* shares the same root, for the Church fathers had always implied in this order: *prudentia* (contemplative wisdom), *justitia* (consistency with Natural Law), and *fortitudo* (fortitude).[36] But revolutionary Protestant moralists, many of whom had read Machiavelli, rejected this notion of virtue as inadequate to the task of reconstructing civilization on Christian lines. The times called less for quiet submission to ancient custom and more for confronting evil courageously. Machiavelli spoke for many when he said:

Our religion [as represented in the Scholastic theory of virtue] . . . demands that you be fit to suffer rather than to do something strong. . . . This . . . appears to have rendered the world weak and given it up in prey to criminal men who can manage the world with safety seeing that the large majority, in order to enter Paradise, think more of bearing their beatings than of avenging them.[37]

In the Machiavellian literary genre, prudence, the mother of the virtues, was reinterpreted to mean practicality in a narrow worldly sense—don't take undue risks in combat, you may hope for the best but expect the worst from your opponent. (Mutual trust, upon which medieval chivalric restraint in war depended, was destroyed along with the confessional unity of the Church during the Reformation.) In the second place, Machiavellianism taught that to overcome the Devil's resistance in war, the righteous must first learn and then adapt their tactics to the laws of nature. But in the Protestant mind, these were not understood to be Aquinas's *Jus Naturale*, the just creature's participation in Divine Law. Rather, they came to be viewed as something closer to Francis Bacon's causal laws (or Machiavelli's *necessità*) of political-military affairs. The implication of this reconstitution of political virtue is that it excluded nothing in principle from the military arsenal of the righteous (including the appearance of justice where "reasons of religion" recommended it). Freed from the moral constraints of the Church, Protestant revolutionaries rarely hesitated to use any conceivable tack or tool, any organizational invention that promised success in holy war. "Where the safety of the country depends upon the resolution to be taken, no considerations of justice or injustice, humanity or cruelty, nor glory or of shame, should be allowed to prevail."[38]

These are the dimensions of the religious-meaning structure of warfare—the holy war myth and the *Kriegethik*—peculiar to the cult of the transcendent god. The following chapters will examine these dimensions in the cases of ancient Hebraism, Islam, and Reformation Protestantism.

NOTES

1. Rudolf Smend, *Yahweh War and Tribal Confederation*, trans. by Max G. Rogers (Nashville, Tenn.: Abingdon Press, 1970), pp. 27-29, 42.

2. There are no authorized non-Arabic renditions of the Qur'an. Unless otherwise specified in the text, we rely upon the English translation by Hashim Amir-Ali, *The Message of the Qur'an Presented in Perspective* (Rutland, Vermont: Charles Tuttle, 1974). We have also consulted J. M. Roswell's colorful rendition, *The Koran* (Sydney, Australia: E. W. Cole, n.d.) and Majid Khadduri's translations as they appear in *War and Peace in the Law of Islam* (Baltimore: Johns Hopkins University Press, 1955). This last volume will henceforth be referred to as *War*.

3. "Fight ye those who believe not in Allah, nor in the final Day, who do not make taboo that which has been made taboo by Allah and His Apostle; who follow not the teachings true among the Peoples of the Book —until they willingly offer *jizya* [tribute] and are quite subdued" (Qur'an 9:29).

4. The reader may wish to reread comments on this subject at the beginning of chapter 5.

5. Evelyn Underhill, *Mysticism* (New York: E. P. Dutton, 1911), pp. 405-6.

6. Ibid., pp. 380-412.

7. These notions are not unique to Catholicism. Frank W. Sandford's, *The Art of War for the Christian Soldier* (Amherst, N.H.: Kingdom Press, 1966), a publication of his sermons to the Bible School at Shiloh, Maine at the close of the nineteenth century, contains an intriguing esoteric interpretation of the Jewish conquest of the Promised Land, including the exterminations, absolute authority relations, and the deceptions employed by the victors. The conquest shows the reader the tactics he must use if he is to overcome the "Amorite within himself."

The sermons of the late Reformation preachers were filled with associations of fighting and struggling with authentic Christianity: "Fight the good fight of the Lord" (Seward); "If no soldier, no Christian" (Everard); "Above all He honors warlike and martial design" (Sutton); "The condition of the child of God is military life" (Taylor). It should be noted that besides being calls to personal saintliness, these were also exhortations to revolutionary violence.

8. This may be contrasted with a favorite Hindu creation story found in the "Brhadaranyaka Upanishad" or Great Forest Book (ca. 700 B.C.). Atman or True Self, upon becoming conscious, experienced fear and desire. To escape from loneliness, Atman split itself in half, becoming male and female. They mated and produced the human species. Feeling shame at having been known by man, woman turned herself into a cow. Pursuing her, man became a bull. They mated and produced the race of cattle. Subsequently, the cow turned herself into a mare, then an ewe, and so on,

becoming finally an ant. At each transformation the male followed suit first as a stallion, then as a ram, and so on, coupling with her in each form, until all life was created. In the end, Atman could proclaim: "I, indeed, am this creation, for I emitted it all from myself." The commentator agrees: "The world is his, indeed he [Atman] is the world itself." Thus, is the world called *srstih* in Sanskrit, "that which is poured forth" from God ("Brhadaranyaka Upanisad," in *The Thirteen Principal Upanishads*, trans. by R. E. Hume (London: Oxford University Press, 1921), 1:6.1-17, 4:4, 5-6. See the commentary by Joseph Campbell, *The Masks of God*, vol. 2, pp. 84-87.

9. This is Peter Berger's term. See *The Sacred Canopy*, p. 116.

10. Biblical scholars hold that the Akkadian creation story, abstracted by the Israelites of its color, was the basis of the first chapters of Genesis. The story opens with an epic struggle between Marduk, the sun god, and his mother, goddess of the night. Out of the timeless waters, Tiamat has given birth to the epitomy of evil: eleven types of monsters, scorpion-men, vipers, and mad dogs, all armed with poisoned fangs. From among the most revolting of her retainers, she has chosen the fire-breathing snake, Kingu, as her favorite. Marduk, with his four horses—Killer, Pitiless, Tramper, and Flier—destroys the cosmic mother and then produces the world from her remains: "He split her [Tiamat], like a shellfish, in two halves, setting one-half to be the heavens and the lower half the earth." Mankind Marduk makes, not from his own substance, but from Kingu's flesh. *Tehom*, the "deep" mentioned in the first chapter of Genesis, over which Elohim hovered and from which he created the world, is a Hebrew cognate of Tiamat. Furthermore, as Marduk spread the upper half of the mother-body as a roof over the waters, so "Elohim made the firmament and separated the waters that were under the firmament from those that were above the firmament" (*Enuma elish*, trans. and ed. by Alexander Heidel as *The Babylonian Genesis* (Chicago: University of Chicago Press, 2nd ed., 1951), pp. 11-48. For an abridged version see Campbell, *The Masks of God*, vol. 3, pp. 76-85.

11. Thus can Ecclesiastes lament:

"For to him that is joined to all the living there
is hope; for a living dog is better than a dead lion.
    For the living know that they shall die; but the
dead know not anything, neither have they any more a
reward; for the memory of them is forgotten.
    Also their love, and their hatred, and their envy,
is now perished; neither have they any more a portion
for ever in anything that is done under the sun."

. . . .

"Whatsoever thy hand findeth to do, do it with thy
might; for there is no work, nor device, nor knowledge,
nor wisdom, in the grave, whither thou goest" (Eccles.
9:4-6, 10).

12. For the classic statement, see Eric Voegelin, *Israel and Revelation, Order and History* (Baton Rouge: Louisiana State University Press, 1956), vol. 1, pp. 21-35, 111-33.

13. Confucius, *Analects*, XIII: 18.

14. *Shoo King* (*Shu Ching*), V, i, 3.

15. Ibid., V, ii. By the same token, sin and guilt have little significance in Confucianism. Only 3 of the 500 paragraphs of the *Analects* deal with the related subject of shame, and none at all with sin. One may, it was held, certainly be disgraced by the shame (*ch'ih*) that one brings upon himself through intemperateness, obsequiousness, pride, or disloyalty, but he is not thereby morally corrupted. There is no idea of him choosing the regretful course of action as an autonomous being with his own free will. "In vain," Weber tells us, "Christian missionaries sought to awaken a feeling of sin" among the Chinese literati; they refused to be burdened with anything so lacking in dignity (*The Religion of China*, pp. 228-29). For a concurring analysis, see Fingarette, *Confucius: The Secular as Sacred*, pp. 18-36.

16. For comparable exhortations to justice, see Mic. 7:9, Ps. 51:14, Matt. 5:48.

17. For the classic sociological discussion of theodicy, see Weber, *The Sociology of Religion*, pp. 112-15, 138-50. Peter Berger's analysis in *The Sacred Canopy*, pp. 53-80 is based upon this.

18. For a brilliant analysis of Christology, see Berger, *The Sacred Canopy*, pp. 76-80.

19. Albert Camus, *The Rebel*, trans. by Anthony Bower (New York: Vintage Books, 1956) contains perhaps the most valuable treatment of *ressentiment* written in the twentieth century.

20. According to Weber: "In no other religion in the world do we find a universal deity possessing the unparalleled desire for vengeance manifested by Yahweh. . . . In the mind of the pious Jew the moralism of the law was inevitably combined with . . . hope for revenge, which suffused practically all the exilic and postexilic sacred scriptures. . . . To interpret *ressentiment* as the decisive element in Judaism would be an incredible aberration, in view of the many significant historical changes which Judaism has undergone. Nevertheless, we must not underestimate the influence of *ressentiment* upon even the basic characteristics of the Jewish religion" (*The Sociology of Religion*, p. 111f).

21. Fingarette, *Confucius: The Secular as Sacred*, pp. 24-27. This, by the way, is one basis for the dispute between Confucianism and Chinese Legalist philosophy and also between Confucianism and Maoism.

22. For the complete passage, see Friedrich Nietzsche, *Toward a Genealogy of Morals*, trans. by Walter Kaufman (New York: Vintage Books), part I, sec. 10.

23. But see F. Van Trigt, "La Signification de la Lutte de Jacob près du Yabboq," *Oudtestament Studien* 12 (1958): 281.

24. The King James Version reads: ". . . [A]nd trust ye not any brother: for every brother will utterly supplant, . . ." See also Hosea's accusation, 12:2-4 and Van Trigt, "La Signification de la Lutte de Jacob," p. 288.

25. J. L. McKenzie, "Jacob at Peniel," *Catholic Biblical Quarterly* 25 (1963): 75.

26. *The Zend Avesta*, vol. 3, trans. by L. H. Mills (Oxford: Clarendon Press, 1867), Yasna 45:2-3.

27. For the argument that the Islamic conquests were "caused" by ideal motives, see John Bagot Glubb, *The Great Arab Conquests* (London: Hodder & Stoughton, 1963), p. 307 and W. R. W. Gardner, "Jihad," *Muslim World* 2 (1912): 347-57. For the contrary view that the cause was material, see W. Montgomery Watt, "Islamic Conceptions of the Holy War," in *The Holy War*, ed. by Thomas Patrick Murphy (Columbus: Ohio State University Press, 1976), pp. 147-52; Edward J. Jurji, "The Islamic Theory of War," *Muslim World* 30 (October 1940): 332-42; and Weber, *The Sociology of Religion*, pp. 51-52, 87.

28. Khadduri, *War*, pp. 84-86.

29. Abu Ja'fr Muhammad ibn Jarir, *Ta'rikh al Rusu wa al-Muluk* (Leiden: n.p., 1870-1901), Series I, V, 2276-77, quoted in Khadduri, *War*, p. 99. Consider, however, this verse from Abu-Tammâm's *Hamâsah:*

"No not for Paradise didst thou the nomad life forsake;
Rather, I believe, it was thy yearning after bread and dates"
(Philip K. Hitti, *History of the Arabs* [New York: St. Martins Press, 1967], p. 144).

30. For this distinction the reader is referred to Alfred Vagts, *A History of Militarism* (New York: Meridian Press, 1959), pp. 1-22.

31. Niccolo Machiavelli, *The Prince*, trans. by Christian Detmold, ed. by Lester Crocker (New York: Washington Square, 1974), p. 57.

32. Felix Gilbert, "Machiavelli: The Renaissance of the Art of War," in *Makers of Modern Strategy*, ed. by Edward M. Earle (Princeton, N.J.: Princeton University Press, 1961), pp. 3-25.

33. Niccolo Machiavelli, *The Art of War*, vol. 2, *Machiavelli: The Chief*

Works and Others, trans. and ed. by Allan H. Gilbert (Durham, N.C.:
Duke University Press, 1965), pp. 718-19. See Charles Oman, *The History
of the Art of War in the Sixteenth Century* (London: Metheun & Co.,
1937), p. 571 for a note on the influence that these admonitions had on the
Protestant general Maurice of Nassau.

34. Machiavelli, *The Art of War*, pp. 660-62, 691.

35. Ibn-Khaldun, *The Muqaddimah*, vol. 2, trans. by Franz Rosenthal
(New York: Bollingen Foundation Inc., 1958), pp. 73-82.

36. For a readable account of the Thomistic notion of virtue, see Josef
Pieper, *The Four Cardinal Virtues* (South Bend, Ind.: University of Notre
Dame Press, 1966). For the significance of the shift in the meaning of
"virility" during the Renaissance, see Hannah Pitkin, *Wittgenstein on
Justice* (Berkeley: University of California Press, 1972), pp. 308-10. For the
rise of the cult of *virtù*, see Alfred von Martin, *Sociology of the Renaissance*, trans. by W. L. Luetkens, intro. by Wallace K. Ferguson (New
York: Harper Torchbooks, 1963), pp. 15, 39, 69. For a good analysis of the
real meaning of *virtù*, see John Plamenatz, "In Search of Machiavellian
Virtù," in *The Political Calculus*, ed. by Anthony Parel (Toronto: University of Toronto Press, 1972), pp. 157-78.

37. Niccolo Machiavelli, *Discourses on the First Decade of Titus Livius*,
vol. 1, *Machiavelli: The Chief Works and Others*, 3:41.

38. Ibid., 2:2.

9

DIVINE TRANSCENDENCE: THE ANCIENT HEBRAIC MILITARY ETHIC

RITUAL OBLIGATIONS

In the ancient Hebraic world, warfare was a sacred enterprise, a holy obligation.[1] Repeatedly in the Old Testament, Yahweh awakens His nation to the crimes of unrighteousness, and urges it to "gird up thy loins like a man" for battle. But unlike the Christian military sacrament, the Hebraic holy war was rarely used as an instrument for the forcible conversion of nonbelievers. Ideally, it was intended only for expelling the uncircumcised from the villages and farms of Palestine. Not until the world conquests first of Darius and then of Alexander which occurred about 700 to 900 years after the seizure of the Promised Land, did Occidental mythology seriously begin contemplating the possibility of a single universal religion for all men, established by force of arms.

As for sacramental warfare elsewhere, the rules circumscribing the Hebraic military campaign were carefully transcribed. The Old Testament lists five distinct requisites that must be satisfied before Israel will be permitted by God to fall upon His enemies. There first must be a ceremonial summoning of the twelve tribes of Israel by the ram's horn. Once collected at a central location, the potential warriors must be screened to determine their fitness for battle. Those, say the legalists, are exempt from battle who are there for the wrong reasons: to glorify themselves instead of God.[2] Next, the enemy city must be formally offered the choice either peacefully to become tributaries to God's nation, or to fight. If the invitation to surrender is ignored, then Yahweh's favorable will must be discerned by the drawing of lots. Only at the propitious moment can the fifth and final step before battle be taken, the utterance of the collective war cry, the *t'ru'ah:* "Arise, Yahweh, and let thy enemies be scattered!" This is the cry, say the history books, that crumbled the walls of Jericho (Deut. 20:1-12 and Num. 10:1-9).

Upon completion of the contest, the question arises of the division of spoils. Again, the law is explicit. Booty, it is said, is to be divided equally between the soldiers and the community, with a portion taken out for the Levites and Yahweh (Num. 31:25-47). The prizes of war include soldiers and their women and children. Those captives residing outside the boundaries of the Promised Land can either be enslaved, sold, or made concubines, as circumstances permit. (The disposition of those living within the Promised Land will be discussed below.) In any case, before they are allowed entry into Israel, the captives, like the victors themselves, must undergo the purificatory and exclusionary rites recounted earlier because these persons had come into direct contact with death. (Num. 31:19-34).³ For the ancient Hebrew, as among all primitive societies, death and killing were taboo.

In the Torah the relationship of battlefield concubinage can be legally consumated only after seven days. The concubine is not a slave and, therefore, may not be sold. If her master finds her unpleasing, he is obligated by law to set her free (Deut. 21:10-14). Presumably, this applied only to captive women outside the community of Israel. However, there are stories of marriage by rape even among the Chosen People. For example, after its defeat at Gibeah the house of Benjamin took its wives through force, and seized several more virgins in the vineyards at Shiloh because all its original women had been killed (Judg. 21:8-23).

These regulations comprise the *jus ad* and *post bellum* for Yahweh's nation. As for the *jus in bello*—the rules governing the use of certain tactics and weapons—there are none. The ancient Hebraic martial ethic places absolutely no restraints on the use of violence in combat. By contrast, the Hindu *dharmashastras* outlaw the use of barbed, poison, and fire weapons, and place virtually the complete population, apart from the combatants themselves, under immunity from harm. Even the latter can be rightfully attacked only if they are properly armed, are not fleeing from battle, and are not physically injured or in some other way distressed. *The Laws of Manu* expressly proscribe the burning of enemy camps, night attacks, and assassinations. But in ancient Hebraism, God in His transcendent majesty, apart from a desire for prayers and post-battle offerings, is wholly indifferent to the actual conduct of war.

The freedom of Yahweh war from ritual constraints raises the question of whether it can be considered sacred combat in the strict sense of the word. Rudolf Smend, the foremost authority on the subject says this:

The war of Yahweh as such and as a whole can hardly be subsumed under the category of the cultic. . . . The priests are not essentially prominent, and what there is of cultic usage is the preparation which occurs in consecration for a completely uncultic historical action of unique and incomparable force. . . . Even the accompanying music has much improvisation; the wild, charismatic character of Yahweh war cannot attain to the orderly regularity which is otherwise the distinguishing mark of the cultus.[4]

Smend holds that the Israelite conquests were conventionalized by ritual only in writing and then long after the fact, perhaps through Greek influence. The actual conquests themselves, he says, were characterized by uncontrolled violence.[5]

The absence of tactical and weapons restraints cannot be considered due to the primitive level of Israelite tribal organization at the time of the conquests. On the contrary, the anthropology of war indicates that typically communities at a low level of political development place large numbers of sacred proscriptions around armed combat.[6] Our hypothesis is that, as in the Yahweh cult, where the divine is conceived as radically transcending the realm of natural events, then war, as part of that realm, will be experienced as only a means to a higher end. Consequently, it will have few playful, cultic attributes. This does not mean that the Yahweh war is not holy. It most certainly is. But it is not an immanentist-cosmological symbolism of war. It is an altogether different type: an act of violence conducted not to uphold the cosmic order, but to establish God's terrible justice in history in the manner deemed most practical.

MACHIAVELLIANISM IN THE WAR OF YAHWEH

For all its puritanical legalism in the areas of diet and sex, the Old Testament is perfectly compatible with an opportunistic and calculating Machiavellianism. Most, if not all, of Israel's victories over its enemies are attributed to a proud refusal by God's warriors to conform to any standards of chivalry whatsoever.[7] The conquests of both Bethel and Jericho (ca. 1200 B.C.), for example, are said to have resulted from the treachery of "fifth columns." In the latter case a harlot named Rahab is the turncoat-heroine.[8] Jericho, furthermore, is plundered on the day of the Sabbath, when work of any sort is absolutely prohibited by law (Judg. 1:22-26, Josh. 2:1-25). Ambushes after feigned retreats were the bases of the downfalls not only of Ai (Josh. 8:3-19), but also of Saul's victories over the Amalekites and the Philistines about two centuries later (1 Sam. 15: 4-6; 14: 1-23). In the latter case Jonathan, Saul's commander, approached the enemy camp sentries with a peaceful air and then slaughtered them, inducing wild confusion in the camp that eventuated in its rout. Treachery was utilized even in conflicts within Israel itself. Thus Yahweh's Chosen People crushed the tribe of Benjamin in an ambush at Gibeah after having earlier been defeated by them in a fair fight (Judg. 20:29-48). The notorious King Abimelech did the same thing at Shechem when the city rebelled after he murdered the 70 sons of Jerubaal there. Abimelech's night ambush of the city was followed by an unsuspected massacre of the peaceful tillers of the soil in the neighborhood (Judg. 9:32-46). But the most famous night terror attack of all was conducted by Gideon's 300 stalwarts, picked significantly enough for their ferociousness, as indicated by their willingness to lap water like dogs. When reconnaissance revealed that morale was already low in the Midian camp, Gideon ordered his men to sneak upon the camp hiding their torches in jars until the trumpets sounded so that they could descend en masse upon the horrified sleepers (Judg. 7:6-8, 16-22).

Machiavellian perfidiousness, as the case of King Abimelech suggests, is not limited to the battlefield in the Old Testament. The Benjaminite champion Ehud is applauded for skulking into the tent of Eglan, the king of Moab, and then killing him (Judg. 3:15-20). Jael is celebrated in the bloody Song of Deborah and Barak for her murder of the Canaanite General Sisera by hammering a tent peg through his brain while he slept (Judg. 4:17-22). Five hundred years later around 600 B.C., the beautiful widow Judith temporarily staved off the Assyrian conquest through a similar assassination of General Holofernes (Jth. 13:4-12).

The insidiousness of Jael's act can be appreciated only by comparing it to the ancient Bedouin custom of asylum (Arabic *dakhâla*). For while Holofernes was attempting to seduce Judith in his own tent, Sisera had sought protection in Jael's abode under the auspices of the right to hospitality, considered by analysts to be among the most obligatory of all nomadic folkways. Asylum is explicitly stated as a law of God both by Moses in Exodus (25:9)[9] and by Muhammad.[10] Abraham, it is said, welcomed three complete strangers to his tent and provided them with food, drink, and perhaps even his own wife, Sarah (Gen. 18:1-31). The Benjaminites at Gibeah failed to treat the Levite from Ephraim with the same degree of respect and as a result were harshly punished by Israel centuries later (Judg. 19:11-30). The significance of Jael's act, is that when it comes to achieving military victory in the Old Testament, apparently no law, even the most sacred, is so binding that it cannot be transgressed.

THE EXTENT OF THE HEBRAIC HOLY WAR

The military history of ancient Judaism includes a period lasting longer than the time between the Hundred Years' War and World War II. Naturally, it would be impossible to attempt to derive all the various battles, weapons, and tactics from a single military tradition. In fact, a careful analysis of the Bible reveals two distinct military ethics: the one just depicted, which is characterized in the books of Joshua and Judges, and another more "civilized" ethic, introduced in the books of Kings, Samuel, and Chronicles.

The first tradition reflects Israel's nomadic past, a period lasting from about 1250 to 1020 B.C., during which the Chosen People had few arms, even less armor, and no siege weapons at all. (In Deborah's and Jael's day, for example, there was "not a shield or spear among the forty thousand [sic] men of Israel" [Judg. 5:8].) The only way this poorly armed host could deal effectively with Philistine chariots, fortresses, and iron-armed phalanxes was by means of tricks and subterfuge on the part of small groups of carefully picked warriors. Attacking (*karr*, Arabic) when faced with inferior opposition, then employing spies, poison, and retreat (*farr*) when confronted with superior force, avoiding the enemy except in mountain defiles and lava outcrops, or fighting only at night: This is the strategy that became idealized as the manner in which a truly holy, God-pleasing war should be fought.[11]

After the split in the monarchy in 926 B.C., this older ethic reasserted itself in the kingdom of Israel while under the rule of the house of Benjamin, until it was extinguished in 721 B.C. by Assyria. One of the greatest Israelite kings, Ahab (reigned 874-853 B.C.), is pictured in biblical accounts as a typical Machiavellian nomadic warrior chieftain. As a case in point, when his spies reveal that Ben-Hadad II of Damascus and his troops are drunk, Ahab attacks and routs them at midday, instead of waiting until they have sobered and are capable of a fair fight (1 Kings 20:16-18). The following year, knowing that Ben-Hadad expects an engagement in the mountains since "Yahweh is a god of the mountains," Ahab instead surprises and defeats him on the plains (1 Kings 20:28-29). Three years later, Ahab finally fell at Ramoth-Gilead to his long-time adversary: this in spite of his unsporting refusal to don his royal uniform in battle, as kings were then required by chivalric custom to do (1 Kings 22:29-38).

The house of Judah, however, adhered to a more courtly military ethic. Judah was always much closer culturally to the settled agricultural folk of Palestine than Benjamin, offering little resistance to religious practices such as the field magic and fertility goddess worship that were to scandalize the prophet Jeremiah. And the second Judaic patriarch, David (ca. 1010-970 B.C.), served as a mercenary captain in the Philistine army for two years during his struggle with the Benjaminite elder, Saul, for control of Yahweh's nation. Consequently, after his victory over Benjamin at the Battle of Gibeon, a Philistine-inspired military ethic replaced nomadic custom in Israel, until Jerusalem itself was sacked and its population deported to Nineveh in 586 B.C.

After its conquest of Israel, Judah erected fortified towns at Megiddo, Gezer, Beth-Horon, Baalath, and Tamar. These were later to be cursed by Isaiah, Jeremiah, and Micah as symbolizing

Judah's lack of trust in God.[12] In addition, it staffed these fortresses with professional chariot-riding soldiers, whereas Yahweh's preferred battle array, as taught in the Torah and exalted in the Song of Deborah, was the mule-riding people's militia.[13] The prophets rebuked these soldiers, variously calling them "lions" and "wolves." Notably, unlike Deborah's day when apparently weapons of any sort were rare, David's champions were armed "with warlike weapons of every kind." And more significantly still, we read of them "drawing up their line of battle" against their foes and "standing strong" in the face of severe resistance, instead of resorting to the ancient nomadic tactic of *karr* and *farr* (1 Chron. 19:10-12). During David's time the common freemen fell into a mere reserve status[14] and were later disarmed altogether when both the professionals and volunteers were replaced by an army of conscripts. But a military draft not only necessitated ignoring the customary summons of tribes, but required an accurate census. And census-taking is absolutely prohibited in the Bible (Josh. 13:19). God alone, we are told, will keep a register of who shall live or die.

David's transgressions of sacred military law alone were many. He built a permanent residence for Yahweh, when for centuries the god of the nomads had preferred a movable tent. Furthermore, he had intercourse with Uriah's wife Bathsheba, while his forces were in the field, rendering himself unclean and endangering the whole campaign. Later, he sought to palliate the horror of his misdeed by offering Uriah the same opportunity to do wrong. But the latter refused, citing God's law. Finally, in a futile attempt to cover up his crime, David had Uriah killed in battle (2 Sam. 11).[15] But more important than either of these singular acts, was that under David's leadership the whole meaning of combat began changing radically, from a means to glorify God's majesty, to a vehicle of self-display for individual warriors. This is indicated most clearly by the adoption of the Philistine custom of having individual champions (*'ish ḥabbenaym*, literally, "the man for combat between two") duel with enemy representatives to decide the outcome of battle, in lieu of an all out melee by a complete host of soldiers.

The classic example of the biblical duel, of course, is that to which David owed his own rise to eminence, the legendary combat between himself and Goliath in the Valley of Elahl (1 Sam. 17). But there are many others reported in the history books. David is challenged by Dodo at Gob, but Abishai intervenes and destroys the Philistine champion (2 Sam. 21:15-17). There were in fact several duels at Gob that day: Sibbecai fought Saph, Elhanan defeated another Goliath, "the shaft of whose spear was like a weaver's beam," and David's nephew killed another giant who had twenty-four fingers and toes. Benaiah, son of Jehoiada, was one of the most renowned of David's champions. At different times he slew two Champions of Moab in the same combat, killed a lion by hand that was harassing the visitors to a water cistern, and in single combat, armed with only a staff, slaughtered a huge Egyptian "five cubits" tall with his own spear.[16]

The most revealing case of the courtly joust is related in 2 Sam. 2: 14-16, where twelve of David's knights take on an equal number of Saul's in the traditional manner, each holding the hair of his opponent with one hand while wielding a short sword in the other. This took place at Gibeon while David was still a Philistine mercenary. Abner, Saul's general, understanding the Philistinian preference for the sporting duel, challenged the commander of Judah in the following words: "Let the young men now arise and *play* before us" (King James Version). Obviously, we should not make too much of the word "play." In the Jerusalem Bible this same line is translated: "Let the young soldiers come forward and hold a contest before us." Nevertheless, as Johan Huizinga has shown, there is no mention in the original Hebrew scripture of this affair *not* being playful. The Hebrew text uses a form of the verb *sahaq* in describing the incident, meaning "to laugh," "to act jestingly," or "to dance."[17] Therefore, it can safely be considered indicative of the degree to which warfare, by David's time, had evolved into an enterprise quite contrary to the intent and practice of the clearly nonplayful Yahweh war. It seems to have become primarily a vocation for professional military adepts to flaunt their skills, an end in itself to be conducted fairly and courteously.

To return to our story, at Gibeon, all twenty-four champions met their deaths, necessitating a standard engagement to settle the dispute. The Tribe of Benjamin was about to be wiped out when its general, Abner, again in recognition of Philistine chivalry, reminded General Joab that it was not fair to pursue a fleeing enemy: "Shall the sword devour forever? . . . Bid the people ere from following their brethren." (A truly Machiavellian commander, as Abner seems in other respects to have been, even if unsporting himself, will request that the opposition refrain from breaking the rules of the game if things are going badly for himself.) All of Abner's other requests for leniency, his promises, and even his threats to "smite" his pursuers, had already fallen on deaf ears. But this last pleading, an honorable warrior could hardly refuse. Joab allowed him to flee the field unharmed with the remnants of his army.

IRRATIONAL ELEMENTS IN THE YAHWEH WAR

In martial ethics where warfare is understood to be an end in itself, the possession of the soldier by divine spirits, and the frenzy associated with this, is encouraged. But in the cult of the transcendent god, self-deification is considered an abomination. Saul's warriors eat raw flesh with blood after their defeat of the Philistines and are condemned by Yahweh (1 Sam. 14:32-34). David dances naked before the Ark when it is brought into the citadel at Jerusalem, and his wife Michal, daughter of Saul and thus a Benjaminite, "despises him in her heart" (2 Sam. 6: 16-17, 20-22). Many of the prohibitions in the Pentateuch, and the Qur'an as well,[18] including the taboos against wine and pork, the restrictions against nudity and all manner of "unnatural" sex acts, and perhaps even the use of circumcision before battle (Josh. 5:2) can be accounted for in part by the fear of warrior frenzy in Judaism and Islam.[19]

Down through the first caliphs it was said of the members of the Muslim military consociation that "they are horse riders during the day and monks during the night."[20] Adultery, for example, was frowned upon. This was very likely one reason for the institution of the concept of "temporary marriage" (Arabic *muta*) in Muslim military law. The renowned General Khalid ibn al-Waleed and the Egyptian conqueror Amr ibn al-Assi (who flourished in the seventh and eighth centuries A.D.) both lost their positions in disgrace because of their failures to abide by the puritanical restrictions of

TABLE 6: Chronology from Judges to the End of the Kingdom of Judah (ca. 1250-587 B.C.), Showing When the Ethic of Yahweh War and the Military Ethic of the Philistines Prevailed in Ancient Judaism.

1. Prevalence of the Yahweh war ethic (ca. 1250-1020 B.C.).
   Conquest of the Promised Land and the siege of Jericho.
   Deborah and Barak defeat the Canaanites when Jael breaks the law of hospitality.
   The time of Gideon, Abimelech, and Samson.
   The time of the Benjaminite crime against hospitality and its punishment by Israel.
2. Saul of the house of Benjamin reigns over Israel (ca. 1030-1010 B.C.) and is defeated at Gibeon by the Philistine mercenary, David of the house of Judah.
3. David captures Jerusalem and introduces Philistine military ethic, including the use of duels to determine the outcome of battle (ca. 1000-970 B.C.).
4. Solomon reigns over Israel (ca. 970-931 B.C.).
5. Schism and the establishment of the dual kingdoms of Israel and Judah (926 B.C.).

Israel	Judah
a. Ahab reigns from 874-853 B.C. and apparently practices Yahweh war ethic.	a. Jehoshaphat reigns from 870-848 B.C. and seeks to exterminate idolatry.
b. First prophecies of doom (ca. 780-740 B.C.).	b. Calls of Micah and Isaiah (ca. 740 B.C.).
c. Israel extinguished by Assyria (721 B.C.).	c. First revision of lawbooks and history books (720 B.C.).
	d. Capture of Jerusalem by Assyria and its population deported (587 B.C.).

Islam. Not without justification does Max Weber compare the discipline of the Islamic and Benjaminite warrior barracks with that of a monastery.[21]

To be sure, like nomadic peoples elsewhere, Israel was familiar with warrior ecstasy, a moderate, but enduring sense of the certainty of Yahweh's aid in the field. This was the case particularly for the Nazarites or "separated ones"; military virtuosi apparently consecrated "from the womb" to the calling of war. They were distinguished by their ascetic regimen and disheveled hair. (The reader will recall that Samson, the Nazarite, was slain when he allowed Delilah to shear his locks [Judg. 16:17-21]. Samson epitomizes the biblical warrior berserk: capable of slaying, say the legends, a thousand men armed with only the jawbone of an ass.)

But the foregoing comments must be qualified lest biblical martial enthusiasm be confused with something it is not. Weber distinguishes between two types of religious ecstasy: (1) the acute mental aberration induced "by music and dance; by sexuality; or by a combination of all three—in short by orgies," and (2) a "chronically heightened religious mood," a mild euphoria experienced as an active ethical conversion.[22] It is clear that the martial ecstasy of the Nazarite is closer to the second type than it is to the first. Nor does the call of the Nazarite result in an amoral, worldly-indifferent serenity, as do the disciplines of *bushido* or *karma yoga*: rather, it eventuates in an impassioned scream against immorality. The experience of Yahweh's voice, that is to say, becomes visible in an ethical predisposition, in a mission to conquer the fallen charnel house of the world and to transform it into a kingdom for God.[23]

THE RITE OF ANATHEMA

Our previous discussion of the ritual obligations of Yahweh war touched only upon the treatment of prisoners residing in towns *outside* the Promised Land. They were to be divided among the soldiers and community as slaves and concubines. But quite another rule applied to those villages which fate placed *within* the boundaries of Yahweh's abode: "As regards the towns of those peoples which Yahweh your God gives you as your own inheritance, *you must spare not the life of any living thing* [my italics] . . . Thou shalt utterly destroy them." The only exception, says the law, is to be the fruit tree. After all, "is the tree in the field human that you should besiege it too?" (Deut. 20:15-20 JB).[24] In none of the scriptures of the other major world religions, the Mahabharata included, is there such a terrifying commandment as this.

Technically, this admonition is called *herem*, the anathema or ban. The Hebraic term is derived from the infinitive "to separate," meaning the taking of a thing out, consecrating it, and then offering it as a sacrifice to God.[25] According to biblical accounts, the Hittites, Amorites, Canaanites, Perizites, Hivites, and Jebusites were all "preserved" and then consumed by Yahweh in this way. By my own very conservative count, this comes to approximately twenty cities.

Yahweh held His nation to the sacred obligation of *herem*. Saul's failure to kill King Agag, together with the Amalekite population, for instance, is the reason given for his destruction at the hands of David. Although he repents and butchers Agag in the end, he still loses favor in Yahweh's eyes (1 Sam. 15:7-23). God is similarly enraged when Achan steals some gold and hides it in his tent after Israel has been commanded to destroy everything in Jericho. For his transgression he is stoned to death and his family immolated by fire. Such is the seriousness with which the law of *herem* is viewed in the Old Testament.

There is, naturally, a good deal of debate concerning the question of whether the ritual of the ban was really ever enacted in fact. Both Eric Voegelin and Weber point out correctly that the lawbooks together with Joshua and Judges were all written about 550 years after the reputed conquest of Palestine. And they were composed during a period when Israel had already been conquered by Assyria and Judah was nearing the same end. The doctrine of *herem* is, they argue, a completely fabricated product of *ressentiment* on the part of an impoverished and virtually demilitarized people. "The utopian phantasies of their [Judaism's] champions were saturated the more with bloody images of Yahweh's heroic feats the more unmilitary they had become in fact."[26]

However, several facts bear consideration before coming to such a conclusion prematurely. In the first place, concrete evidence exists that other Semitic nations during the biblical period also practiced a form of the ban in honor of their patron gods. Historically, the Semitic pantheon had a voracious appetite for its enemies. Roland de Vaux, for example, cites a ninth century B.C. nonbiblical inscription attributed to the king of Moab, Masha by name, which boasts that the entire population of Nebo was anathemized (ḥrm).[27] Furthermore, the Assyrians, who in biblical genealogy are said to have descended from Noah's first grandson, also used a ban of sorts following their sieges. "By these things which were done," says King Ashurbanipal, explaining the horrible savagery with which he customarily punished conquered cities, "I satisfied the hearts of the great gods, my lords." His enemies, he continues, had practiced idolatry: "They have uttered curses against Asshur my god, and devised evil against me . . . his worshipper." Because of this "their tongues I pulled out."[28] "I cut off their heads, I burned them with fire, a pile of living men and of heads against the city gate I set up, men I impaled on stakes, the city I destroyed and devastated, I turned it into mounds and ruin heaps."[29] There is little empirical justification for believing that Israel, which so clearly exemplified other aspects of Semitic culture, was not also as bloodthirsty in its own holy wars as other Semitic nations were in theirs.[30]

We also have direct evidence that the ḥerem was more than simply a romantic ideal of frustrated Jewish scribes. During the periods of legal reform under Jehu and the Rechabites (ca. 841 B.C.) and the Maccabees (166-60 B.C.) the anathema was employed with a vengeance not only on foreigners, but on Jewish communities accused of apostasy as well. We can have confidence in the veracity of these biblical reports, as the books of Kings and Maccabees were written contemporaneously with the events they depict. In addition to this, the violent fury of the Maccabean revolt is confirmed by the independent account of the Jewish general Flavius Josephus (A.D. 37-100?).[31] This revolt is interesting in another respect too, for together with the ritual of the ban—we count the sons of Baean, the cities of Borzah, Carnaim, Ephron, and the populations of scores of other fortresses such as Idumaean, Gezer, and Gilead as all exterminated—the other obligations of the holy war are also reported to have reappeared.[32] Among these were the ancient military summons with the ram's horn, excluding those volunteers who did not meet the Deuteronomic criteria, the use of the fast and continence in the field, and the long-forgotten war cry: "Arise, Yahweh, and let thy enemies be scattered!"[33]

The bloody purges, fratricides, and liquidations committed first by the Maccabees, then by the Pharisees, then by the Sadducees, and then again by the Pharisees during the last century before the birth of Jesus, lent a certain credence to the prophecies of doom. It was after the last wars of the Pharisees that a small sect calling itself the Essenes withdrew to the Dead Sea, where as a remnant of Yahweh's people, they prepared themselves for the promised Armageddon between the Messiah and the Sons of Darkness. The Dead Sea Scrolls, in which are recorded their millennarian hopes, bear directly on the present discussion, because once more they explicitly affirm the ancient Hebraic concept of the holy war. Except now it is imbued with the Zoroastrian theme that the upcoming war will be the Battle of the Apocalypse when the Son of Light will destroy every last faithless one who has disregarded His covenant.

All of which brings us to an immensely important conclusion. Whether or not the blood described in Joshua actually flowed or not, is to a great extent irrelevant in a study of Occidental martial ethics. For the fact is, that the idea of Yahweh placing an absolute ban on His enemies has repeatedly been taken by those who consider the Bible to be the authentic Word of God, as a commandment binding on themselves. It is only by understanding this that we can account for the otherwise inexplicable violence done in apparent good conscience by fundamentalist Christians, Catholic and Protestant alike, to heretics and nonbelievers throughout history, from the Albigensian Crusade to the siege of Jerusalem, from Charlemagne's conversion of Germany, to the religious wars of the sixteenth and seventeenth centuries. In all these cases and in others besides—the Jewish pogroms, the inquisitions, the Hussite revolt, Jan Bockelson's theocracy, Jan Zizka's armies, and we might add, the Islamic Assassins, the Wahhabis, Almoravids, and Almohads —both Christian and Muslim alike were essentially reenacting the ancient Hebraic mythology of the ban. They were playing out the mythological tale, recalling in their collective memories the belief that this world, relative to the transcendence of God, is utterly fallen and must be cleansed of darkness so that the reign of light can prevail at last. "Fight them, then, until there is an end of doctrinal strife, and there is no other religion than God's," says Muhammad (Qur'an 8:39 Khadduri). So Thomas Muntzer, the Anabaptist revolutionary, organized a military force of 300 peasants corresponding to Gideon's legendary array, and called them the League of the Elect. Their responsibility is to prepare the earth for the millennium of Christ, "a new Jerusalem purified of all uncleanliness." It is "harvest time," he tells his followers; You the Elect will serve as God's terrible scythe: "Go at them, and at them, and at them! It is time. . . . Don't be moved to pity. . . . At them, and at them while the fire is hot! Don't let your sword get cold! . . ."[34]

NOTES

1. "Hebraic holy war" and "Yahweh war" are used interchangeably in this chapter. They will be contrasted with the Philistine art of war as practiced by the house of Judah.

2. For these criteria, see our discussion of the motives for war in the previous chapter.

3. See note 23 chapter 2.

4. Rudolf Smend, *Yahweh War and Tribal Confederation*, trans. by Max G. Rogers (Nashville, Tenn.: Abingdon Press, 1970), pp. 36-37.

5. Ibid., pp. 36-42. Gustav von Rad, *Der Heilege Krieg im alten Israel* ~~Gerhard~~ (Zurich: n.p., 1951), pp. 6, 14, 29, 31.

The later Bronze and early Iron Age Greeks were coming to dominate the Aegean just about the time that the Amorites, Moabites, and Hebrews were overrunning Canaan. The legends celebrating the Greek victories in the *Iliad* and the Semitic victories in the Book of Joshua were composed contemporaneously and contain many of the same themes.

6. An excellent bibliography of anthropological studies of primitive combat confirming this proposition is found in *War*, ed. by Leon Bramson and George W. Goethels (New York: Basic Books, 1968), pp. 431-32.

7. Cf. Roland de Vaux, *Ancient Israel: Its Life and Institutions*, trans. by John McHugh (New York: McGraw-Hill, 1961), p. 217. The most extreme denunciation of biblical Machiavellianism by an established scholar

in the field is found in Albrecht Alt, *Kleine Schriften zur Geschichte des Volkes Israel*, vol. 1, (Munich: Beck, 1953), pp. 190-91. For a theological apology for Old Testament violence, see G. Ernest Wright, "The Conquest Theme in the Bible," in *A Light unto My Path*, ed. by Howard Bream, Ralph Heim, and Carey Moore (Philadelphia: Temple University Press, 1974), pp. 509-18.

8. Rahab, the Wild Sea Beast, goes by several names in the Old Testament: Leviathan (Job 41:1-8), Behemoth (Job 40:15), and the Fleeing Serpent (Job 26:13), for example. She is the archetypal symbol in Hebraism of Femininity, destroyed by Yahweh in primordial combat (Job 7:12 and 9:13). (Cf. our comments in note 10 of chapter 8.) Although this Rahab is spelled slightly differently in Hebraic than the Rahab of Jericho, it is nonetheless clear that the latter, particularly in her role as (temple?) prostitute, has the same demonic character as the former. In attributing the fall of Jericho to "Rahab," the author of Joshua seems to recognize the evil employed by Israel in its conquest of the Promised Land. If our analysis is true, this would correspond to the esoteric meaning of Jacob's wound in Genesis, obtained in his fight with the angel of God.

9. See also Numbers 35:9-34.

10. Qur'an 11:72; 15:51; 51:24.

11. This is Max Weber's argument in *Ancient Judaism*, trans. by Hans H. Gerth (New York: Free Press, 1952), pp. 105-17. It is based upon the classic analysis of K. Budde, "Das nomadische Ideal im alten Testament," *Soloweitschick, M. vom Buch das tausend Jahre wuchs* (Berlin: n.p. 1932 [1896]), pp. 89-112.

Ibn-Khaldun's analysis of nomadic tactics written in the fourteenth century has yet to be superseded. See *The Muqaddimah*, vol. 2, pp. 73-89. The interested reader will also wish to consult Yigael Yadin, *The Art of Warfare in Biblical Lands*, trans. by M. Pearlman (Jerusalem: International Pub. Co. Ltd., 1963), esp. vol. 2, and D. R. Hill, "The Role of the Camel and Horse in the Early Arab Conquests," in *War, Technology and Society in the Middle East*, ed. by V. J. Parry and M. E. Yapp (London: Oxford University Press, 1975), pp. 32-43.

12. Cf. Isaiah 22:9-12; Jeremiah 5:17; 21:13-14.

13. Cf. Isaiah's mock of the charioteers (30:15-16).

14. See, for example, the battle at Rabah (2 Sam. 12:29).

15. For penetrating analyses of David's compromises with the law of Yahweh war, see Voegelin, *Israel and Revelation*, pp. 261-65, 273-82 and Weber, *Ancient Judaism*, pp. 96-102.

16. For these and other duels, see 2 Sam. 21:18-22; 2 Sam. 23:8-23; 1 Chron. 2:23; 11:23.

17. See Huizinga's discussion in *Homo Ludens*, p. 41.

18. Cf. Qur'an 17:32; 2:219.

19. Weber, *Ancient Judaism*, pp. 91-92.

20. Quoted in Khadduri, *War*, p. 99.

21. Weber, *From Max Weber*, p. 258.

22. Weber, *The Sociology of Religion*, pp. 157-58.

23. Ibid., pp. 166-83. See also Weber's discussion of ethical prophecy in *Ancient Judaism*, pp. 267-335.

24. Cf. Levit. 27: 28-29.

25. Roland de Vaux, *Ancient Israel*, p. 260.

26. Weber, *Ancient Judaism*, p. 111.

27. Roland de Vaux, *Ancient Israel*, p. 261. However, de Vaux agrees with Voegelin and Weber that the *ḥerem* was rarely if ever practiced in fact (p. 256).

28. Zenaide A. Ragozin, *Assyria: From the Rise of the Empire to the Fall of Nineveh* (London: T. Fisher Unwin, 1867), pp. 8-9.

29. A. T. Olmstead, *History of Assyria* (Chicago: University of Chicago Press, 1923), p. 97, quoted from an official stele of Ashur-Nasir-Apal. See also pp. 84, 87, 88, 92, 111, 112, 113, 114 and 136 for other gruesome entries.

30. The classic sociology of Semitic peoples is by W. Robertson Smith, *The Religion of the Semites: The Fundamental Institutions* (New York: Schocken Books, 1972 [1888-91]).

31. Flavius Josephus, *The Wars of the Jews*, in *The Life and Works of Flavius Josephus*, trans. by William Whiston (Philadelphia: John C. Winston Co., 1954), pp. 604-875.

32. For example, see 1 Mac. 5:5, 28, 35, 44, 51; 2 Mac. 11:23, 35-38.

33. Campbell, *The Masks of God*, vol. 3, pp. 281-86.

34. *Thomas Muntzer's Briefwechsel*, ed. by Bohmer and Kirn (Leipzig; n.p., 1931), pp. 109-11, quoted in Norman Cohn, *The Pursuit of the Millennium* (New York: Oxford University Press, 1970), pp. 247-48.

Appropriately a chapter on the *jihad*, the Muslim holy war, follows a discussion of the Hebraic notion of sacred combat. Jewish scholars have long proclaimed Israel's abhorence of Bedouin life, which had its origin, they say, in Cain, the criminal exiled to the desert following his murder of Yahweh's favorite son, Abel (Gen. 4:1-16). The Muslim, however, traces his religious heritage back to Ishmael, Abraham's son by Hagar, Sarah's Egyptian maid-servant. Ishmael, say the legends, was the patriarch of the northern Arabic tribes, one clan of which was the Qur'aish. Muhammad, whom believers consider the "seal" of the great prophets, is taught to have been a son of this clan (Qur'an 3:60-61, 4:123), and like Jeremiah, Ezekiel, Isaiah, and Jesus, he was called by God to bring man to *aslama*, literally to obedience to His covenant. It is held that the paradigmatic case of submission to divine will is Abraham's sacrifice of his second son Isaac (Qur'an 2:157; 48:29. Cf. Gen. 22:1-19).

Genealogical arguments aside, there are empirically compelling reasons for treating ancient Hebraism and ancient Islam as exemplars of similar, if not identical, religious traditions. In both cults there is one true god, an uncreated creator (Qur'an 2:27-28; 2:256; 3:1; 16:3-77), who is absolutely omniscient and omnipotent (Qur'an 2:100-1; 3:25-27; 6:59-62; 13:9-17), and whose attributes of love are overshadowed by his might (Qur'an 59:23-24). In both, sin is action contrary to God's word (*kalâm*), and includes not just the shirking of religious duties, but more importantly, disobedience of God's moral commandments; drinking wine, being sexually immodest, committing infanticide, being ungenerous to orphans, widows, and the aged, or gambling—in short, being unrighteous. Furthermore, demonstrating its continuity with apocalyptic Christianity, Islam holds that there will be a Day of Judgment, wherein every man's actions "shall be laid before him [like] a wide-opened book," and he will be either condemned to the everlasting fires of Hell or be granted eternal life in Heaven (Qur'an 15:35-36; 17:13, 22:5; 30:56; 82:17-18). And finally, like both Hebraism and Christianity, Islam has its ritual enactment in anticipation of the Lord's Day: the holy war to destroy the Other, the *harbies*, those alien to God's chosen innocents.

TOLERANCE IN THE JIHAD

It will be recalled that Yahweh war was not to be employed as a vehicle of forcible conversion. The *jihad* shares this feature with Hebraism. "Allah is the Patron for all Believers," teaches the Angel Gabriel through the mouth of the Prophet (Qur'an 2:257). "Why wrangle over that which you know not; try to excel in good works; when you shall return to God, He will tell you about that which you have differed."[1]

Although Islam was, and to this day still is, motivated by a universalizing tendency, the *jihadists* were customarily satisfied if conquered peoples simply accepted their "protection" (*dhimma*) in exchange for paying a land tax (*kharaj*) and a poll tax (*jizya*) of one *dinar*, a measure of wheat, and some honey and vinegar every year. On the whole, especially when compared to medieval Christianity, it was tolerant of what it called "Peoples of the Book" within *dar al-Islam*, the abode of Islam. These persons were required only to proclaim upon capture "there is no God but Allah!" Other than this, as long as they did nothing to embarrass the Islamic brotherhood, the *dhimmiyûn* or *protégés* of the Prophet were free to worship God in their own way. The only major exception to this was the second caliph Umar's declaration in A.D. 635 that the Arabian peninsula itself shall be inhabited solely by Muslims.

"Maintain the protection (*dhimma*) that I accorded my non-Muslim subjects," admonishes a legally binding *hadîth* or teaching attributed to Muhammad. "The blood of the *dhimmi* is like the blood of the Muslim" agrees the fourth caliph Ali (d. A.D. 661).[2] Accordingly, throughout Muslim history, the person of the *dhimmi* has been considered inviolable, his tombs, schools, and convoys respected, and even his own laws continued. Until recently in

Egypt, for example, civil disputes between Christian *protégés* were judged by a Muslim cadi justice in accordance with Christian law. Of course, particularly during times of crisis, the protected minorities could suffer severe humiliations and even death at the hands of their hosts, although formally persecution is contrary to sacred law. In the nineteenth and twentieth centuries, Christians and Jews experienced a series of massacres in Ottoman Turkey, the most infamous of which was the extermination of the population of Smyrna in September 1923, when an estimated 120,000 died.[3] During the reigns of caliphs al-Mutawakki (A.D. 847-61) and al-Hakim (A.D. 996-1020), *dhimmiyûn* were required to give way to Muslims on the street, were prohibited from either riding camels or building their houses to the same height as Muslim residences, and obligated to wear special marks on their shoulders (*shi'ar*) for purposes of identification—the Christians blue, yellow for Jews, and black or red for Zoroastrians.

Raisons d'état promoted an Islamic policy of religious tolerance. Muslims were required to pay one nominal tax, a sort of legal alms called a *zakât*, consisting of 2½ percent of their annual income (Qur'an 2:40; 9:5). But this was insufficient to preserve the financial solvency of the Brotherhood. Caliph Umar (reigned A.D. 634-644) therefore invented the idea that those who submit voluntarily to Islamic rule be given the right to follow their own religion, if they pay the two taxes, the *jizya* and *kharaj*, mentioned at the beginning of this section.[4] There is more. In keeping with its Bedouin heritage, Islamic law forbade believers from engaging in either commerce in precious metals, in banking, or in some maritime pursuits. These occupations, essential to the economic well-being of any advanced civilization, were necessarily relegated to Christians or Jews, whose heterodox religious customs were thus protected. Customarily, a properly licensed non-Muslim traveler, diplomat, or caravanist received an annually renewable written guarantee (*amân*) from the caliph of safety from harassment. While he held this document he was exempt from taxation.

But beyond these political-economic considerations, there are authentic religious grounds for religious tolerance during the *jihad*. Authorities believe that the institution of *dhimma* evolved directly from the Abrahamic tradition of hospitality, *dakhâla*, spoken of in the previous chapter.[5] In *dakhâla*, even the enemy guest (*harbie*) is held sacred. Upon the utterance of the phrase, "O [name of host], I place myself under your protection [*dakhîl*]," and the host's response, "You are under my protection, hand over your arms," the supplicant has the right to expect care from the host to the best of his power for a minimum of three days.[6] The only real difference between this and outright military surrender, is that in the *jihad* the captor is not legally bound automatically to grant the captive's request for *dakhîl*. If he does, however, his promise of protection is considered inviolable.

THE RULES OF THE JIHAD

Originally the *jihad* was illegal unless first declared by proper authority—the caliph (later the Turkish sultan), the viceregent of Allah, after consultation with his advisors on sacred law. There is evidence that in the beginning, Islamic armies could fight only on auspicious days. Muhammad seems to have preferred Thursdays, specifically, Thursdays of the proper months, for initially the four sacred months at the beginning and end of each year were devoted exclusively to prayer and trade (Qur'an 9:2).[7] However, this was abrogated by the following more general revelation: "Fighting in them [i.e., in the proscribed months] is a grave matter, but ambushing on the paths of Allah, sacrileges in the Sacred House of Prayer, expelling its inhabitants—these are matters still more grave in the sight of Allah. Such harassment is worse than killing." (Qur'an 2:217).

Before combat commenced, the enemy was to be given an "invitation," as it was called, either to join the Islamic brotherhood, the *umma*, or, if they were Peoples of the Book, to accept Islamic political rule. "Nor do We ever punish a people until We have first sent to them a Messenger to warn them" (Qur'an 17:15; 8:33). Those who voluntarily proclaim that there is no other God but Allah, are to be "secure in their blood and property."[8] If after three days the opponent has not relented, then, following noon prayers, the battle array is formed and the order to charge given.

This is followed by the *takbir*, "Allah is the greatest," repeated collectively four times.[9]

Four-fifths of the spoils of war is the exclusive right of "those who witnessed the battle," to be divided in different proportions to horse and foot soldiers, depending upon which school of law one consults.[10] The remaining one-fifth "is at the disposal of Allah and His Apostle" (and after Muhammad's death, of the caliph), to dispense with as he sees fit (Qur'an 8:41). In a strict sense booty (*fay'*) is comprised of nothing but movable assets, Bedouin tradition knowing little of private property in terms of land. In Islamic law, as in nomadic civilization generally, land is in principle considered the inalienable possession of the military fraternity (in this case, the religious brotherhood) as a whole. Even in the Old Testament, we read that "land must not be sold in perpetuity" (Lev. 25:23-24). And those that did appropriate land from Israel as their own were condemned by Isaiah (5:8). As in the Bible, so in Islam, the power to collect "taxes" or "rents"—it being virtually impossible to distinguish between the two in such a situation—was assigned to a tribe, a clan, or an individual as a grant (*iqtâ*), but only on the authority of the ruling house. Its "owner" had little if any say over its disposition on his death.

As to the movable goods seized as prizes of war, included in them were *sabi* (women and children) as well as captured combatants (*asra*). *Asra* could either be killed, enslaved, or exchanged for ransom as the circumstances allowed. The women, if handsome, were "married" or joined in concubinage in the field; this was according to ancient Bedouin custom.[11] Contrary to the case for ancient Hebraism, there seem to have been no lustral rites prerequisite to the assimilation of either human or material war prizes into the Islamic brotherhood.

The story of Muslim slavery is notoriously long and black, and we need not dwell on it except to mention that for many centuries it was the primary source of recruitment for both the harem system and the *mamluk* (literally, "owned") armies which played such essential roles in Muslim history and legend. It is, however, important to appreciate that Muhammad himself frowned upon slavery, saying at one time that "there is not an act more acceptable to

God'' than the freeing of one's bondsmen. To this end, part of the *zakât* was originally intended for use as a form of public ransom. Typically, however, slaves were granted freedom by their owners, ostensibly to conform with Qur'anic inujunctions, only when their feebleness or age made them economic liabilities.

THE BRUTALITY OF THE JIHAD

The *jihad* evolved from the *ghazw* (*razzia*), the caravan or oasis raid. This is revealed most clearly in an etymology of the term *ghazi*, "warrior for the faith." Originally it meant "he who partakes in the *ghazw*." Nevertheless, it is essential to appreciate that the *ghazw* and the *jihad* are identical neither in terms of their meanings to the participants nor in their conduct. The *jihad*, ideally, was never simply a religiously sanctified camel raid.

The *ghazw* was primarily a stage for the Bedouin male to demonstrate his endurance, daring, and skill, so as to secure public confirmation of his *muruwwa*, his manliness.[12] When done well, it was a sporting contest between equals, played during the dry season when the herds grazed some distance from the main camp, and were thus susceptible to theft at little danger to humans. Above all, the *ghazi* sought not to lose face (*wajh*).

Contrast this Bedouin tradition with Islam and its preferred form of military violence. In the first place, far from lauding *muruwwa*, booty, and tribal and clan loyalty, and the associated Bedouin virtues (or "vices") of male sexual promiscuity, gambling, and drinking, Islam promotes instead *dîn*, religious piety. Indeed, some authorities have gone so far as to argue that Islam is a "victory of urban norms over nomadic ones and city over desert power."[13] In Islam the brotherhood of all believers (*umma*) replaces the idea of exclusive tribal bonds (*asabiyya*). Furthermore, each believer is enjoined to pardon those who have transgressed against him, even those who have "blackened" his face by making a fool of him (Qur'an 3: 133-4). And the *ghazw*, with its personal vengeance and ego-parading, is relegated in revelation to Jahiliyah, the Time of Ignorance and barbarism. The *jihad* that takes its place is a struggle for righteousness, to establish a world consistent with Allah's ethical commandments. It is conducted not at the level of public approbation and shame, but at that of morality, conscience, and sin. It serves not simply as a proving ground for a young man's courage, but as a vehicle for spreading *aslama*, obedience, across the earth. Those who partake in the *jihad* merely for booty and personal notoriety are rebuked as *munâfiq* (hypocrites). While those who fight for neither clan nor self are celebrated in scripture as authentic *mu'min* (believers). The real *jihadist* is "the instrument of the religion of Allah. A servant of God who purifies the earth from the filth of polytheism, [he] is the sword of God . . . the protector and the refuge of the believers."[14]

In the ancient *ghazw*, the camel incursion, the losers experienced temporary ridicule, while the victors took pleasure in an equally tenuous heightened self-esteem. But in the *jihad*, although thoughts of shame and honor are still entertained, Allah's warriors are more than proud. They are ipso facto innocent. The infidel is considered not just shameful, but guilty, the embodiment of that which is alien to *aslama*. Whereas, in the *ghazw*, one's opponent might very well be his neighbor or his own brother, in the *jihad* he is a *harbie*, a stranger with a being radically opposed to that of the believers. If in the *ghazw*, therefore, a premium is placed on chivalric restraint, in the *jihad* there are no limits on either weapons or tactics. Allah is indifferent to the manner in which *dar al-harb* (the abode of the alien, the enemy) is cleansed, as long as it is done effectively. Thus, when a one-time Wahhabi fanatic who had fought in the 'Ikhwan rebellion in the Najd Desert in 1925 was asked why the terrible atrocities, he confessed:

We were infected by a great sickness. The Imam [Bin Sa'ud, the commander-and-chief as well as prayer leader] had so filled us with rage and bitterness against all mankind, who were not of our faith, and especially those holding the Shi'ah creed, that we were literally mad, and quite incapable of forming proper judgement. We had again and again been told of the great reward that would come to us from God for every infidel we slew, and we believed what we were told implicitly. Nay more, we were promised immediate Heaven and glorious *hûris* [houris] there, if we were fortunate enough to get killed.[15]

The *jihadists* are allowed to employ siege tools, cut canals, and flood the abode of the alien. Poison and fire-arrows are legally permitted, even if, says Abu Hanafi, they may result in death to believers being held hostage. (Hanafi was the founder of the school of law defining canon in the Ottoman Empire, the Mughal Empire, Iraq, and Syria).[16] "Against [the enemy], all is permitted," contends the French scholar Clement Huart. "The general is at liberty to employ any combat technique, 'any manner that he thinks will give more advantage to the believers and be more noxious to the enemy' [to quote al-Mawerdi in his eleventh-century legal treatise, *The Principles of Sovereignty*]; for example, the devastation of enemy territory by smoke and fire, by surprise at day or night, or by pitched battle."[17]

It is true that in the Qur'an, the Prophet teaches that "verily, Allah loveth not the treacherous." Nevertheless, he is also reputed to have said in two legally binding *hadîths* that "war is trickery" and "many a trick is worth more than a tribe."[18] Furthermore, he qualifies this Qur'anic *sura* by adding that if the enemy himself is thought to be acting deceitfully, then "throw their compact (in their faces) so that ye may be as equals" (Qur'an 8:58). But since the *harbie* by definition is deceitful, then Muhammad's caution does not in practice mitigate the ferocity of the *jihad*.[19]

There is considerable debate about the existence of immunities in the law of the *jihad*. Pro-Muslim commentators cite the first caliph Abu Bakr's "ten rules to keep by heart," read at the inauguration of the first Syrian campaign (A.D. 630) to dispute the argument that the holy war knew no restrictions on violence. These rules forbade his soldiers from killing either "a child or aged man or woman" a shepherd or monastic, or from destroying palm or fruit trees, beehives, or herds.[20] In fact, however, the major schools of sacred jurisprudence (the Hanafi, Shaf'i, and the Maliki) greatly limited the applicability of these prohibitions. The college of Malikites, for example, reduced the immunities to include only the herds and the beehives. Abu Hanafi went even further than this. For it is said: "It is not meet that the Apostle take prisoners [and thereby burden his campaign] until he has subjected the land: think ye only of the present" (Qur'an 8:67). ". . . [W]hen ye meet in battle those who disbelieve, then let there be the striking off of heads until ye have slaughtered them" (Qur'an 47:4-5 Khadduri). "Slay the polytheists wherever ye may find them" (Qur'an 9:5 Khadduri).[21]

In practice little was exempt from military destruction in the *jihad*. State goods, private property, and even the lives of private citizens were all at the mercy of the victor. "Nor could the prisoner of war delude himself in imagining that his life would be spared, for by custom of combat any infidel who fell under the power of the Muslim could be slaughtered [if, of course, he had not already been promised protection under the principle of *dhimma*]. . . . This was a general rule and one can speak of it as dominating the history of the Muslim wars."[22] This is the precedent that legitimized, even if it did not exclusively cause, the military horrors committed by Babur the Great (1483-1530), the first Mughal commander, and by the self-styled Muslim military judge and liberator Timur Lenk (1336-1405), whose emblems were towers of heads and walls of live bodies bound with brick and mortar.

Having established this, it is important in order to maintain a balanced perspective, to keep in mind that the *jihadist* was, at least in theory, encouraged to remember in the case of women, infants, and the aged the example of Allah's mercy. "He is compassionate," says the Qur'an; so too should his warriors be (Qur'an 8:69-70). "Be not prone to kill (merely) because (you are) permitted" (Qur'an 17:33). Unless they directly face one in battle, it was taught, these categories should be treated liberally. Only the rigidly fundamentalist and heterodox Khariji-Shiite sects (for example, the Assassins and the Almoravids) and the Wahhabis declared that all resisting nonbelievers are anathema to Allah, and thus subject, after the biblical precedent of *ḥerem*, to liquidation.[23]

CONCLUSION

A worshipper of an absolutely transcendent, all-powerful god, the *jihadist* was a believer also in divine predestination.[24] "When you were aiming arrows it was not you who aimed," he had been taught, "it was Allah who aimed. It was not you who slew them it was Allah who slew them" (Qur'an 8:17)! Since "nothing can befall us save that which Allah doth decree . . ." (Qur'an 9:51), it was perhaps inevitable, then, that the *jihadist* be improvident with his own life in combat. If caution does not avert the decree of fate, why not "when ye are face to face with the enemy, stand ye fast and concentrate on Allah so that you succeed" (Qur'an 8:45), tranquilly confident that He who sent rain from the skies to rescue you from thirst, will likewise deliver the infidel into your hands (Qur'an 8:11 and 14)?

It is understandable, then, that when massed for attack, the *jihadists* would present a terrifying spectacle to their less faithful and more worldly enemies. "*Il vero nervo*," says one Christian commander about the Ottoman Janissary footmen. "The Turkish troops are very ardent and intrepid," agrees another. "Crying with all their might 'Allah, Allah, God, God,' they would descend upon their enemies, like bulls with their heads down."[25]

With religious fanaticism, unity of command, and obedience to superiors guaranteed by patrimonial conscription, the lance, scimitar, and bow-wielding Islamic warriors were the scourge of Christian civilization for nearly a millenium. Constantinople was sacked with the aid of artillery in 1453, most of Hungary seized from 1526 to 1543, and Vienna itself besieged in 1529 and 1532, precisely at the high point of Martin Luther's revolt. Luther was not the only Reformationist who saw in the Ottoman conquests the hand of God punishing the Church for her worldly compromises.

The tactics of the *sipahi* cavalry, the main arm of the Ottoman forces—first harassing, then fleeing in feigned retreat, and then ambushing—were well suited to exploit the chivalric impetuousness of the European knight. And once these were destroyed, the Janissary footmen would charge and usually scatter the Christian infantry.[26] Around the middle of the sixteenth century, however, with the introduction of the bureaucratic standing army by the Habsburgs, the military tide began its inexorable turn in favor of the soldiers of the Christian god. For all their religious ardor as individuals, the Turkish cavalry as a whole was helpless before the overwhelming fire power of the muskets and field guns of this new type of army. The massed, coordinated fire would first drive off the *sipahi*, and then the Christian cavalry would charge into the midst of the Janissary guard, who would respond too slowly and too individually to prevent a massacre.[27]

NOTES

1. This is an *hadîth*, a saying attributed to the Prophet, and as such, is legally binding. It is quoted in Syed Ameer Ali, *The Spirit of Islam: A History of the Ideals of Islam* (New York: Humanities Press, 1974), pp. 212-13.

2. Ibid., p. 268. The charter granted to the Jews at Medina and the Christians at Najran by Muhammad, is quoted on p. 273.

3. George Horton, *The Blight of Asia* (Indianapolis: Bobbs-Merrill Co., 1926) contains a well-documented, if admittedly clearly biased description of Turkish violence through the nineteenth century. A list of Turkish mass liquidations of non-Muslim minorities committed between 1822 and 1904 is found on pp. 19-20.

4. Hitti, *History of the Arabs*, pp. 224-39. See also Maurice Gaudefroy-Demombynes, *Muslim Institutions (New York: Barnes & Noble, 1961)*.

5. Louis Massignon, "Le Respect de la Personne Humaine en Islam, et la Priorité du Droit d'Asile sur le Devoir de Juste Guerre," *Revue Internationale de la Croix-Rouge* 420 (1952): 460-64, 467-68.

6. H. R. P. Dickson, *The Arab of the Desert* (London: George Allen & Unwin Leg., 1949), pp. 118-39, 349.

7. Khadduri, *War*, p. 91.

8. This *hadîth* is quoted in Khadduri, *War*, pp. 96-97. For comparable admonitions from the Qur'an, see 8:33 and 9:3-4.

9. Khadduri, *War*, p. 91.

10. For a careful analysis of the rules of booty division, see Clement Huart, "Le Droit de la Guerre," *Revue du Monde Musulman* 2 (1907):336-38. See also Khadduri, *War*, pp. 119-23.

11. For elaboration on all these points, see Khadduri, *War*, pp. 126-31.

12. Raphael Patai, *The Arab Mind* (New York: Charles Scribner's Sons, 1973), pp. 79-81. See also Hitti, *History of the Arabs*, p. 25.

13. Bryan S. Turner, *Weber and Islam: A Critical Study* (London: Routledge & Kegan Paul, 1974), pp. 35-36, 104-6.

14. Quoted in Paul Wittek, *The Rise of the Ottoman Empire* (New York: Burt Franklin, 1971 [1938]), p. 14.

The notion of the religiously motivated *ghazi* (*jihadist*) won an audience not only among the Bedouins, but also among the Turkish mercenaries living on the Arabian-Byzantine frontier, as early as A.D. 700. Wittek argues that because the *jihad* integrated the notion of heavenly salvation with the possibility for worldly plunder, the Turkish steppe-warrior was particularly responsive to the Prophet's teachings.

Mahmud of Ghazna, the Seljuk emir who led the initial Muslim thrusts into the heart of Hindu civilization during the tenth century, is said to have drawn upon as many as 20,000 Turkish archers in his campaigns. The *ghazi* fanatic played an equally significant role in the victories of the Ottomans in Anatolia about two and a half centuries later. By approximately 1200, under Caliph al-Nasir, the idea of the religiously oriented *ghazi* had evolved into a formal corporation, comparable, says Wittek, to Frankish knighthood. Membership was preceded by a formal investiture wherein the candidate received a scimitar from his spiritual advisor with vows like: "With this club will I first subdue all my passions and then kill all enemies of the faith" (ibid., p. 37). The duly ordained *ghazi* wore a distinctive outfit, including in Ottoman Turkey, special trousers and a white hat, the latter signifying his purity. This is where the phrase, "put on the white cap for the *ghazw* (*jihad*)," had its source.

15. Dickson, *The Arab of the Desert*, p. 348.

16. Khadduri, *War*, pp. 105-6.

17. Huart, "Le Droit de la Guerre," p. 340.

18. Ibn-Khaldun, *The Muqaddimah*, vol. 2, pp. 86, 131. See also Khadduri, *War*, p. 92.

19. Mutilation of the dead is, however, strictly forbidden in the Qur'an. The heads of the vanquished may not be carried on the victors' lances (Khadduri, *War*, pp. 106-7). This is not insignificant since mutilation was a common Semitic practice, if we can believe the Assyrian frescoes and certain Old Testament legends. David, it is said, won Saul's daughter Michal for his wife when, after killing a hundred Philistines, he presented their foreskins as an offering to the Benjaminite king (I Sam. 18:25).

20. Abu Bakr's ten rules are quoted in Khadduri, *War*, p. 102.

21. Hashim Amir-Ali's versions are somewhat less bloodthirsty: "So when ye meet those who oppose truth, strike out valiantly until you have subdued them" and ". . . drive ye out the Pagans wherever ye may find them—seize them, beleaguer them, and close to them all roads." For similar Qur'anic injunctions, see 4:91-93; 8:39 and 57; 17:13.

22. Huart, "Le Droit de la Guerre," pp. 340-41, 44.

23. Khadduri, *War*, pp. 76-77.

24. Patai, *The Arab Mind*, pp. 150-55.

25. C. E. de Warnery, *Remarques sur le Militaire des Turcs* (Leipzig: n.p., 1770), p. 24, quoted in V. J. Parry, "La Manière de Combattre," in *War, Technology and Society in the Middle East*, p. 246.

26. For a still excellent history and description of Turkish military institutions, see Oman, *History of the Art of War in the Middle Ages*, vol. 2, pp. 336-60.

27. Parry, "La Manière de Combattre," p. 243.

THE PROTESTANT ETHIC AND THE SPIRIT OF VIOLENCE

11

INTRODUCTION

The century from 1560-1660 was a watershed period in military history.[1] Pitirim Sorokin estimates that war casualties in the seventeenth century increased by more than one hundred percent over what they appear to have been in the previous one hundred years.[2] Germany's population alone was reduced anywhere from (the most conservative estimates) two-thirds its original size of sixteen million to (the most liberal estimates) a quarter of the original number during the Thirty Years' War.[3] By the Treaty of Westphalia (1648), German farmland had been ravaged, its schools closed for lack of teachers, more than half its houses destroyed, and its capacity for economic development delayed perhaps a generation.[4]

Three men are customarily credited with inspiring the seventeenth century military revolution. All of them were Protestants: Maurice of the House of Orange of the Netherlands (1567-1625), an orthodox Calvinist; Gustavus Adolphus, the great Swedish "Innovator" (1591-1632), a Lutheran; and his English admirer Oliver Cromwell (1599-1658), a neo-Calvinist Independent. (We can add to this list the name of Frederick William I (1688-1740) of Germany, a devoted Lutheran.) Our intention in this chapter is to show that the shared religion of these three or four men was not merely coincidental; that, on the contrary, Protestantism introduced the European mind to a military symbolism radically different from that associated with Catholic genius, a symbolism which encouraged military invention.

It is probably worthwhile to remember that our concern is not to uncover causal relations between religion and war. In other words, our argument is not that Protestantism and its promotion of cold-

TABLE 7: Sorokin's Index of War Intensity

COUNTRY*	CENTURY					
	12th	13th	14th	15th	16th	17th
France	3	12	35	44	84	1152
Austria	7	11	7	155	273	2830
Great Britain	6	8	50	60	61	156
Russia	11	19	50	52	155	161
Spain					159	599
Netherlands						279
Italy						16
Totals	27	50	142	311	732	5193

*Data for Germany and Sweden not available.

Sorokin's index is a weighted composite measure of five factors related to the "intensity" of war: its duration, the sizes of the forces involved, the numbers killed and wounded, the number of participating countries, and the proportion of combatants to the total population of the society. The larger the index score, the more "intense" the wars fought during the specified century. By themselves the scores have no meaning. But they are useful for making approximate comparisons of the relative intensity of violence across centuries. Over all, Sorokin would say, seventeenth-century wars were about seven times more intense than those of the previous century. And the rate of increase of war intensity from the sixteenth to the seventeenth centuries was two to three times greater than any previous period.

Adapted from Quincy Wright, *A Study of War* (Chicago: University of Chicago Press, 1965), Table 49, p. 655.

hearted and righteous opportunism was the sole cause of the European military revolution. As pointed out in chapter 1, we view the *Kriegethik* of a society and its dominant religion as dialectically related, as representing the two aspects of a single military-religious meaning structure.

THE CATHOLIC AND PROTESTANT MILITARY ETHICS CONSTRASTED

As we observed in chapter 5, the ascendancy of Gregory VII to the papacy in 1073 signaled the inauguration of the Church's efforts to reform the world after the dictates of canon law. The *treuga Dei*, the *pax Dei*, the papal restrictions against the use of archery and crossbows, and those forbidding the enslavement of Christians in war, the establishment of the monastic military orders, and finally the bloodthirsty Crusade cult: All were symptomatic of the clergy's attempts to harness military force for spiritual ends in the subsequent centuries. Within two hundred years, warfare and politics had evolved into divine callings, *officia* within the *corpus Christianum*. Society had come to be viewed by theologians as a sort of visible church; each of its estates, including the *fideles beati Petri* (the vassals of Saint Peter) was considered a distinct organ of the Christian body and each was charged with a unique responsibility for the realization of that body's true end—the attainment of the Beatific Vision by every confessor in proportion to his ability.

Of course, based as it was upon the doctrine of spiritual transcendence, Christian theology had always recognized that the material world with its violence and inequality was not wholly of the spiritual order. And this appreciation continued even during the period when the Church came to control the European armed nobility. As the Scholastic philosophers came to understand it, there are two types of law. There is first Natural Law, or better yet because of man's sin, "relatively" Natural Law, governing man's affairs on earth. There is also "New Law," *Lex Christi*, the commandment of universal love overseeing the spiritual realm. The first law is the manifestation of reason on earth and is exemplified in the Decalogue. But the second is the realization of God's grace itself, in the second Person of the trinity, Jesus Christ. Even if man could act perfectly consistently with Natural Law, it was held, his final purpose for existence—the attainment of the vision of God in heaven—would still be unsatisfied, for this comes only through grace and not through the intellect. Martin Luther more or less agreed with all this, being after all an Augustinian monk and very much a child of the medieval *Zeitgeist*. But Scholastic theology went ever further by maintaining that while Natural Law and the Law of Christ are logically *distinguishable*, they are not *separable* in fact. The former is a preparation for the latter, the latter a fulfillment of the former. Luther seems to have rejected this concept.

In his theology, the difference between the (relatively) natural and the spiritual became not merely an analytical distinction but an empirical assertion: the basis of the notion that church and state have unalterably opposed purposes.

The Church, says Luther, should deal exclusively with the individual's *private* experience of faith, with the Law of Christ; that is, the Church should preach the Word so that it might be an occasion for the grace-filled realization that despite man's utter corruption, he is "justified." He is saved. However, as the mistress of the natural world with its trappings of political power, the Church has been rendered incapable of meeting this, her sole responsibility. Lutheranism in theory therefore relinquishes all the symbolism and paraphernalia of ecclesiastical sanction. In principle, it renounces the inquisitional device and abandons the institution of canon law and all the apparatus of religious compulsion. Or more correctly, the state provides for them through lay-clergy consistories (*das landesherrliche Kirchenregiment*). The reformed Church, in other words, takes Christ's teachings literally and "renders unto Caesar what is Caesar's" (Luke 20:25). She purifies herself of all sin and occupies herself exclusively with her single calling. But in so doing—and this is the crucial point—Lutheranism by implication also liberates the state of all spiritual and all private moral obligations. It frees the state from the fetters with which the Church had sought to encompass it for a half a millennium. The effect that this implication had on political thinking and practice was revolutionary.

Because of his congenital sin and disobedience of the Decalogue, says Luther, man in his natural condition would live in a state of perpetual anarchy were it not for the fact that God in His infinite mercy has ordained that there be princes to quell violence.[5] Despite God's mandate, however, the state's duty resides solely in this world. It deals only with the profane. "It is," in other words, "sinful power to punish sin." The state is "God's rod and the devil's servant."[6] As such, the state should follow the imperative of doing what is "natural" or more strictly, what is "relatively natural." And above all what is natural and rational for the state is to augment and consolidate its own power. In realizing this end, neither it nor the public official *qua* public official need heed the commandment to love his neighbor. For this is appropriate only to the spiritual realm, to the dimension of the sacred, which is to say, to the private individual and to the Church. To this extent Luther can claim that the Turkish hordes and ancient Persians in spite of, indeed *because* of their brutality, understood Natural Law better than the Greeks or Romans.[7] By the same token in a strict sense (unlike the case for Catholicism) there can be no "holy war" in Lutheranism, this being a self-contradiction. The Church alone deals with the holy and uses "spiritual weapons," the state alone deals with force and violence; the Church with love and forgiveness, the state with war.

But . . . you should understand that you are not fighting the Turk for the reasons the emperors have been urged to go to war . . . as head of Christendom and as Protector of the Church and defender of the faith, to wipe out the Turk's religion . . . not so! The emperor is not the head of Christendom or the defender of the gospel or the faith. . . . The emperor's sword has nothing to do with the faith; it belongs to physical worldly things.[8]

But this does not mean that a devout Christian must renounce war. As we have just pointed out, although they are only of this fallen world and not of the spiritual realm, "war and killing along with all the things that accompany wartime and martial law have been instituted by God. . . . The hand that wields the sword and kills with it is not man's hand but God's; and it is not man, but God, who hangs, tortures, beheads, kills and fights."[9] The Lutheran is not allowed to withdraw from the world into the safety of monastic life. On the contrary, the truly pious man will completely submit himself to the state's authority even if it is tyrannical (although he may hope and pray that it be just). For only in his personal life, his spiritual life, is he free. His body belongs to the state.[10]

Let every man be subject unto the higher powers. . . . [For] the powers that be are ordained by God. Whosoever therefore resisteth the power, resisteth the ordinance of God: and they that resist shall receive to themselves damnation. . . . For he is the minister of God, a revenger to execute wrath upon him that doeth evil (Rom. 13:1-4; cf. 1 Pet. 2:13-14).[11]

This excerpt from Paul's letters to the Romans contains the kernel of Luther's political philosophy. This is clear: Just as Lutheranism glorifies the purity of the Church, so it exhalts the craven power of the state. No one has so "highly praised" the virtue of the state since Paul, says Luther of himself.[12] This is the outlook that provided the foundation for unblinking Prussian *Realpolitik* and its last major spokesman, Heinrich von Treitschke.[13]

When the northern European princes began arrogating to themselves the police functions of the Church—appointing pastors, enforcing both tithes and conformity to faith and morals, and punishing heretics—this may have relieved the Church of certain unpleasant duties, but she ended up essentially as a puppet whose strings were pulled by political officials, as a department, so to speak, of the royal government with the responsibility to legitimize and in some cases actually implement state policy.[14] During the Thirty Years' War the pulpit was used to disseminate military propaganda, and pastors were employed as tax assessors, collectors, and even as draft board officials, the local board for administrative convenience being made identical to parish boundaries.[15] Political officials of the period boasted that reformed doctrine provided both scope and divine sanction for acts true Christians could never have countenanced.[16]

Consequently it was left to the Baptist sects and their Calvinist offspring, such as the English Brownists and Barrowists, to fulfill historically Luther's wish for a true separation of church and state. Again, the idea was that the "church" (for we are no longer dealing strictly with churches as such, but with sects) should concern itself only with the inward power of the spirit. But to allow each soul to experience fully the operation of grace in his life, all manner of outward religious expression should be completely voluntary. The state should have absolutely no authority over the church, nor the church over the state, except for the loose requirement that it be "Christian."[17] Although the Baptists initially renounced all forms of external compulsion including in rare cases even that issuing from the inequality of wealth, the horror of persecution by the established churches drove them for a while to preach millenarianism and to advocate the apocalyptic violence of the Last Days. It is important, however, to appreciate that this was alien to the original principles of the Baptists. We must distinguish between the revolutionary violence of the Taborites, the Hussites, and Thomas

Muntzer's "League of the Elect" (as that unhappy and short-lived venture was called) and the essential pacifism of Anabaptism.[18] Nonetheless, Baptist chiliasm plus the notion of full independence of church from state (and vice versa) penetrated English Calvinism in the form of the Independence movement, the cadres and chaplains of which came to make up Oliver Cromwell's New Model Army.[19]

In the Calvinist cantons of Switzerland, France, and the Netherlands, the Saints explicitly repudiated the Baptist theory of church independence. Instead the ideal was the establishment of a Christocracy, modeled after Israel and ruled by a board of discipline made up of carefully examined elders, according to the standards of the Covenant.[20] While in principle this might have enabled the Church to severely restrict political-military practice, mitigating the Machiavellianism permitted by Luther and acquiesced to by the Baptists, in fact it had just the opposite consequences. For along with the sexual and various other moral proscriptions of the Pentateuch, Calvinism reaffirmed as well the Judaic concept of holy war with all its associated scheming, deception, and ferociousness. In Calvinist theology, God appears in all his biblical transcendence, and relative to His awesome majesty the means of politics and warfare are seen as mere tools, any of which can be used without hesitation if they can be shown to serve His Will. But since the divine Will is inscrutable and can only be deciphered de facto, this means that that policy is right, morally and practically, which works. Might makes right![21] That method of force which best realizes God's Purposes on this earth is not just permitted, it is commanded: "Good brother, we must bend unto all means that give furtherance to the Holy Cause."[22] This is why Troeltsch can say that "Calvin himself [who by training was not a monk but a lawyer] writes and acts like a most practiced and accomplished politician, and like a military strategist who has weighed all the risks."[23]

Originally Calvin adopted the Lutheran position in regard to war. A holy war, he says, is logically inconceivable. The use of armed violence is exclusively a secular affair, hopefully only a last resort and then only in self-defense.[24] But he also recognized that if the Church was to accomplish its mission to impose a Christian commonwealth on France, something stronger than Luther's "spiritual weapons" would have to be employed. So in the end the religious war became not simply a right but a duty incumbent upon all the Saints. "For the devil can not abide that they [the Calvinists] should preach the Word of God purely, but will resist it. . . . Therefore we must be ready to fight."[25] Christ and the Apostles did not resort to violence admits Theodorus Beza, Calvin's greatest disciple. This was because it would have been morally wrong for them to do so, not because violence is ethically disallowed per se, but because the first Christians were *private* individuals and as such were obligated to submit to even pernicious authority. Only *public* officials legally charged with the responsibility of force are justified and then when so ordered by the Church presbyters, to use it in resisting evil. Since God has granted to the Church a readily available public military arm in the guise of the French nobility (later in Holland, the citizen's militia), then its use in furthering His cause is morally unobjectionable.[26]

THE PROTESTANT MILITARY REVOLUTION

The Protestant commanders Maurice, Adolphus, and Cromwell and their respective officer corps and civilian advisors demonstrated a remarkable capacity to adapt for the purposes of war the latest European materiel and organizational inventions. There was, as we have already suggested, no one cause for this, but it can hardly be doubted that their openness to military innovation was explicitly legitimized by the desacralized *Kriegethik* of Calvinism, Lutheranism, and neo-Calvinist Independency.[27] In other words, calculating ruthlessness in the pursuit of the power interests of the state or party was without question encouraged by the meaning that Reformation Protestantism gave to military affairs as part of the natural, fallen order. This was all unintentional, of course. The original purpose of the Reformation was not to surrender this world to the propagators of evil, but to renew it with the mystical joy, certitude, and love of Christ. The aim was not to make profane this world, but to celebrate Christ's atonement of man's sins. But the ironies of history are such that man often accomplishes the opposite of that which he consciously intends.[28]

It remains open to further investigation to what degree Machiavelli himself directly influenced political thinking in Protestant Europe.[29] To be sure, the juridical and political structures of what became the Protestant countries were unsuited to the Florentine notion of the *polis*, comprised of independent citizens, acting calculatedly on the basis of their own interests, instead of in unthinking obedience to sacred tradition. However, by the middle of the sixteenth century, at least in England, those sitting in Commons or administering law in the shires and boroughs were coming into intimate contact with secular humanism at Oxford and Cambridge and in the private inns of the court. These very individuals—the gentry—made up the vanguard of the Puritan revolt, and in some cases served as officers in Cromwell's army. They also became England's first "Machiavellian" theorists.[30] By 1600, political opportunism, or to use the more legitimate term, "Tacitus-like counsel," was flourishing even in conservative royal circles. Francis Bacon (1561-1626) wrote more than once of how"we are beholden to Machiavel, and writers of that kind" for accurately depicting the "evil arts" of public life.[31] It was Bacon who popularized for Englishmen the Italian ditty—*Tanto buon che val niente*, "so good that he is good for nothing"—affirming Machiavelli's suggestion that Scholasticism with its insistence on virtue had emasculated the European man. The appearance of virtue, Bacon argued, might indeed be helpful to a king, "but use of [virtue itself] is an impediment." In the second chapter to the eighth book of *The Advancement of Learning* (1603-5), Bacon proposes a "science of success in life," where like the author of *The Prince*, he speaks of friendship as only a means to self-aggrandizement and advises the reader on the manipulative use of informal discourse.

The heightened Puritan experience of God's spiritualized transcendence, and by implication the profligacy and moral corruption of English political life, merely augmented an already present disposition to view Machiavelli (the scientist, if not the moralist) in a favorable light. Notwithstanding its judgment that Machiavelli was *the* "politicke villain," Puritanism with its requirement that saintliness be expressed outwardly in industriousness, sober clear-headed rationality, and "prudence" relative to "reasons of religion" (a contemporary pun on *raison d'état"*), in fact was highly congenial to political opportunism whatever its name. The Puritan doctrine of divine election was perfectly suited to justify illegal scheming and conspiracy by those who, wishing to forge new destinies on the basis of their own strength, their own *virtù*, their own personal charisma, could not find grounds for their rebellions in ancient law or in divinely sanctioned custom. "Yee talk of Lawes, Lawes," said Hugh Peters, a prominent New Model Army chaplain, in a revealing sermon. "The kingdome is not to be maintained by Lawes, but by perfect men."[32] What he had in mind, of course, were those like the English revolutionaries who would first unseat and then execute the traditionally rightful English monarch, Charles I, or men like the brothers Nassau or Orange, the Vasa family in Sweden, or the French Huguenots.

If one is rational, as indeed he must be if he is to thrive in a wholly natural world, he will, urges John Saltmarsh, another of Cromwell's preachers, "be a wolf in sheep's clothing" and "strike when the iron is hot" and plot dissension among his enemies while maintaining a facade of piety.[33] That is, he will act on the basis of what past experience shows to be the most practical way, regardless of moral scruples or honored custom. But the facts known to the sixteenth century demonstrated that of all the peoples of history, it was the Romans who were the most successful militarily. Thus by implication it was supposed that the most rational military policy would be one modeled after that of the Caesars. It was exactly this and not a yearning to wallow among the antiquated ruins of the past that drew Reformation writers in droves back to the Roman military strategists.

The library of the typical well-read Elizabethan gentleman-warrior was based upon the work of four Roman authors: Frontinus and his *The Strategemes, Sleythtes and Policies of Warre* (English translation, 1539), Onosander, *Of the Generall Captaine and His Office* (1563), Caesar, *The Eyght Bookes of Caius Julius Caesar Conteyning His Martiall Exploytes in Gallia* (1565) and Vegetius, *The Four Bookes of Martiall Policye* (1572).[34] These were supplemented by Machiavelli's classic volume on the subject which was based upon these same sources updated with observations on the Swiss phalanx. From these sources the instigators of the Protestant military revolution—which we now appreciate was not nearly as "revolutionary" as first supposed—received the fundamental axioms of what were soon to become and what remain today standard Occidental military science.

ROMAN THEORY AND PROTESTANT PRACTICE

It is necessary to understand how much more complicated Roman field tactics were to those used by the ancient Greeks in order to grasp the full significance of the innovations introduced by the Protestant model armies. The Greek phalanx was a concentrated mass of highly individualistic heroes, hoplites, which relied upon shock at the weak points of the enemy line to defeat its foes. It was more or less the model for the Swiss phalanx or later the French "legion" or the Spanish "hedgehog," *tercio*.[35] While the phalanx (legion and *tercio*) worked well on expanses of flat ground, in hilly regions it was apt to break up, rendering the foot soldier vulnerable to cavalry. Thus Roman tacticians broke it into approximately forty smaller units called cohorts. These were juxtaposed in ranks in such a way that they could move readily to the front when another cohort faltered. But for the Roman system to be employed successfully in battle, to maintain the attack and fill gaps in the line, three conditions had to be met: There had to be flexible, prudent leadership, lengthy drill, and most importantly, absolute obedience to the commander. To promote authoritarian discipline, the Romans instituted a number of policies including the drafting of nonprofessional citizen soldiers, uniform dress, regular payment of a money salary, veteran's benefits, a system of supply magazines, meticulous record-keeping, and a harshly enforced set of military statutes.[36]

The Protestant "innovators," as they came to be called, used without exception every one of these Roman artifices in constructing their "new model" armies. Maurice of Nassau, unsuccessfully confronting the massive *tercios* of the Habsburgs, thought after his reading of Vegetius to break his own brigades into smaller eighty-man companies so that his armies might be more responsive to his commands and make a less enticing target for Spanish cannon. Maurice reduced the ranks in his companies from fifteen to five and increased the proportion of arquebusiers to pikemen to approximately twice that of the *tercio*.[37] Unless our calculations are wrong, assuming that the average Dutch brigade was broken into six smaller companies, it had a fire power 150 percent greater than a similarly sized *tercio*. In addition, Maurice ordered his pikemen to stand a yard apart so that the arquebusiers could flee into their ranks when pursued by cavalry, and he arranged his companies into the ancient Roman pattern so that they could exchange places while under fire. Both innovations entailed coordination and precision of movement, calling for hours of drill in march step to drum cadence. Furthermore, it required a body of technically trained officers and NCOs. The Spanish sergeant-major had to learn how to "embattle by the square root." Maurice's captains not only had to master this or the "quadrant" as it was called, but a great number of other complex evolutions based on Roman examples such as the wedge, the tongs, the saw, and the globe.[38] In 1617, the Dutch established the first modern military academy at Siegen where the Protestant engineers of violence learned to apply the latest scientific discoveries to the practice of war: algebra and geometry to calculate camp size, to requisition and allocate supplies more rationally, to increase the accuracy of artillery fire, and to construct the bridges, canals, trench works, and fortifications that frustrated the Spanish sieges for years; and cartography, chemistry, and metallurgy to develop an arsenal of new instruments—mines, fragmentation bombs, hand grenades, corned powder, wheel-lock guns, and regimental field guns—with which the Protestant armies horrified their less ingenious Catholic foes.[39]

With its systematic training and intense drill, Maurice's army evolved from a brute mass of men into an articulated organism each part of which responded automatically and unthinkingly to impulses from above. And whenever disobedience threatened the integrity of this carefully wrought instrument of destruction, Maurice ruthlessly crushed it. He was the first European commander to reintroduce the Roman practice of executing officers for failure to abide by strict rules regarding the treatment of noncombatants.[40] This action was the inspiration for Gustavus Adolphus's famous "Swedish Discipline," issued just prior to the invasion of Germany in 1625.[41]

Article IV of the "Swedish Discipline" states that "Death is the penalty for plundering or outrage," while the first article provides for courts-martial, each brigade having its own court presided over by the commanding colonel together with his picked assessors. The office of provost-marshal is charged with the power of arrest, but not with the execution of punishment (Article II). A unit found guilty of cowardice in battle is punished collectively in accordance with ancient Roman precedent. Every tenth man selected by lot is killed or mutilated and the other nine live outside the camp "until they have wiped out their disgrace by a bold deed" (Article IV). That Roman military law is not the sole source of the "Swedish Discipline" is indicated by certain other provisions which could only have had a basis in Reformation enthusiasm: Morning and evening prayer is required in every regiment daily, with full services on Sundays. To this end a soldier's Prayer Book was distributed to everyone. "Despising divine service," say the statutes, is punishable by death (Article's VI and VII). Cromwell's moral police were later to extend Adolphus's edicts to include masturbation, sexual intercourse, cursing, gambling, dice playing, and drinking. In short, the Protestant soldier was directed to fight effectively, but soberly.

The reader will recall our discussion of the soldier-ascetic of Saint Bernard's Knights of the Temple in chapter 5. But in Calvinism, as Weber has pointed out, the monastic rule became democratized to include even the common lay-soldier.[42] The army of the Huguenots was modern Europe's first fully disciplined armed force, anticipating the Scottish Presbyterian army and Cromwell's New Model army. It is true that in the latter Huguenot campaigns, as mercenaries came increasingly to the fore, spartan self-control disappeared,[43] but the Calvinist success in subduing the romantically independent spirit of the French nobleman should be considered a remarkable accomplishment. The fact that Maurice of Nassau was capable of imbuing his almost exclusively mercenary force with enough discipline to defeat the Spanish at Tournhout (1597) and Nieuport (1600) is equally noteworthy.[44] In all cases it was the obedience they could command, when compared to the disorder of their opponents—for example, the unreliability of Charles I's English barons in the Civil War (1642-1646) or the mutinous propensity of the hired soldier—that explains the victories that the small, impoverished, and poorly armed Calvinist hosts won in France, the Netherlands, and in England over their foes. The Puritan discipline of Cromwell's regiment of horse soldiers, which came to be known as the Ironsides is, of course, legendary: "No man swears but he pays his twelve pence; if he be drunk he is set in the stocks or worse; if one calls the other 'Roundhead' he is cashiered; insomuch that the countries where they come leap for joy of them, and come in and join with them."[45] Consider the following incident. On January, 1645 the Parliament determined that six thousand horsemen and foot soldiers should be sent under the command of one William Waller to regions west of London. Virtually all the troops refused the order because of arrears in the payment of salaries, but not Cromwell's dragoons. They marched to Wiltshire where, against Colonel Long's Royalists, Cromwell experienced one of his greatest successes.[46]

Gustavus Adolphus was the innovator par excellence. He was responsible for establishing the first nationalized selective service system, the *Indelning*, after Roman example, with rational selection criteria and exemptions. Contrast this with the typical draft of serfs by the local mercenary captain. As he and not the central government, was the sole source of the inductee's support the captain naturally became the object of whatever loyalty the inductee had (which was notably little).[47] Sweden also introduced the first reliable system of salary payment directly from the state treasury. The French, Spanish, and English had all formally implemented this practice as early as 1490; but so lax were the offical exchequers in meeting their obligations that troops under the pay of states were commonly more unruly than mercenary hirelings.[48] When the Swedish soldier was not in the field, his "salary" took the form of upkeep on a private farm which in some cases was his own. The owner was allowed to deduct one-eighth his yearly tax for each soldier so provided.[49] This avoided the costly mustering-out fee payable to each soldier when armies, as was customary, were disbanded during the winter. The Swedish, for the first time in modern history, used the closed season for training, and even in minor cases for campaigns. (Maurice's greatest victory, that at Tournhout, was achieved in January.) Adolphus is also credited with being the first to clothe his troops in uniforms, again following Roman precedent. Mercenaries had up to this time always resisted the imposition of standardized clothing, as it hindered their propensity to change sides at times of acute danger.[50] Furthermore, the Swedish army was clothed, sheltered, and fed from magazines, all of which were run by specially trained commissary staffs. Meanwhile his opponents, Wallenstein's mercenaries, were employing the traditional practice of devastating the surrounding region in order to sustain themselves.[51] Lastly, to augment the accountability of his officers to his personal will, Adolphus reintroduced the use of written orders after the original Roman outline. "Gustavus' orders are a model of which the modern staff officer might be proud," contends B.H. Liddell-Hart, "the paragraphs numbered, each short, crisp, and embodying one specific point; the whole in a logical sequence that is reminiscent of modern practice —information as to the enemy, intention of the commander, and method of execution first, then administrative arrangements, and finaly intercommunication."[52]

Gustavus Adolphus molded the Swedish soldiers into the most powerful land force the world had yet seen. It was comprised of the same peasants John of Nassau had found sulky and slack in drill and disinclined to war: the same nobility who, he said, were of little use except "to plague peasants;" the same soldiers who had experienced disastrous defeats in 1605 and 1611 at Karkholm and Klusino at the hands of the Russians and Poles, and who caused John to leave for Holland in disgust after a frustrating year of attempting to upgrade them.[53] The bayonet which would finally render obsolete the pikeman had yet to appear, the bolt-action carbine and the machine gun which would permit Adolphus's three ranks to be collapsed into one had still to be invented, and the self-propelled tank that would replace the horse was still three centuries away in the future. Except for these things, the Lutheran innovator was the first to employ in concert modern Europe's fundamental implements of collective violence.[54] Yet these tools would have meant much less than they eventually did for subsequent military history had not the "Lion of the North" introduced still another concept into European thinking; had he not attempted to annihilate the Habsburg dynasty through "grand strategy," by manipulating seven armies simultaneously from the Oder River to Italy. Adolphus's designs of world conquest (or liberation) and his ruthless, systematic manner of carrying them out remind one, says Michael Roberts, of Genghis Khan. They far surpassed in both scope and complexity anything contemplated by either Hannibal or Alexander, the only other comparable Occidental generals.[55] His efforts would not be matched in scale until the times of Napoleon, General Grant, and the totalitarian wars of the twentieth century. In fact, it was the invention of "totalitarian" warfare, all things considered, that Gustavus Adolphus accomplished. By this we mean a technique of violence whereby, within the existing technological limits, the pursuit of victory results in the methodical mobilization of the society's total resources, human and natural, scientific and religious.

In Sweden during the Thirty Years' War, five-sevenths of the total tax appropriation went to the war effort, and the state initiated the practice of rationing food supplies to the civilian population so as not to interfere with the state's long-range strategic goals. The total male citizenry from ages fifteen to sixty was subjected to conscription and those not drafted were "channeled" by exemptions into roles supportive of the war effort. The standardization of weapons, powder, and dress drove the Swedish to establish armaments monopolies. And ingenious financial apparatuses were created to underwrite the tremendous expenses of recruiting, training, and supplying troops stationed overseas, namely, currency debasement, the sale of monopolies, the appropriation of private farms and their sale as crown lands, and the sale of war bonds.[56] It was not merely the Swedish state that penetrated the social life of the community. With the bureaucratization of the Swedish armed forces hosts of clerks, accountants, lawyers, chaplains, medical workers, teamsters, and secretaries were drafted. Just as the effect of the Gregorian reforms at the end of the first Christian millennium was to blur the distinction we now take for granted between church and society, sacred and secular, the military reforms of the seventeenth-century Protestant armies confused the boundaries between the state and society. Whereas in the Middle Ages every calling including that of the knight could be viewed as a liturgical ministry of the *corpus Christianum*, after the wars of the Reformation, all men including the clergy could see themselves as functionaries of the state.[57]

PROTESTANT MYSTICISM AND VIOLENCE

Protestantism in general and the protests of Luther, Karlstadt, Muntzer, Sebastian Franck, John Saltmarsh, and all the other reformers had their origin in Christian mysticism. Even Calvinism with all its puritanical legalism was deeply affected by the mystical spirit. By "Christian mysticism" we are referring to the direct inward experience of being "justified" in God; the experience with all its fathomless ecstasy of being saved. This can be contrasted with the outward, objective formal certification or assurance that one is redeemed. (Although the latter too can certainly be an occasion for mystical experience. Inward experience and outward certification can be considered ideal types.) In other words, the Reformation had its beginning in a reaction of loose congeries of charismatic individuals to what they considered spiritually stultifying rituals of the established medieval Church. While the Church before and since then had been able to accommodate charismatic protest within the institution of monasticism, she was either unwilling or incapable of doing it in the case of the individuals mentioned above. Others have dealt extensively with this issue; here we wish to examine what influence Protestant mysticism had on the contemporary military ethic. It is not sufficient merely to study the legitimizing impetus Protestantism gave to the secularization of politics and war, as this ignores the tremendous energy, the world-reforming zealousness, the enthusiasm (literally, the state of being "filled with god") with which it colored the practice of war.

Terms like "entirely passive," "resigned," "flowing with," "dying to self," "stilling," "surrendering," and the like are admittedly universal to the vocabulary of mysticism wherever it has flourished East or West. But it is wholly inaccurate, as both Rudolf Otto and Evelyn Underhill in their seminal studies of the subject have shown, to suppose that mysticism of all forms, the direct experience of the *numinosum* in one's own life, leads as such to inaction, passivity, silence, and their associated virtues or vices. The mysticism of Luther, Muntzer, Hans Hutt and John Saltmarsh was violent in tone. It screamed its outrage at the injustices and the pathos of the human condition; for "when the perfect is known, one despises what is imperfect" (1 Cor. 13:10).

Luther's god and that of Muntzer and Hutt, of Denck, and of the English revolutionary chaplains was not the god of pantheism nor the god of the worldly indifferent Hindu yogi or the serene Zen master. The mystical *experience*, which they all seem to have had, should not be confused with the *mythos* of divine immanence which all of them viciously rebuked.[58] On the contrary, the god of Protestant mysticism was the transcendent god of Calvin, a god who in his undecipherable power does not simply permit but compels the criminal to act and then in his matchless righteousness condemns him though he was helpless to do otherwise. Compared to this spiritualized transcendence, anything not of the spirit (which is to say, anything of the material world) including the affairs of earth and its chief denizen, man himself, are inexorably Evil.

Even infants themselves, as they bring their condemnation into the world with them, are rendered subject to punishment of their own sinfulness. . . . For though they have not yet produced the fruits of their iniquity, yet they have had the seed of it in them. Their whole nature is, as it were, a seed of sin and therefore cannot but be odious and abominable to God.[59]

Christian mythology had always appreciated God's transcendence and by implication the fallen state of man. But in the world view of the Catholic church fathers, man's sin was sublimated into a larger divine harmony. It became *felix culpa*, our "happy fault."

For without it there would have been no Mary, no infant Jesus, no Church, and no sacraments. *Malum est non ens* proclaims Thomas Aquinas in the *Summa Theologica*; Evil is nonexistence. All appearance of evil is a lack of being. In a strict sense it has no existence in and of itself. But in Protestantism, the sacraments, the intricate rituals, the lush music, and literal pictorial devices are greatly reduced, and the infinite gulf between the Creator and the creature, between holiness and sin, reappears in all its starkness. Thus although the mysticism from which Protestantism arose was a subjective consciousness of salvation, an indwelling of the Holy Spirit, it would have been inconceivable that this was the experience of divine union with God. Becoming one with a god such as this would be impossible.[60] Nor did the Protestant religious experience induce in the mystic cosmic tranquility, coolness, peace and stillness in God. Not even in Luther, who yearned to retire into a personal spirituality, into the private citadel of absolute freedom, was the experience of "justification" reveled in for its own sake alone, for the joy and rapture it brought him and for nothing else. This would have been idolatrous deification of the creature. Reformation Protestantism was filled with a consciousness of a divine mission; of its being an instrument for the glorification of God's will.

To say it in another way: In Protestantism the heightened religious experience must be authenticated. It must be validated. It must manifest itself in ethical activity in the world; or to use Weber's favorite term, in "inner worldly asceticism."[61] "What we have gathered in prayer, we must give out in love," so the lesson goes. But this love is not the Greek *eros*, the sensual enjoyment of beauty, but *agapé*, the absolute giving of oneself for the enhancement of others. As we have already said, the Protestant god is not the Oriental deity of amorality, but the god of Jewish ethical propehcy. And like the Jewish prophets, the Protestant whose spirit is seized by God will strike out at evil with all the impassioned frenzy that they did. His life on earth will be pictured as it was by Thomas Sutton, another of the Independent chaplains, as "a continual battalion and bloody skirmish . . . against the devil. . . . Whoever is a professed soldier, he is a professed Christian." "Above all creatures God loves the soldier,"[62] for "God crowns but well-tried wrestlers" (Calvin). "Without running, fighting, sweating, wrestling, heaven is not taken" (Samuel Rutherford). This, finally, explains the "divine hatred," so to speak, that filled the Reformation Protestant. We say "divine" hatred because the Protestant mystic did not himself strictly hate, any more than he truly acted; rather, his wrath was that of God's. God acted through him. Man, after all, as it was taught, could will nothing himself but evil. God alone is righteous. The will of the truly righteous man is thus but the will of God become manifest in his body.

The divine anger of the righteous man, of course, is not peculiar to Reformation Protestantism. Recall again the legends of the warrior-berserks Samson, Gideon, Saul, and Jashobeam (a captain of David's Thirty) "who wielded his battle-axe against three hundred whom he killed at one time" (1 Chron. 11:11). A same sort of martial ecstasy became manifest as well in the heart of the fervent Protestant soldier. This is precisely why Oliver Cromwell (like Maurice and Adolphus before him) preferred "men as had the fear of God before them and made some conscience of what they did" in his own regiment. At first those in Parliament complained bitterly of his method of officer selection. It tended to ignore "men of estate," they cried, in favor of "common men, pore and mean of parentage," who had only "visions" and "revelations" to recommend them. But these protests turned to cheers when the Ironsides won repeated victories over the royal Cavaliers.[63]

We are cognizant of the fact that professional sociological consensus has maintained since Weber [64] that the individual Calvinist was imbued not so much with martial courage, as with an acute sense of foreboding and anxiety concerning his own election. It is this uncertainty, the argument goes, that drove him to compulsive industriousness. But this convoluted interpretation of Weber's reasoning is both superfluous and probably incorrect as a characterization of the early Protestant mind. The simple fact is that the experience of faith alone, the certitude that one has been saved by God from eternal damnation, can still, as it did centuries ago, provide an immeasurable source of inner psychological strength to the believer. It was this very assurance, and not some early twentieth-century version of existential *angst*, that filled the Protestant soldier with the courage and determination to fight the anti-Christ until the Last Days.

NOTES

1. Michael Roberts, *The Military Revolution 1560-1660* (Belfast, Ireland: Queens University Press, n.d.).

2. Quincy Wright, *A Study of War* (Chicago: University of Chicago Press, 1965), p. 656.

3. Ibid., p. 244.

4. John U. Nef, *War and Human Progress* (London: Routledge & Kegan Paul, 1950), pp. 65-88.

5. Martin Luther, *Luther: Selected Political Writings*, ed. by J. M. Porter (Philadelphia: Fortress Press, 1974), pp. 53-57.

6. Ibid., pp. 60-64.

7. Troeltsch, *The Social Teachings of the Christian Churches*, vol. 2, p. 532. It is worth noting that the Ottomans returned the compliment by lauding Lutheranism as a return to authentic monotheism and a rejection of idolatry (See K. M. Setton, "Lutheranism and the Turkish Peril," *Balkan Studies* 3 [1962]: 136-65).

8. Luther, *Selected Political Writings*, p. 130. See Troeltsch, *The Social Teachings of the Christian Churches*, vol. 2, pp. 549-51, 865-67 n. 261.

9. Luther, *Selected Political Writings*, p. 103.

10. Troeltsch, *The Social Teachings of the Christian Churches*, vol. 2, pp. 539-44.

11. The monk from Wittenberg thus finds himself, inspite of his legendary magnanimity, advocating burning, decapitation, and the wheel against the rebellious peasants of Thuringia. See Luther, *Selected Political Writings*, pp. 85-88, 89-99 and Troeltsch, *The Social Teachings of the Christian Churches*, vol. 2, pp. 532-33, 857-58 n. 246.

12. Luther, *Selected Political Writings*, p. 102.

13. Troeltsch, *The Social Teachings of the Christian Churches*, vol. 2, pp. 528-32.

14. Karl Holl, "Die Bedeutung der grossen Kriege für das religiöse und kirchliche Leben innerhalb des deutschen Protestantismus," *Gesamm. Aufsätze zur Kirchengeschichte* 3 (1917): 338-47, 374-82.

15. Michael Roberts, *Gustavus Adolphus: A History of Sweden 1611-1632*, vol. 1, (London: Longmans, Green & Co., 1953), pp. 351-416.

16. Troeltsch, *The Social Teachings of the Christian Churches*, vol. 2, p. 698.

17. Ibid., pp. 656-77.

18. Ibid., pp. 703-5, 953-55 n. 454.

19. Leo Solt, *Saints in Arms: Puritanism and Democracy in Cromwell's Army* (New York: AMS Press, 1971).

20. Troeltsch, *The Social Teachings of the Christian Churches*, vol. 2, pp. 598-602, 617-28.

21. Michael Walzer, *The Revolution of the Saints* (Cambridge, Mass.: Harvard University Press, 1965), p. 38.

22. Ibid., p. 17.

23. Troeltsch, *The Social Teachings of the Christian Churches*, vol. 2, pp. 599-601.

24. Ibid., pp. 650-51, 919-20 n. 397.

25. Walzer, *The Revolution of the Saints*, p. 65 n. 108.

26. Ibid., pp. 68-87, 90-91, 100-9. Cf. Troeltsch, *The Social Teachings of the Christian Churches*, vol. 2, pp. 651-52, 921-22 n. 399. Notice that in Calvinist casuistry the Lutheran distinction between public and private life reappears.

27. Walzer, *The Revolution of the Saints*, pp. 272-75.

28. There are indications that the horrors of Protestant military practice during the Thirty Years' War unintentionally resulted in heightened skepticism regarding the possibility of war being holy (Holl, "Die Bedeutung der grossen Kriege," pp. 315-16, 353-55). In other words, the heretofore unheard of violence of combat had as one consequence its further desacralization in the eyes of the masses. Increasingly during the seventeenth century, as in German Pietism, religion came to be seen popularly as the province of private experience; public affairs were correspondingly relegated to the profane realm. This, perhaps, further augmented the tendencies toward Machiavellianism in warmaking and added still more to the violence of war.

29. For the different receptions of Machiavelli's works in Catholic and Protestant countries, see Felix Raab, *The English Face of Machiavelli* (London: Routledge & Kegan Paul, 1964), pp. 52-53.

30. J. G. A. Pocock, *The Machiavellian Moment* (Princeton, N.J.: Princeton University Press, 1975), pp. 333-53. Cf. Walzer, *The Revolution of the Saints*, pp. 127-60.

31. Raab, *The English Face of Machiavelli*, pp. 73-76.

32. For these and other quotes, see Solt, *Saints in Arms*, p. 83.

33. Ibid., pp. 84-86.

34. Henry J. Webb, *Elizabethan Military Science* (Madison: University of Wisconsin Press, 1965), p. 6.

35. For good discussions of these issues, see F. E. Adcock, *The Greek and Macedonian Art of War* (Berkeley: University of California Press, 1957); Charles C. Oman, *History of the Art of War in the Sixteenth Century* (London: Metheun & Co., 1937), pp. 59-61; Roberts, *Gustavus Adolphus*, vol. 2, pp. 172-76.

36. Hans Delbrück, *History of the Art of War within the Framework of Political History*, vol. 1, trans. by W. J. Renfroe Jr. (Westport, Conn.: Greenwood Press, 1975), pp. 283-90.

37. Oman, *History of the Art of War in the Sixteenth Century*, pp. 568-69. See also Roberts, *Gustavus Adolphus*, vol. 2, pp. 182-86.

38. Roberts, *The Military Revolution 1560-1660*, p. 10.

39. For descriptions of these inventions, see Oman, *History of the Art of War in the Sixteenth Century*, pp. 569-71; Roberts, *The Military Revolution*, pp. 26-28; George Clark, *War and Society in the Seventeenth Century* (London: Cambridge University Press, 1956), pp. 79-82.

40. Oman, *History of the Art of War in the Sixteenth Century*, p. 571.

41. For a translation of the "Swedish Discipline," see C. R. L. Fletcher, *Gustavus Adolphus and the Thirty Years' War* (New York: Capricorn Books, 1963), pp. 299-301.

42. Max Weber, *The Protestant Ethic and the Spirit of Capitalism*, trans. by Talcott Parsons (New York: Charles Scribner's Sons, 1958), pp. 118-24.

43. Oman, *History of the Art of War in the Sixteenth Century*, pp. 400-3.

44. Ibid., pp. 542-49.

45. C. H. Firth, "The Raising of the Ironsides," *Transactions of the Royal Historical Society* 13 (1899): 58.

46. Ibid., pp. 59-60.

47. Roberts, *Gustavus Adolphus*, vol. 2, pp. 201-12.

48. Oman, *History of the Art of War in the Sixteenth Century*, pp. 373-74, 547, 549.

49. Roberts, *Gustavus Adolphus*, vol. 2, pp. 214-15.

50. Roberts, *The Military Revolution 1560-1660*, p. 12.

51. Ibid., p. 16.

52. B. H. Liddel-Hart, "Gustavus Adolphus—Founder of Modern War," in his *Great Captains Unveiled* (Freeport, N.Y.: Books for Libraries Press, Inc., 1967), pp. 99-101.

53. Roberts, *Gustavus Adolphus*, vol. 2, pp. 194-97.

54. Those interested in examining in detail the alterations Adolphus brought to each of the three main combat arms—infantry, cavalry, and artillery—may wish to consult the following: Webb, *Elizabethan Military Science*, pp. 93-95; Otto Laskowski, "Infantry Tactics and Firing Power in the XVI Century," *Teki Historyczne* 4 (1950): 106-15; Oman, *History of the Art of War in the Sixteenth Century*, pp. 86-87; and especially, Roberts, *Gustavus Adolphus*, vol. 2, pp. 171-72, 223-25, 228-34, 260-61, 270-71.

55. Roberts, *The Military Revolution*, p. 13.

56. Clark, *War and Society in the Seventeenth Century*, pp. 61-71.

57. Hans Speier, *Social Order and the Risks of War* (New York: George W. Stewart, 1952), pp. 230-39, 254-60.

58. Otto, *Mysticism East and West*, pp. 7-8, 141.

59. John Calvin, *On God and Man*, ed. by F. W. Strothmann (New York: Frederick Ungar, 1956), p. 26.

60. Otto, *Mysticism East and West*, pp. 181-87. Max Weber equivocates on this point, see *The Protestant Ethic and the Spirit of Capitalism*, pp. 112-14.

61. According to Evelyn Underhill in her unsurpassed work, external validation of religious experience is the sine qua non of all true Christian mysticism, Catholic as well as Protestant (*Mysticism*, pp. 429-32). All of the Catholic mystics including Francis of Assisi, John of the Cross, Theresa of Avila, Ignatius of Loyola, Bernard of Clairvaux, and Catherine of Siena were canonized as saints in the Church not simply for their mystical gifts, but for their great reformist activity. It may be that the only difference between Catholic and Protestant mysticism is that, as a rule, the former was restricted primarily to the monasteries and convents, whereas the latter was available to the average lay confessor.

62. Walzer, *The Revolution of the Saints*, pp. 278-79, 290-95.

63. Firth, "The Raising of the Ironsides," pp. 21-24.

64. Weber, *The Protestant Ethic and the Spirit of Capitalism*, pp. 109-15.

HOLY WAR AND THE QUESTION OF ETHICS

12

Holy wars are staged during times of anomie when people begin to lose conviction in what they once held to be eternal verities. Holy war is a teaching technique. It resubstantiates a person's beliefs, "re-nomizing" human existence. It preserves the cosmic world from nothingness or it eradicates absurdity by bringing justice into historical reality. In either case, the holy war is an armed confrontation with Evil. It is, in the realm of the public, the first and most rudimentary ethical act.

Although originally born from a profound sense of moral responsibility for history, the Judeo-Christo-Muslim type of holy war became a self-contradiction when, in the seventeenth century, it evolved from its own symbolic structure the ethic of totalitarian violence. With each successive military crisis, it has become agonizingly clearer that the goal so grandly proclaimed in the myth of the Occidental holy war (whether in its pure or in its desacralized forms)—to establish justice in history—is incompatible with the *Kriegethik* it legitimizes; a *Kriegethik* in which transcendent ends are compartmentalized from worldly means; and issues of moral gravity are reduced to questions of practical expediency; an ethic where, apart from all lovely intents, right is operationalized as might.

The contradiction between the myth of the Occidental holy war and its ethic, between the yearning for a just world and the tools employed in its implementation, poses a dilemma for Westerners that cripples their capacity to respond effectively to evil: They know that if corruption, tyranny, and violence are ignored or passively surrendered to, there is the threat of all human values being annihilated. But they also know that the fight against evil can itself corrupt, tyrannize, and persecute. When the choice is between two equally undesirable acts—to be, as Sartre has written, either a victim of evil or a perpetrator of it—the spirit of rebellion is paralyzed.[1] We need not recite the familiar litany of political nihilism and private escapism symptomatic of ths paralysis in contemporary culture.

Ressentiment and its child, rebellion, are good. Albert Camus tells us that there are in effect only two possible worlds for mankind, that in which good and evil are viewed as childish attachments to ego, and the world of rebellion. To renounce the possibility of rebellion that does not inevitably destroy human community, he says, is to deny our roots as offspring of Greco-Judaic culture. Moreover, *ressentiment* is born from an intuitive sense of oneself or another being wronged fundamentally. It is the voice of the human heart crying out against atrocity. Rebellion is the outraged "no" to this wrong, a damnation of deeds that have transgressed certain inviolable limits defining what it is to be human. It is, thus, an affirmation of a universal human nature, of human rights that supersede conventional moralities. When the myth of rebellion is crippled, humanity is denied one of the vehicles by which it rediscovers its higher significance.[2]

Our intention in these last pages is to reexamine the Occidental holy war myth with an eye to placing its most morally important component, divine *ressentiment*, on firmer ground. This shall be accomplished by suggesting that rebellion be informed by one of the tenets of ancient military wisdom: The righteous are themselves blemished. Therefore they must be merciful and moderate lest they be the occasion of even darker crimes than those against which they fight.

THE TRANSFERENCE OF EVIL IN THE TRANSCENDENT-HISTORICAL HOLY WAR MYTH

The Occidental holy war seeks to cleanse the world of darkness and to establish the reign of light. It takes place in two ideal-typical forms: Esoterically, as a conscious struggle by the individual ascetic to suppress his own propensity to sin, his tendency to act contrary to an idealized conventional morality; and exoterically, as a public campaign to exterminate the sin of others. Both types of battle are fought in a dualistic world. And in both, the warrior experiences the realities of goodness or sin in an alienated manner. That is, as potentialities they are abstracted from his own being and simultaneously deposited upon an Other that is a stranger to him.[3]

In the esoteric combat, the ascetic is overwhelmingly cognizant of his own creatureliness. He is ego-*de*flated, transferring all goodness to a divine Person existing independent of himself and proclaiming: "I am naught, Thou art all." In the exoteric campaign, the combatant identifies his own ego with conventional morality and is ego-*in*flated, possessed by a sense of his own goodness. In this case, sin instead of goodness is transferred to a person or group, imaginary or real, independent of himself. In the esoteric battle, the ascetic will crush himself so as to establish an authentic relationship with the good Other. In the exoteric battle, the crusaders will destroy the bad Other so as to remain unconscious of their own sin. In either case, the severity of the punishment will reflect the fear and hatred of sin in the minds of the combatants. And as self-doubt can arouse these emotions to limitless heights, then both the esoteric and exoteric holy wars are commonly associated with atrocities. The flagellations, starvings, and solitary confinements the ascetic imposes upon his own body parallel the tortures and murders committed by the crusader to the bodies of the sinners. "Wonderful things were to be seen," writes Raymond du Aguilers of the investment of Jerusalem during the First Crusade; "numbers of the Saracens were beheaded . . . others were shot with arrows, or forced to jump from the towers; others were tortured for several days and then burned in flames. In the streets were seen piles of heads and hands and feet." The horses, he continues, waded in blood up to their bridles. "It was a just and wonderful judgement of God that the same should receive the blood of those whose blasphemies it had so long carried up to God."[4]

The ritual transference of evil either to an invisible spirit, to an inanimate object, a plant, an animal, an individual, or a group, represents an essential stage in the evolution of human consciousness. Accordingly, it is found not only in the Levitical rite of the scapegoat, but universally among settled peoples: for example in the Central European "Burning Out of Witches," in the Greek

Thargelia, or in the ancient European folk custom of "Carrying Out Death," wherein during Spring, an effigy of death was taken outside the city walls in a processional and then burnt and buried.[5] It is, nonetheless, a primitive magical drama. The public identification, parading and expulsion of evil is usually taken literally by the audience. Only rarely is it viewed symbolically as representing a subjective process through which each individual must go to become more fully conscious. Rather, it is a collective experience that occurs externally and to which the masses remain largely passive spectators. To be sure, even the spectator undergoes a vicarious release from anxiety and an ecstatic joy when evil is clearly embodied and then banished or killed. This, perhaps, explains the orgiastic celebrations that often accompany the successful conclusion of the rite, whether the rite takes the form of a criminal prosecution or a victorious political-military campaign. But this point aside, in its ritual objectification, evil becomes a stranger to the community from which it is exiled. And the community can, therefore, take pride in the knowledge of its own righteousness, committing even barbaric acts against the evil one in "good conscience."

THE REDISCOVERY OF VIRTUE

Technological progress comes at a price. For each expansion granted people in their freedom to act as a result of new technical skills, there must be either a corresponding development in humankind's ethical sensibilities or disaster may result. Nowhere is this seen more clearly and tragically than in modern warfare. Given the modern technology of violence, people can no longer afford to revel in the false consciousness created and sustained by means of the ritual transference of evil. Humankind's almost inconceivable technical power to destroy life calls on each of us to carry a far heavier ethical burden than that with which we are familiar. What is the nature of this burden?

Self-righteous rage, rage that transfers all evil to the enemy "out there," subjectively inducing a certainty of soul, thought, and intention, as emotionally satisfying as it might be, can be an instrument of the most horrible crimes if it is not informed by prudence. By prudence, we mean seeing all things, including oneself, as they truly are.[6] The recognition of human totality implies preeminently, the recognition of the human capacity to evil. Rebellion, at the same time that it affirms a good nature common to mankind must, if it is to remain true to its origins, also acknowledge a common human inclination to evil.

The phrase *tat tvam asi*, "that art thou," has become banalized by contemporary hucksters of painless and immediate enlighten- ment, as a vehicle of morally irresponsible pride and selfishness: I am the mountain, the mountain is I; I am the sun, the sun is I; I am the true, the good, and the beautiful and they are myself. But there is another more complete and accurate rendering of the phrase, exemplified in Hindu military wisdom. This is the sobering truth depicted in the Mahabharata which is discovered by the white- skinned Pandu brothers, the righteous defenders of *dharma*, after they attain victory over the black-skinned Kurus through resort to treachery and unfair weapons: I am the evil one, the evil one is I; I am the ugly one, the ugly one is I. I am the brother of unrighteous- ness. *Tat tvam asi.* Typically, wisdom of this sort makes its visita- tion when one's conscious defenses are down, and the capacity for justifying personal cruelty, indifference, and deception is suspended momentarily. Solitude is such a time; another is deep sleep. Further- more, such a revelation often appears in the form of startling pri- mordial images. So it was for the Pandu brothers. Recall the vision which appeared to them after they had fallen into an unconscious postbattle swoon:

The warriors in the Pandava camp beheld Death-night in her embodied form, black, of bloody mouth and bloody eyes, wearing crimson garlands and smeared with crimson unguents, attired in a single piece of red cloth, with a noose in hand, and resembling an elderly lady, employed in chanting a dismal note and standing full before their eyes, and about to lead away men and steeds and elephants all tied with a stout cord.[7]

It should be obvious from this example that prudence, as defined above, involves much more than a detached intellectual admission of one's own capacity to harm others. On the contrary, it neces- sitates a full cognitive and emotional *acceptance* of one's personal limitations. By its very nature, prudence entails at least two types of psychological "death": First, a deeply wounding experience of one's own perversity and depravity, a confrontation with one's personal "shadow"; and second, a "digestion" and assimilation of this shadow into one's own life, a painful, sacrificial renunciation of the possibility of perfection in oneself, in others, and in social reality.[8]

Given this price, it is understandable why teachings since ancient times indicate that without courage there can be no real prudence, but merely its clever and cautious facade. For this same reason it can be seen why the attainment of prudence should be universally represented by military symbolism. The ultimate esoteric meaning of holy war mythology everywhere is the courageous no-holds-barred confrontation with, and grappling with, truth. It is this and nothing else that distinguishes the legendary military hero of epic literature, whether he be Arjuna or Jacob, from ordinary mortals. Just as the psychic wounds of both the Pandu hero and of Israel's first son brought them to new life in sight of the divine, so may our own dying to the ethic of moral purity and perfection bring us closer to our own human nature, to a life of excellence (*areté*) in the Greek sense. "Man, if thou knowest what thou doest, thou art blessed, but if thou knowest not, thou art accursed and a transgressor of the law."[9]

The Occidental holy war is based on the premise that the world should be just and that each should be given his due. But this premise by itself is an incomplete basis for ethical behavior. Without exception every utopia of perfect justice, from Plato's *Republic* to Zamiatin's *We* (where even the thought of an irrational number is a crime), ends in a nightmare of "we are innocent" coupled with systematic human degradation and spiritual impoverishment. Justice without sight of prudence, in other words, is simply an excuse for tyranny by the strong, clear-sighted, and pure of heart.[10]

We do not wish to be misunderstood as suggesting that mercy alone is a sufficient basis for public policy. Mercy without justice, as Thomas Aquinas once showed, is the mother of dissolution. For the Jew, the Muslim, and the Christian, there is objective evil in the world against which he has a responsibility to rebel. Nevertheless, the meting out of justice without mercy is cruelty; even a computer can be programmed automatically to give each his due. Human beings, it seems, are called to be more than perfectly rational machines. But sympathetic understanding and merciful treatment of the quirks, perversions, and even the crimes of the decrepit, the misformed, and the socio-pathic—in short, the enemies of *nomos*, against whom the exoteric holy war is fought—presupposes that the judge accepts himself as he truly is, capable of both good and evil. This is why in those symbolisms of sacred combat—Nahuatlism, Hinduism, medieval Christianity, Confucianism, and Zen *bushidō* —in which the protagonists ritually identify themselves with their opponents, the conduct of battle is carefully tempered, and little harm is done by either side. And by the same token, why in those symbolisms of holy war—Hebraism, Islam, and Reformation Protestantism—in which the antagonist is ritually associated with the *ḥarbie*, with what is absolutely alien to the protagonist, battle is liberated from all constraints, and violence tends to become totalitarian.

Contemporary events confirm this interpretatation as well. Precisely as existential phenomenology of the personal blemish and the music and art-forms of atonality, irrationality, and conventional scandal have grown in popularity (in exactly those circles where the poetic revelation of man's finitude touches the human heart), there is a corresponding "liberalism" in welfare, mental health, and criminal policy. We may be thankful that the subject of sin has once again found a respectable social-scientific audience.[11] And we may hope that this spirit will begin to penetrate the discussion of foreign policy before the next holy war.

NOTES

1. Albert Camus, "Neither Victims nor Executioners," trans. by Dwight MacDonald, in *Seeds of Liberation*, ed. by Paul Goodman (New York: George Braziller, 1964). Camus asks the reader to "suppose that certain individuals resolve that they will consistently oppose to power, the force of example; to authority, exhortation; to insult, friendly reasoning; to trickery, simple honor. They would be preparing the future. Who can fail to see the positively dazzling realism of such behavior?" (p. 40). Sartre responds: "A fine sight they are too, the believers in nonviolence, saying they are neither victims nor executioners. Very well then, if you're not victims when the government which you've voted for, when the army in which your younger brothers are serving without hesitation or remorse

have undertaken race murder, you are without a shadow of a doubt, executioners. And if you choose to be victims and to risk being put in prison for a day or two, you are simply choosing to pull your irons out of the fire'' (Jean-Paul Sartre, "Preface," Frantz Fanon, *The Wretched of the Earth*, trans. by Constance Farrington [New York: Grove Press, 1968], p. 25).

2. For the finest discussion of the subject of rebellion in modern literature, see Camus, *The Rebel*, particularly the first and last chapters.

3. The classic statement of the phenomena of religious alienation will be found in Ludwig Feuerbach, *The Essence of Christianity*, trans. by George Eliot, intro. by Karl Barth (New York: Harper & Row, 1957).

4. Quoted in Durant, *The Age of Faith*, p. 592.

5. Frazer, *The Golden Bough*, pp. 624-79. An important addition to the literature of scapegoating is René Girard's, *Violence and the Sacred*, trans. by Patrick Gregory (Baltimore, Md.: Johns Hopkins University Press, 1977).

6. Pieper, *The Four Cardinal Virtues*, pp. 10-23.

7. *Sauptika-parva*, viii. To repeat the point made in chapter 8, the reappropriation of sin back to oneself is not unique to Oriental religion. All the major prophets assail not only the guilt of foreign nations, but with increasing fervency over time, that of Israel herself. The sense of foreboding over impending punishment characteristic of Judaic prophecy clearly implies a feeling of responsibility for the world's sin. This is a wound no less severe than that suffered by the Pandus. Indeed, the books of the prophets are, apart from their calls for revenge, a virtual orgy of national self-recrimination; an anticipation of Paul's notion of Original Sin wherein there is nothing redeemable in humanity (Rom. 3:10-19).

The critical power of these prophetic observations, however, is practically undercut by the equally common use of the literary device of the "remnant" who are not guilty in God's eyes, or who are "justified by faith" in Christ.

8. These points are based on Erich Neumann, *Depth Psychology and a New Ethic*, trans. by Eugene Rolfe (New York: G. P. Putnam's Sons, 1969).

9. *Codex Bezae*, Luke 6:4, quoted in ibid., p. 15.

10. It is not commonly enough appreciated how closely Camus's own studies of virtue (although he did not use the term) parallel ancient discussions of the subject. Besides *The Rebel*, which constitutes a rich source for the theoretical ethicist, several of his novels also deal with the issue; most notably *The Plague*.

11. For example, see Stanford Lyman, *The Seven Deadly Sins* (New York: St. Martin's Press, 1978).

BIBLIOGRAPHY

GENERAL WORKS ON RELIGION, MYTHOLOGY AND ETHICS

Berger, Peter L. *The Sacred Canopy*. Garden City, N.Y.: Doubleday and Company, 1969.

———. "Second Thoughts on Substantive and Functional Definitions of Religion." *Journal for the Scientific Study of Religion* 13 (1974): 125-33.

Bulfinch, Thomas. *Bulfinch's Mythology*. New York: Random House, n.d.

Campbell, Joseph. *The Hero with a Thousand Faces*. New York: Meridian Press, 1956.

———. *The Masks of God*. 4 vols. New York: Viking Press, 1970. Vol. 1 *Primitive Mythology*; Vol. 2 *Oriental Mythology*; Vol. 3 *Occidental Mythology*; Vol. 4 *Creative Mythology*.

———. *The Mythic Image*. Princeton, N.J.: Princeton University Press, 1974.

———. *Myths to Live By*. New York: Viking Press, 1972.

Camus, Albert. "Neither Victims nor Executioners." In *Seeds of Liberation*. Edited by Paul Goodman. New York: George Braziller, 1964.

———. *The Rebel*. Translated by Anthony Bower. New York: Vintage Books, 1956 (1947).

Feuerbach, Ludwig. *The Essence of Christianity*. Translated by George Eliot, introduced by Karl Barth. New York: Harper & Row, 1957.

Frazer, James G. *The Golden Bough: A Study in Magic and Religion*. New York: Macmillan, 1951 (1922).

Huizinga, Johan. *Homo Ludens: A Study of the Play Element in Culture*. Boston: Beacon Press, 1955.

Lyman, Stanford. *The Seven Deadly Sins*. New York: St. Martin's Press, 1978.

McNamara, Patrick H., ed. *Religion American Style*. New York: Harper & Row, 1974.

Mills, C. Wright and Hans H. Gerth. "The Sociology of Motivation." *Character and Social Structure*. New York: Harcourt, Brace and World, 1964.

Neumann, Erich. *Depth Psychology and a New Ethic.* Translated by
     Eugene Rolfe. New York: G.P. Putnam's Sons, 1969.

_____. *The Great Mother: An Analysis of the Archetype.* Translated by
     Ralph Manheim. Bollingen Series 47. New York: 1955.

Nietzsche, Friedrich. *Toward a Genealogy of Morals.* Translated by Walter
     Kaufman. New York: Vintage Books, 1967.

Otto, Rudolf. *The Idea of the Holy.* Translated and introduced by John
     W. Harvey. London: Oxford University Press, 1973 (1923).

_____. *Mysticism East and West: A Comparative Analysis of Mysticism.*
     Translated by Bertha L. Bracey and Richenda C. Payne. New York:
     Macmillan, 1932.

Pieper, Josef. *The Four Cardinal Virtues.* South Bend, Ind.: University of
     Notre Dame Press, 1966.

_____. *Leisure the Basis of Culture.* Translated by Alexander Dru. New
     York: Random House, 1963.

Ryan, Joseph Michael. "Ethnoscience and Problems of Method in the
     Social Scientific Study of Religion." *Sociological Analysis* 39 (Fall
     1978): 241-49.

Sartre, Jean-Paul. "Preface." Frantz Fanon's *Wretched of the Earth.*
     Translated by Constance Farrington. New York: Grove Press, 1968.

Slotten, Ralph. "Exoteric and Esoteric Modes of Apprehension." *Socio-
     logical Analysis* 38 (1977): 185-208.

Stark, Werner, *The Sociology of Religion.* 3 vols. New York: Fordham
     University Press, 1967.

Tillich, Paul. *Dynamics of Faith.* New York: Harper & Row, 1958.

Underhill, Evelyn. *Mysticism.* New York: E.P. Dutton, 1911.

Weber, Max. "The Social Psychology of the World Religions." In *From
     Max Weber: Essays in Sociology.* Translated, edited, and introduced
     by Hans H. Gerth and C. Wright Mills. New York: Oxford Univer-
     sity Press, 1958.

_____. *The Sociology of Religion.* Translated by Ephraim Fischoff. Bos-
     ton: Beacon Press, 1963.

Yinger, J. Milton. *The Scientific Study of Religion.* New York: Macmillan,
     1970.

GENERAL WORKS ON VIOLENCE AND RELIGION AND WARFARE

Aho, James A. "Suffering, Redemption and Violence: Albert Camus and
     the Sociology of Violence." *Rendezvous* 9 (Spring 1974/Winter
     1974-75): 51-62.

Baron, Salo. "Impact of Wars on Religion." *Political Science Quarterly* 57 (December 1952): 534-72.

Bramson, Leon and George W. Goethels eds. *War.* New York: Basic Books, 1968.

Cohn, Norman. *The Pursuit of the Millennium.* New York: Oxford University Press, 1970.

Coser, Lewis. "The Dysfunctions of Military Secrecy." In Lewis Coser, *Continuities in the Study of Conflict.* New York: Free Press, 1970.

Dumézil, Georges. *The Destiny of the Warrior.* Translated by Alf Hiltebeitel. Chicago: University of Chicago Press, 1970.

Girard, René. *Violence and the Sacred.* Translated by Patrick Gregory. Baltimore, Md.: Johns Hopkins University Press, 1977.

Gray, J. Glenn. *The Warriors: Reflections on Men in Battle.* New York: Harcourt Brace, 1959.

Laffont, Robert. *The Ancient Art of Warfare.* 2 vols. Paris: International Book Society, 1974.

Nef, John U. *War and Human Progress.* London: Routledge and Kegan Paul, 1950.

Schneider, Joseph. "Primitive Warfare: A Methodological Note." *American Sociological Review* 15 (1950): 772-77.

Speier, Hans. *Social Order and the Risks of War.* New York: George W. Stewart, 1952.

Toynbee, Arnold. *War and Civilization.* New York: Oxford University Press, 1950.

Vagts, Alfred. *A History of Militarism.* New York: Meridian Press, 1959.

Wright, Quincy. *A Study of War.* Chicago: University of Chicago Press, 1965.

GRECO-ROMAN MYTHOLOGY AND WARFARE

Adcock, F.E. *The Greek and Macedonian Art of War.* Berkeley: University of California Press, 1957.

Daniels, C. M. "The Role of the Roman Army in the Spread and Practice of Mithraism." *Mithraic Studies* vol. 2. Edited by John Hinnels. Oxford Road: Manchester University Press, 1976: 249-74.

Delbrück, Hans. *Antiquity.* Vol. I of *History of the Art of War within the Framework of Political History.* Translated by W. J. Renfroe Jr. Westport, Conn.: Greenwood Press, 1975.

The Iliad of Homer. Translated and introduced by Richmond Lattimore. Chicago: University of Chicago Press, 1951.

AZTEC WARFARE AND RELIGION

Bandelier, Adolf F. "The Art of War and Mode of Warfare of the Ancient Mexicans." *Peabody Museum of American Archeology and Ethnology* 10th Annual Report 2 (1877): 95-161.

Braden, Charles S. *Religious Aspects of the Conquest of Mexico.* New York: AMS Press, 1966 (1930).

Burland, C. A. *Montezuma: Lord of the Aztecs.* New York: G. P. Putnam's Sons, 1973.

Caso, Alfonso. *The Aztecs: People of the Sun.* Translated by Lowell Dunham. Norman: University of Oklahoma Press, 1958.

"Codex Ramirez." Translated by Paul Radin. "The Sources and Authenticity of the History of the Ancient Mexicans." *University of California Publications in American Archeology and Ethnology* 17 (1920): 67-123.

Coe, Michael D. *Mexico.* New York: Frederick A. Praeger, 1962.

Davies, Byam Nigel. *The Aztecs: A History.* New York: G. P. Putnam's Sons, 1974.

———. *Los Senorios Independientes del Imperio Azteca.* Mexico City: Instituto Nacional de Anthropologiae Historia, 1968.

Diaz del Castillo, Bernal. *The Discovery and Conquest of Mexico.* Translated by A. P. Maudslay. New York: Noonday Press, 1966.

Diego de Duran. *Historia de las Indias de Nueva España e Islal de Tierra Firma.* 2 vols. Edited by Angel M. Garibay K. Mexico: Editorial Porrua, 1967 (1867-1880).

Florentine Codex. 13 vols. Translated from Nahuatl by A. J. O. Anderson and Charles E. Dibble. Sante Fe: Monographs of the School of American Research; Salt Lake City: University of Utah Press, 1952. This is based on Bernardino de Sahagún, *Historia General de las Cosas de Nueva España.*

Garibay K., A. M., ed. *The Broken Spears.* Translated by L. Kemp, introduced by Miguel León-Portilla, Boston: Beacon Press, 1962.

Harner, Michael. "The Ecological Basis for Aztec Sacrifice." *American Ethnologist* 4 (Feb. 1977): 117-35.

León-Portilla, Miguel. *Aztec Thought and Culture: A Study of the Ancient Nahuatl Mind.* Translated by J. E. Davis. Norman, Okla.: University of Oklahoma Press, 1963.

Morgan, Lewis H. "Montezuma's Dinner." *North American Review* 122 (April 1876): 265-308.

Noguera, Eduardo. "Las Guerras Floridas." *Mexico Prehispanico: Culturas, Deidades, Monumentos* (1946): 361-64.

Paz, Octavio. *The Labyrinth of Solitude: Life and Thought in Mexico.* Translated by Lysander Kemp. New York: Grove Press, 1961.

Prescott, William H. *History and Conquest of Mexico.* 3 vols. New York: Harper and Brothers, 1843.

Sanders, William T. and Price, Barbara J. *Mesoamerica: The Evolution of a Civilization.* New York: Random House, 1968.

ANCIENT INDIAN RELIGION AND WARFARE

Armour, W. S. "Customs of Warfare in Ancient India." *Transactions of the Grotius Society* 8 (1922): 71-88.

Basham, A. L. *The Wonder That Was India.* London: Sidgwick and Jackson, 1954.

Bhagavad-Gita. Translated by Sarvepalli Radhakrishnan. In *A Sourcebook in Indian Philosophy.* Edited by Radhakrishnan and C. A. Moore. Princeton, N.J.: Princeton University Press, 1957.

Chakravarti, P. C. *The Art of War in Ancient India.* Ramma, Dacca: University of Dacca Press, n.d.

The Edicts of Asoka. Translated by N. A. Nikam and Richard McKeon. Chicago: University of Chicago Press, 1959.

Elliot, Henry M. *The History of India as Told by its Own Historians.* 8 vols. Edited by John Dowson. London: n.p., 1877.

History and Culture of the Indian People. 11 vols. General editor R. C. Majumdar. Bombay: Bharatiya Vidya Bhavan, 1951.

Hopkins, Edward. *The Social and Military Position of the Ruling Caste in India.* Durga Kund, Varanasi: Bharat-Bharati, 1972 (1889).

Hymns to the Goddess. Translated by Ellen and Arthur Avalon. London: Luzac and Company, 1913.

Kautilya's Arthashastra. Translated by R. Shamasastry, introduced by J. F. Fleet. Mysore: Mysore Publishing House, 1960 (1915).

Law, Narendra Nath. *Interstate Relations in Ancient India.* London: Luzac and Company, 1920.

The Laws of Manu. Translated by Georg Bühler. New York: Dover Books, 1969 (1886).

The Life of Hiuen Tsiang. Translated by Samuel Beal. Westport, Conn.: Hyperion Press, 1973 (1911).

Mahabharata. 18 vols. Translated by Pratap Chandra Roy. Calcutta: Datta Bose and Company, 1919-1933. Volumes consulted in this research: Vol. 1 *Adi-parva*; Vol. 2 *Sabha-parva*; Vol. 3 *Aranyak-parva*; Vol.

4 *Vairata-parva*; Vol. 5 *Udyoga-parva*; Vol. 6 *Bhishma-parva*; Vol.
7 *Drona-parva*; Vol. 8 *Karna-parva*; Vol. 9 *Salya-parva*; Vol. 10
Sauptika-parva; Vol. 11 *Stree-parva*; Vol. 12 *Santi-parva*.

Majumdar, Bimal Kanti. *The Military System in Ancient India*. 2nd rev.
edition. Calcutta: Firma K. L. Mukhopadhyay, 1960.

Sacred Laws of the Aryas: Part 2 Vasishtha and Baudhyana. Translated by
Georg Bühler. Delhi: Motilal Banarsidass, 1969 (1882). This volume
contains both "Vasishtha's Dharmasastra" and "Baudhyana's
Dharmasastra."

Sarkar, Jadunath. *Military History of India*. New Delhi: Orient Longmans,
1960.

The Thirteen Principal Upanishads. Translated and edited by R. E. Hume.
London: Oxford University Press, 1921.

Van Nooten, B. A. *The Mahabharata*. New York: Twayne Publishers Inc.,
1971.

Weber, Max. *The Religion of India: The Sociology of Hinduism and Buddhism*. Translated by Hans H. Gerth and Don Martindale. Glencoe,
Ill.: Free Press of Glencoe, 1956.

MEDIEVAL EUROPEAN WARFARE AND RELIGION

Ackerman, Robert W. "The Knighting Ceremonies in Middle English
Romances." *Speculum* 19 (July 1944): 283-313.

Barber, Richard. *The Knight and Chivalry*. New York: Charles Scribner's
Sons, 1970.

Blake, E. O. "The Formation of the 'Crusade Idea'." *Journal of Ecclesiastical History* 21 (1970): 11-31.

Bloch, Marc. *Feudal Society*. 2 vols. Translated by L. A. Manyon. Chicago:
University of Chicago Press, 1970.

Bonet, Honoré. *The Tree of Battles*. Translated and edited by G. W.
Coopland. Liverpool: Liverpool University Press, 1949.

Brundage, James A. "Holy War and the Medieval Lawyers." In *The Holy
War*. Edited by Thomas Patrick Murphy. Columbus: Ohio State
University Press, 1976.

Cowdrey, H. E. J. "The Genesis of the Crusades: The Springs of Western
Ideas of Holy War." In *The Holy War*. Edited by Thomas Patrick
Murphy. Columbus: Ohio State University Press, 1976.

_____. "The Peace and Truce of God of the Eleventh Century." *Past and
Present* 66 (Feb. 1970): 42-67.

Durant, Will. *The Age of Faith*. Vol. 4 of *The Story of Civilization*. New
York: Simon and Schuster, 1950.

Erdmann, Carl. *Die Entstehung des Kreuzzugsgedankes.* Stuttgart: W. Kohlhammer, 1935.

Hatto, A. T. "Archery and Chivalry: A Noble Prejudice." *Modern Language Review* 35 (1940): 40-54.

Keen, M. H. "Chivalry, Nobility and the Man-At-Arms." In *War, Literature and Politics in the Late Middle Ages.* Edited by C. T. Allmand. Liverpool: Liverpool University Press, 1976.

_____. *The Laws of War in the Late Middle Ages.* London: Routledge and Kegan Paul, 1965.

Lovejoy, A. O. *The Great Chain of Being.* Cambridge, Mass.: Harvard University Press, 1936.

Oman, Charles. *The Art of War in the Middle Ages.* 2 vols. New York: Burt Franklin, 1969 (1924).

Patch, H. R. *The Goddess Fortuna in Medieval Literature.* Cambridge, Mass.: Harvard University Press, 1927.

Postan, M. M. "The Costs of the Hundred Years' War." *Past and Present* 27 (1964): 34-53.

Robinson, I. S. "Gregory VII and the Soldiers of Christ." *History* 58 (1973): 169-92.

Seward, Desmond. *The Monks of War.* London: Archon Press, 1972.

Troeltsch, Ernst. Vol. 1 of *The Social Teachings of the Christian Churches.* Translated by Olive Wyon, introduced by Richard Niebuhr. New York: Harper & Row, 1969 (1911).

Vale, G. A. "New Techniques and Old Ideals: The Impact of Artillery on War and Chivalry at the End of the Hundred Years' War." In *War, Literature and Politics in the Late Middle Ages.* Edited by C. T. Allmand. Liverpool: Liverpool University Press, 1976.

Verbrugen, J. F. "La Tactique Militaire des Armées des Chevaliers." *Revue du Nord* 29 (1947): 161-80.

Ward, Robert. *An Enquiry into the Foundation and History of the Law of Nations in Europe from the Time of the Greeks and Romans to the Age of Grotius.* 2 vols. Introduced by Carlisle Spivey. New York: Garland Publishers Inc., 1973 (1795).

Wright, N. A. R. "The Tree of Battles of Honoré Bonet and the Laws of War." In *War, Literature and Politics in the Late Middle Ages.* Edited by C. T. Allmand. Liverpool: Liverpool University Press, 1976.

CONFUCIAN MYTHOLOGY AND WARFARE

The Analects of Confucius. Translated and annotated by Arthur Waley. New York: Random House, 1938.

Bloodworth, Dennis and Bloodworth, Ching Ping. *The Chinese Machiavelli: 3000 Years of Chinese Statecraft.* New York: Farrar, Straus and Giroux, 1976.

Britton, Roswell S. "Chinese Interstate Intercourse Before 700 B.C." *American Journal of International Law* 24 (1935): 615-35.

Chen, Shin-tsai. "The Equality of States in Ancient China." *American Journal of International Law* 35 (1941): 641-50.

The Chinese Classics. 5 vols. Translated, edited, introduced, and interpreted by James Legge. Hong Kong: Hong Kong University Press, 1970. Vol. 1 *Doctrine of the Mean* (1892), *The Great Learning* (1892), *The Analects of Confucius* (1892); Vol. 2 *The Works of Mencius* (1895); Vol. 3 *The Shoo King (Shu Ching)* or *Book of Historical Documents* (1865); Vol. 4 *The She King (Shi Ching)* or *Book of Poetry* (1871); Vol. 5 *Ch'un Ts'ew with the Tso Chuen (Ch'un Ch'iu with Tso Chuan)* or *Spring and Autumn Annals with Commentaries by Tso Chuan* (1872).

Creel, Herrlee G. *The Western Chou.* Vol. 1 of *The Origins of Statecraft in China.* Chicago: University of Chicago Press, 1970.

Fairbank, John K. "Varieties of the Chinese Military Experience." *Chinese Ways of Warfare.* Edited by Frank A. Kierman Jr. and John K. Fairbank. Cambridge, Mass.: Harvard University Press, 1974.

Fêng Yu-lan. *A History of Chinese Philosophy.* 2 vols. Translated with notes by Derk Bodde. Princeton, N.J.: Princeton University Press, 1952.

Fingarette, Herbert. *Confucius: The Secular as Sacred.* New York: Harper & Row, 1972.

Grousset, René. *The Rise and Splendour of the Chinese Empire.* Translated by Anthony Watson-Gandy and Terence Gordon. Berkeley: University of California Press, 1958.

Hamburger, Max. "Aristotle and Confucius: A Study in Comparative Philosophy." *Philosophy* 31 (1956): 324-57.

Hsün Tze: The Moulder of Ancient Confucianism. Translated by Homer H. Dubs. London: Probsthain, 1927.

The I-Li or Book of Etiquette and Ceremonial. Translated and introduced by John Steele. London: Probsthain and Company, 1917.

Kierman, Frank A. Jr. "Phases and Modes of Combat in Early China." In *Chinese Ways in Warfare.* Edited by Frank A. Kierman Jr. and John K. Fairbank. Cambridge, Mass.: Harvard University Press, 1974.

Li Chi: Book of Rites. An Encyclopedia of Ancient Ceremonial Usages. 2 vols. Translated by James Legge. Edited with an introduction and study guide by Ch'u Chai and Winberg Chai. New Hyde Park, N.Y.: University Books, 1967 (1885).

Mao Tse-tung. *Selected Military Writings*. Peking: Foreign Languages Press, 1967.

Martin, Desmond. *The Rise of Ghingis Khan and His Conquest of North China* Baltimore, Md.: Johns Hopkins University Press, 1950.

Martin, W. A. P. "Traces of International Law in Ancient China." *International Review* 14 (1883): 63-77.

Sun Tzu. *Art of War*. Translated and introduced by Samuel Griffith. New York: Oxford University Press, 1963.

Wade, T. F. "The Army of the Chinese Empire: Its Two Great Divisions, the Bannermen or National Guard, and the Green Standard or Provincial Troops; Their Organization, Locations, Pay, Condition, &c." *Chinese Repository* 20 (1851): 250-80, 300-40, 363-422.

Walker, Richard Louis. *The Multi-State System of Ancient China*. Camden, Conn.: Shoe String Press, 1953.

The Way and Its Power: A Study of the Tao Tê Ching and Its Place in Chinese Thought. Translated, introduced with notes by Arthur Waley. New York: Grove Press, 1958.

Weber, Max. *The Religion of China: Confucianism and Taoism*. Translated by Hans H. Gerth, introduced by C. K. Yang. New York: Macmillan, 1964.

Welch, Holmes. *Taoism: The Parting of the Way*. Boston: Beacon Press, 1966.

TOKUGAWA JAPANESE RELIGION AND MILITARY ARTS

Anesaki, Masaharu. *History of Japanese Religion*. New York: Charles Tuttle, 1963 (1930).

Bellah, Robert. *Tokugawa Religion*. New York: Free Press, 1957.

Dautremer, J. "The Vendetta or Legal Revenge in Japan." *Asiatic Society of Japan Transactions* 13 (1885): 82-90.

Draeger, Donn F. *Classical Budo*. Vol. 2 of *The Martial Arts and Ways of Japan*. New York and Tokyo: Weatherhill, 1973.

Haines, Bruce A. *Karate's History and Traditions*. Tokyo: Charles Tuttle, 1968.

Hall, J. Carey. "Teijo's Family Instruction: A Samurai's Ethical Bequest to His Posterity (1763)." *Japan Society Transactions and Proceedings* 14 (1915): 128-58.

Hashimoto, Minoru. "The Keystone of Medieval Bushido." *Cultural Nippon* 4 (1936): 263-72, 345-54.

Herrigel, Eugen. *Zen in the Art of Archery.* Translated by R. F. C. Hull. New York: Vintage Books, 1971.

Iwado, Z. Tamotsu. "'Hagakure Bushido' (The Book of the Warrior)." *Cultural Nippon* 7 (1937): 33-55.

Kitigawa, Joseph. *Religion in Japanese History.* New York: Columbia University Press, 1966.

Lewis, A. R. *Knights and Samurai: Feudalism in Northern France and Japan.* London: Temple Smith, 1974.

Merton, Thomas. *Zen and the Birds of Appetite.* New York: New Directions Books, 1968.

Nitobe, Inazo. *Bushido: The Soul of Japan.* Rutland, V.: Charles Tuttle, 1969 (1899).

Ratti, Oscar and Westbrook, Adele. *Secrets of the Samurai: A Survey of Feudal Japan.* Tokyo: Charles Tuttle, 1973.

Razan, Hayashi. "On Mastery of the Arts of Peace and War." In *Sources of Japanese Tradition.* Edited by William Theodore de Bary. New York: Columbia University Press, 1958.

Sakai-Atsuhara. "The Memoirs of Takeda-Shingen and the Kai-no-Gunritsu." *Cultural Nippon* 8 (1940): 83-107.

Sansom, George, *A History of Japan.* 3 vols. Stanford, Calif.: Stanford University Press, 1958.

Seward, Jack. *Hara Kiri: Japanese Ritual Suicide.* Tokyo: Charles Tuttle, 1968.

Soko, Yamaga. "Way of the Samurai." In *Sources of Japanese Tradition.* Edited by William Theodore de Bary. New York: Columbia University Press, 1958.

Suzuki, D. T. *Manual of Zen Buddhism.* London: Rider and Company, 1935.

_____. *Zen Buddhism.* Edited by William Barrett. Garden City, New York: Doubleday and Company, 1956.

ANCIENT SEMITIC AND HEBRAIC RELIGION AND WARFARE

The Babylonian Genesis. Translated and edited by Alexander Heidel. 2nd edition. Chicago: University of Chicago Press, 1951.

Benedict, Marion J. *The God of the Old Testament in Relation to War.* New York: Columbia University, 1927.

Budde, Karl F. R. "Das nomadische Ideal im alten Testament." In *Solo-weitschick, M. vom Buch das tausend Jahre wuchs.* Berlin: n.p., 1932 (1896).

The Holy Bible. King James Version, 1611. Self-pronouncing edition.

The Jerusalem Bible, General editor Alexander Jones. Garden City, New York: Doubleday & Co., 1966.

Josephus, Flavius. *The Wars of the Jews.* In *The Life and Works of Flavius Josephus.* Translated by William Whiston. Philadelphia: John C. Winston, 1954.

McKenzie, J. L. "Jacob at Peniel: Gn 32, 24-32." *Catholic Biblical Quarterly* 25 (1963): 71-76.

Olmstead, A. T. *History of Assyria.* Chicago: University of Chicago Press, 1923.

Rad, Gustav von. *Der Heilege Krieg im alten Israel.* Zurich: n.p., 1951.

Ragozin, Zenaide A. *Assyria: From the Rise of the Empire to the Fall of Nineveh.* London: T. Fisher Unwin, 1867.

Smend, Rudolf. *Yahweh War and Tribal Confederation.* Translated by Max G. Rogers. Nashville, Tenn.: Abingdon Press, 1970.

Smith, W. Robertson. *The Religion of the Semites: The Fundamental Institutions.* New York: Schocken Books, 1972 (1888-1891).

Van Trigt, F. "La Signification de la Lutte de Jacob près du Yabboq Gen. XXXII 23-33." *Oudtestament Studien* 12 (1958): 280-309.

Vaux, Roland de. *Ancient Israel: Its Life and Institutions.* Translated by John McHugh. New York: McGraw-Hill, 1961.

Voegelin, Eric. *Israel and Revelation.* Vol. 1 of *Order and History.* Baton Rouge: Louisiana State University Press, 1956.

Weber, Max. *Ancient Judaism.* Translated by Hans H. Gerth. New York: Free Press, 1952.

Wright, G. Ernest. "The Conquest Theme in the Bible." In *A Light Unto My Path.* Edited by Howard Bream, Ralph Heim and Carey Moore. Philadelphia: Temple University Press, 1974.

Yadin, Yigael. *The Art of War in Biblical Lands.* 2 vols. Translated by M. Pearlman. Jerusalem: International Publishing Company Ltd., 1963.

The Zend Avesta. 3 vols. Translated by L. H. Mills. Oxford: Clarendon Press, 1867.

ISLAM AND WAR

Ali, Syed Ameer. *The Spirit of Islam: A History of the Ideals of Islam.* New York: Humanities Press, 1974.

Ayalon, David. "Preliminary Remarks on the *Mamluk* Military Institution." In *War, Technology and Society in the Middle East*. Edited by V. J. Parry and M. E. Yapp. London: Oxford University Press, 1975.

Dickson, H. R. P. *The Arab of the Desert*. London: George Allen and Unwin Leg., 1949.

Gardner, W. R. W. "Jihad." *Muslim World* 2 (1912): 347-57.

Gaudefroy-Demombynes, Maurice. *Muslim Institutions*. New York: Barnes and Noble, 1961.

Glubb, John Bagot. *The Great Arab Conquests*. London: Hodder and Stoughton, 1963.

Grunebaum, Gustav E. von. *Medieval Islam*. 2nd edition. Chicago: University of Chicago Press, 1953.

Hill, D. R. "The Role of the Camel and Horse in the Early Arab Conquests." In *War, Technology and Society in the Middle East*. Edited by V. J. Parry and M. E. Yapp. London: Oxford University Press, 1975.

Hitti, Philip K. *History of the Arabs*. New York: St. Martin's Press, 1967.

Horton, George. *The Blight of Asia*. Indianapolis, Ind.: Bobbs-Merrill Company, 1926.

Huart, Clement. "Le Droit de la Guerre." *Revue du Monde Musulman* 2 (1907): 331-46.

Ibn-Khaldun. *The Muqaddimah*. 3 vols. Translated by Franz Rosenthal. New York: Bollingen Foundation Inc., 1963.

Jurji, Edward J. "The Islamic Theory of War." *Muslim World* 30 (October 1940): 332-42.

Katsh, Abraham I. *Judaism and Islam: Biblical and Talmudic Backgrounds of the Koran and Its Commentaries*. New York: New York University Press, 1954.

Khadduri, Majid. *War and Peace in the Law of Islam*. Baltimore, Md.: Johns Hopkins University Press, 1955.

The Koran. Translated by J. M. Roswell. Sydney, Australia: E. W. Cole, n.d.

Massignon, Louis. "Le Respect de la Personne Humaine en Islam, et la Priorité du Droit d'Asile sur Devoir de Juste Guerre." *Revue Internationale de la Croix-Rouge* no. 420 (1952): 448-68.

The Message of the Qur'an Presented in Perspective. Translated by Hashim Amir-Ali. Rutland, Vt.: Charles Tuttle, 1974.

Parry, V. J. "La Manière de Combattre." In *War, Technology and Society in the Middle East*. Edited by V. J. Parry and M. E. Yapp. London: Oxford University Press, 1975.

Patai, Raphael. *The Arab Mind.* New York: Charles Scribner's Sons, 1973.

Schacht, Joseph. *An Introduction to Islamic Law.* Oxford: Clarendon Press, 1964.

Shaw, Stanford J. *Empire of the Gazis.* Vol. 1 of *The Ottoman Empire and Modern Turkey.* London: Cambridge University Press, 1976.

Turner, Bryan S. *Weber and Islam: A Critical Study.* London: Routledge and Kegan Paul, 1974.

Watt, W. Montgomery. "Islamic Conceptions of the Holy War." In *The Holy War.* Edited by Thomas Patrick Murphy. Columbus: Ohio State University Press, 1976.

Wittek, Paul. *The Rise of the Ottoman Empire.* New York: Burt Franklin, 1971 (1938).

REFORMATION EUROPEAN WAR AND RELIGION

Beza, Theodore. *Concerning the Rights of Rulers over their Subjects and the Duty of Subjects toward their Rulers.* Translated by Henri-Louis Gonin, introduced by A. Van Schelvin, edited by A. M. Murray. Capetown, S.A.: n.p., 1956.

Calvin, John. *On God and Man.* Edited by F. W. Strothmann. New York: Frederick Ungar, 1956.

Clark, George. *War and Society in the Seventeenth Century.* London: Cambridge University Press, 1956.

Eisenstadt, S. N. "The Protestant Ethic: An Analysis." In *The Protestant Ethic and Modernization.* Edited by S. N. Eisenstadt. New York: Basic Books, 1968.

Firth, C. H. "The Raising of the Ironsides." *Transactions of the Royal Historical Society* 13 (1899): 17-73.

Gilbert, Felix. "Machiavelli: The Renaissance of the Art of War." In *Makers of Modern Strategy.* Edited by Edward M. Earle. Princeton, N.J.: Princeton University Press, 1961.

Holl, Karl. "Die Bedeutung der grossen Kriege für das religiöse und kirchliche Leben innerhalb des deutschen Protestantismus." *Gesammelt. Aufsätze zur Kirchengeschichte* 3 (1917): 302-84.

Laskowski, Otto. "Infantry Tactics and Firing Power in the XVI Century." *Teki Historyczne* 4 (1950): 106-15.

Liddel-Hart, B. H. "Gustavus Adolphus—Founder of Modern War." In B. H. Liddel-Hart, *Great Captains Unveiled.* Freeport, New York: Books for Libraries Press Inc., 1967.

Luther, Martin. *Luther: Selected Political Writings.* Edited by J. M. Porter. Philadelphia: Fortress Press, 1974.

Machiavelli, Niccolo. *The Art of War*. Vol. 2 of *Machiavelli: The Chief Works and Others*. Translated and edited by Allan H. Gilbert. Durham, N.C.: Duke University Press, 1965.

———. *Discourses on the First Decade of Titus Livius*. In Vol. 1 of *Machiavelli: The Chief Works and Others*. Translated and edited by Allan H. Gilbert. Durham, N.C.: Duke University Press, 1965.

———. *The Prince*. Translated by Christian Detmold, introduced by Lester Crocker. New York: Washington Square Press, 1974.

Martin, Alfred von. *Sociology of the Renaissance*. Translated by W. L. Luetkens, introduced by Wallace K. Ferguson. New York: Harper Torchbooks, 1963.

Oman, Charles. *The History of the Art of War in the Sixteenth Century*. London: Metheun and Company, 1937.

Plamenatz, John. In Search of Machiavellian *Virtù*." In *The Political Calculus*. Edited by Anthony Parel. Toronto: University of Toronto Press, 1972.

Pocock, J. G. A. *The Machiavellian Moment*. Princeton, N.J.: Princeton University Press, 1975.

Raab, Felix. *The English Face of Machiavelli*. London: Routledge and Kegan Paul, 1964.

Roberts, Michael. *Gustavus Adolphus: A History of Sweden 1611-1632*. 2 vols. London: Longmans, Green and Company, 1953.

———. *The Military Revolution*. Belfast, Ireland: Queens University Press, n.d.

Sandford, Frank W. *The Art of War for the Christian Soldier*. Amherst, N.H.: Kingdom Press, 1966.

Setton, K. M. "Lutheranism and the Turkish Peril." *Balkan Studies* 3 (1962): 136-65.

Solt, Leo. *Saints in Arms: Puritanism and Democracy in Cromwell's Army*. New York: AMS Press, 1971.

"Swedish Discipline." In C. R. L. Fletcher, *Gustavus Adolphus and the Thirty Years' War*. New York: Capricorn Books, 1963.

Troeltsch, Ernst. Vol. 2 of *The Social Teachings of the Christian Churches*. Translated by Olive Wyon, introduced by Richard Niebuhr. New York: Harper & Row, 1960 (1911).

Walzer, Michael. *The Revolution of the Saints*. Cambridge, Mass.: Harvard University Press, 1965.

Webb, Henry J. *Elizabethan Military Science*. Madison, Wisc.: University of Wisconsin Press, 1965.

Weber, Max. *The Protestant Ethic and the Spirit of Capitalism*. Translated by Talcott Parsons. New York: Charles Scribner's Sons, 1958.

INDEX

Hathor, (Isis), 21
Hawkwood, Sir John de, 32
Heang Seuh, 113
Hebraic military ethic: booty in, 155, 166, 175; ecstasy in, 173, 175; enslavement in, 166; extent of, 169-70; extermination in, 175-78, 181; Machiavellianism in, 151, 156, 166-67, 168-69, 170, 179-80; preconditions for war in, 165; rape in, 166; restrictions on war participation in, 155, 165, 178; summons for war in, 165, 178; tactics in, 169-70; warrior taboo in, 28-29, 38, 166
Hebraism, 6, 7, 11; creation in, 146-47, 161; death in, 147; importance of war in, 145; Islam and, 182-83; justice in, 148-50; projection of evil in, 33, 151, 224; ressentiment in, 150, 162. See also Hebraic military ethic; Judaism; Yahweh; particular books of Old Testament
Hedgehog. See Spanish tercio
Henry III (Holy Roman emperor), 95
Henry V (king of England), 88
Herakles Distracted (Lykus), 96
Herem (anathema), 7, 176-77, 190
Herrigel, Eugen, 135, 136, 137
Hindu military ethic. See Dharma dig-vijaya
Hinduism, 6, 8, 11, 14, 16-17, 96, 101; caste in, 61, 69, 73, 74; creation story in, 160-61; epic combat in, 24-27; glorification of war in, 23, 61-62, 71-72, 75, 79; indifference to time in, 102; justice in, 148-149; military weakness and, 72-75; obedience to law in, 73-75; origins of, 69; war as play in, 30-31, 71; war death in, 23, 31, 62, 71-72. See also Bhagavad-Gita; Dharma; Dharma dig-vijaya; Laws of Manu, The; Mahabharata
Hindus, 34, 53, 56; history of, 60-61, 67-68, 69-70, 72, 75, 78-79, 92; military weakness of, 72-75
Hittites, 60, 176

Hiuen Tsang, 68
Holofernes, General, 169
Holy. See Religious experience
Holy war. See particular military ethics; particular wars
Horsemanship: in Japan, 130; in Medieval Catholicism, 95-96
Horse sacrifice. See Asva-medha
Horus, 21, 26
Hospitalers, 84
Hospitality. See Dakhâla
Hring (freemans's assembly), 81
Hsiang, duke of Sung, 107, 112, 121
Hsün Tzu, 103, 115
Huang Ti ("Yellow Emperor"), 101
Huart, Clement, 189
Huexotzinco, 47, 51
Huguenots, 206
Huitzilopochtli, 17, 21, 26, 27, 73, 101; as Black Tezcatlipoca, 43; epic combat of, 42; sacrifice to, 53, 55; versus Quetzalcoatl, 35-36
Huizinga, Johan, 23, 172
Humphrey, duke of Gloucester, 32
Hundred Years' War, 32, 86, 69
Huns, 72
Hussites, 178, 199
Hutt, Hans, 211
Hwa P'aou, 109
Hwae, 109

I, Tribe of, 110, 124
Ibn Abi Waqqas, Sa'd, 155
Ibn al-Assi, Amr, 173
Ibn al-Waleed, Khalid, 173
Ibn-Kasim, Muhamed, 72
Ibn-Khaldun, 158, 180
I-Ching, 117
Ignatius of Loyala, Saint, 142, 217
Ikhwan Rebellion, 188
I-Li, 120
Iliad, 60, 179
Immanentist-cosmological military ethic: astrology in, 35; attitude toward war in, 30-32; fortress architecture in, 34-35; indifference to costs in, 31-32;

Moslems. *See* Islam
Mu, Battle of, 114
Muga (no mind), 133, 136, 141
Muhammad, Prophet, 154, 155, 158, 169, 179, 182, 185, 186, 189
Mu'min (believers), 188
Muntzer, Thomas, 179, 200, 210, 211
Muruwwa (manliness), 187
Muslim military ethic. *See Jihad*
Muslims. *See* Islam
Muta (temporary marriage), 173
Mysticism: Christian, 8, 146; Protestant, 210-13, 217; Zen, 133, 136, 137-38. *See also* Apocalypse, Battle of; Bloodless victory; Death in war; Magical weapons; Religious experience
Mythology. *See* Religious mythology

Nahuatlism, 6, 11, 30, 43, 51, 96; as vegetation cult, 53; as world religion, 16-17; cannibalism in, 55-56; creation in, 54; epic combat in, 41-42, 43; identity of protagonists in, 50, 224; immanentism in, 55-56; sacrifice in, 52-56. *See also* Huitzilopochtli; Quetzalcoatl; Tezcatlipoca; *Xochiyaoyotl*
Naimittakas (astrologers), 64
Nanauatzin, 54
Napoleon, 209
Narayana, 69
Narbonne, Synod of, 94
Navarre, Battle of, 87
Nazarites, 175
Nei-chia (mind boxing), 132
Nestorian Christianity, 6
Netherlands, 194, 200, 201, 205, 207. *See also* Maurice of Orange
New Model Army. *See* Cromwell, Oliver
Nicholas II, Pope, 94
Niebelungenleid, 60
Nietzsche, Friedrich, 150
Nieuport, Battle of, 207
Nihon Genzaisho Mokoroku (A Catalogue of Books Existing in Japan), 139
Nila, 69

Nitobe, Inazo, 5
Nivritti (world renunciation), 71
Nobunaga, Oda, 129
Nogi, General, 137
No mind. *See Muga*
Nomos (law). *See* Anomie
Normans, 81, 85. *See also* Teutons
Numinous experience. *See* Mysticism; Religious experience; Salvation
Nut, 26

Occidental military ethic. *See* Transcendent-historical military ethic
Ocelot warriors, 48, 49, 55
Odin. *See* Wodan
O-dō (way of the king), 127
of the Generall Captaine and His Office (Onosander), 203
Old Testament. *See* particular books
Olmecs, 57
Origen, 146
Original sin, 225
Osiris, 21, 26, 152
Otto, Rudolf, 5-6, 15, 211
Ottomans. *See* Turks

Pandavas. *See* Pandus
Pandus, 24-26, 27, 30, 37, 70, 152, 222, 223, 225. *See also* Arjuna; Draupadi; Krishna; Shikandian; Yudhisthira
Parashara, 25
Parthians, 72
Pas d'armes (tournament), 86
Paul, Saint, 136, 198-99, 225
Pax Dei (peace of God), 95, 196
Peace movement, Chinese, 113. *See also Pax Dei*; *Treuga Dei*
Peniel. *See* Jacob at Peniel
Pentateuch. *See* particular books of Old Testament
Persephone, 53-54
Persians, 23, 60, 64, 155, 198
Peters, Hugh, 203
Pflegan (to play), 23
Phalanx. *See* Greeks, art of war for
Pharisees, 150, 178

About the Author

JAMES A. AHO is Associate Professor of Sociology at Idaho State University at Pocatello. He is the author of *German Realpolitik and American Sociology: The Sources and Political Significance of the Sociology of Conflict.*